Street Map
EXPLORER

بلدية دبي
DUBAI MUNICIPALITY

TOYOTA
PASSION TO LEAD

EXPLORER

DUBAI MUNICIPALITY

Publishing

Publisher — Alistair MacKenzie
Alistair@Explorer-Publishing.com

Editorial

Editors — Claire England
Claire@Explorer-Publishing.com
Jane Roberts
Jane@Explorer-Publishing.com

Writer — David Quinn
David@Explorer-Publishing.com

Research Manager — Tim Binks
Tim@Explorer-Publishing.com

Researchers — Helga Becker
Helga@Explorer-Publishing.com
Yolanda Singh
Yolanda@Explorer-Publishing.com

Design

Senior Designer — Pete Maloney
Pete@Explorer-Publishing.com

Graphic Designers — Jayde Fernandes
Jayde@Explorer-Publishing.com
Zainudheen Madathil
Zain@Explorer-Publishing.com
Sayed Muhsin
Muhsin@Explorer-Publishing.com

Photography — Pamela Grist
Pamela@Explorer-Publishing.com

Sales & Advertising

Media Sales Manager — Alena Hykes
Alena@Explorer-Publishing.com

Media Sales Executive — Laura Zuffová
Laura@Explorer-Publishing.com

Sales/PR Administrator — Janice Menezes
Janice@Explorer-Publishing.com

Distribution

Distribution Manager — Ivan Rodrigues
Ivan@Explorer-Publishing.com

Distribution Supervisor — Abdul Gafoor
Gafoor@Explorer-Publishing.com

Distribution Executives — Mannie Lugtu
Mannie@Explorer-Publishing.com
Stephen Drilon
Stephen@Explorer-Publishing.com
Rafi Jamal
Rafi@Explorer-Publishing.com

Administration

Accounts Manager — Kamal Basha
Kamal@Explorer-Publishing.com

Accounts Assistant — Sohail Butt
Sohail@Explorer-Publishing.com

IT & Web Manager — Joe Nellary
Joe@Explorer-Publishing.com

Printer — Emirates Printing Press

Dubai Municipality

Head of Advertising — Mohamed Al Noori

Advertising Support — Hisham Hammad

Zakeya Karam

Explorer Publishing & Distribution

Zomorrodah Bldg, Za'abeel Rd   Phone (+971 4) 335 3520 Fax 335 3529
PO Box 34275, Dubai   Info@Explorer-Publishing.com
United Arab Emirates   www.Explorer-Publishing.com

First Edition 2004   Reprint 2005   ISBN 976-8182-10-5
Copyright © 2004 Explorer Group Ltd
Maps Copyright Dubai Muncipality © 2004

Dear Reader,

Dubai is a remarkable place, made more so by the fact that it has grown from a small town to a world class city in a single generation. Hence, I am very pleased to introduce this unique guidebook.

The **Street Map Explorer** is Dubai's first official street atlas. It is an attempt to radically change the way people refer to locations, and to make them aware of the official street and road names.

The **Street Map Explorer** is based around a very simple idea. With this book's collection of maps, simple and easy cross referencing, and a comprehensive index, people will be encouraged to put these numbers to use. Now, instead of giving or receiving vague, convoluted directions, you could proudly (and very specifically) say, 'I live on 7B Satwa!'

Happy Navigating

Qassim Sultan
Director General
Dubai Municipality

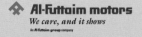

Al-Futtaim motors
We care, and it shows
An Al-futtaim group company

The *Street Map Explorer (Dubai)* is a great initiative – one that I know both residents as well as visitors will find extremely useful. At Al-Futtaim Motors, we care and it shows. So, although finding your way around will be much easier now, please remember to always take care when driving (on and off-road). In this way, we can all contribute to making the roads of Dubai a safer place for everyone.

Colin Leitch
Managing Director, **Al-Futtaim Motors**
Sole Distributors of Toyota in the UAE

Digital Explorer

Web Updates

A tremendous amount of research, effort and passion goes into making our guidebooks. However, in this dynamic and fast paced environment, decisions are swiftly taken and quickly implemented. We will try to provide you with the most current updates on those things which have changed DRAMATICALLY.

1 To view any changes, visit our Website: www.Explorer-Publishing.com

2 Click on **Map Products -> Street Map Explorer (Dubai) -> Updates** to check on any updates that may interest you.

3 All updates are in Adobe PDF format*. You may print in colour or black & white and update your street guide immediately.

4 If you are aware of any mistakes, or have any comments concerning any aspect of this publication, please fill in our online reader response form. We certainly appreciate your time and feedback.

If you do not have Adobe Reader, free reader versions may be downloaded from (www.adobe.com) or use the link from our Website.

Who Are You?

We would love to know more about you. We would equally love to know what we have done right or wrong, or if we have accidentally misled you at some point.

Please take ONE whole minute to fill out the **Reader Response Form** on our Website. To do so:

1 Visit **www.Explorer-Publishing.com**

2 At the top right, click on **RESPONSE FORM**

3 Fill it out and let us know more about you

Explorer Community

Whether it's an idea, a correction, an opinion or simply a recommendation, we want to hear from you. Log on and be part of the **Explorer Community** – let your opinions be heard, viewed, compiled and printed.

Dubai Explorer

For nine years now this has been the undisputed No.1 insiders' guide to Dubai. Meticulously researched and updated by fact-hungry residents living and breathing this vibrant city, it contains all the info you'll ever need on where to eat, sleep, shop and socialise - and a whole lot more.

STREET MAP **EXPLORER**

Table of Contents

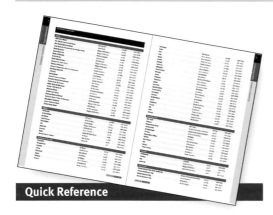

Quick Reference

The quick reference section at the beginning of the book lists all major landmarks and popular destinations. To find a consulate for example, refer to the Embassy/Consulate category and scroll through the list. All the consulates marked on the map are listed along with telephone numbers.

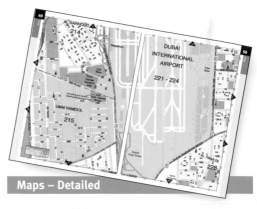

Maps – Detailed

The detailed maps are divided into a grid of rows (1 - 9) and columns (A - M) to allow a more specific and accurate search. The maps are at a scale of 1:15,000 (1cm = 150m).

Dubai Maps 1 - 70   1

Business Location

Banks	x
DEWA	x
Embassies/Consulates	x
Emirates Post	xi
Etisalat	xi
Free Zones	xi
Government Offices	xii
Libraries	xii
Ministries	xii

Educational

Nursery	xiii
Schools	xiii
Colleges/Universities	xv

Emergency

Hospital	xv
Police	xv

Entertainment

Beaches	xvi
Cinemas	xvi
Golf Clubs	xvi
Museums/Heritage	xvi
Parks	xvi

Essential Info

Airports	xvii
Area Names	xvii

Landmarks

Hotels	xviii
Major Developments	xx

Shopping

Malls/Shopping Centres	xx
Markets/Souks	xxi

Index

If you know the precise name (eg, Dubai Courts, Al Maktoum Bridge), use the alphabetical index at the end of the book to find it.

A - Z Index   71

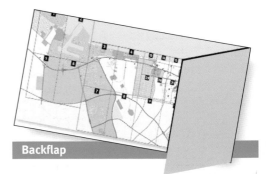

Backflap

Placed at the end of the book, this map provides a quick and convenient view of the entire city, with a legend identifying broad sectors.

Using the Maps

Step 1 Find the location you require in the index and note the map page number and grid reference.

...Al Anz East, 42 **K3**
...Jumeira 1, 22 **M3**
...Jumeira 2, 21 **B5**
...Nadd Al Hamar, 55 **F8**
...Port Saeed, 41 **B2**
...Ras Al Khor Industrial 1, 46 **K8**
...Riggat Al Buteen, 25 **A8**
...Umm Ramool, 49 **A7**
...Umm Suqeim 2, 18 **G3**

10
...Al Garhoud, 41 **C7**
...Al Quoz Industrial 1, 34 **H2**
...Al Quoz Industrial 4, 33 **B6**
...Al Qusais 1, 43 **C7**
...Al Qusais Ind 3, 44 **K7**
...Al Qusais Ind 4, 52 **L2**
...Al Twar 1, 42 **K6**, 42 **L5**
...Al Twar 2, 51 **A3**
...Dubai International Airport, 41 **D6**
..Jumeira 3, 19 **F2**
'Muhaisnah 1, 59 **B3**
'snah 2, 60 **L2.** 6^

Flip to the relevant page and use the grid reference to find your location on the map. **Step 2**

Indicates page number **40** & map number **40**.
Eg, Map Ref **40-K5**

Indicates that this is column **K**.
Eg, Map Ref 40-**K5**

Refers to the section of the book

Indicates that this is road number **17**

Shows a landmark

Indicates the adjacent map page number

The overview map

Indicates that this is row **5**.
Eg, Map Ref 40-K**5**

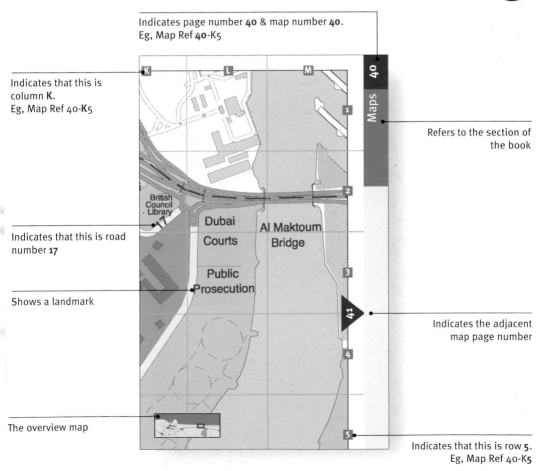

Explorer Insiders' City Guides

These are no ordinary guidebooks. They are your lifestyle support system, medicine for boredom, ointment for obstacles, available over the counter and prescribed by those in the know. An essential resource for residents, tourists and business people, they cover the what, the how, the why, the where and the when. All you have to do is read!

Abu Dhabi Explorer

The ultimate guide to the UAE's capital just got bigger and better. Now covering Al Ain you'll wonder how you ever managed without it.

Bahrain Explorer

The inside track on where and how to experience everything this fascinating gulf state has to offer.

Dubai Explorer

The original, and still the best by far. Now in its 9th year, this is the only guide you'll ever need for exploring this fascinating city.

Geneva Explorer

Your very own personal guide giving the low-down on everything to do and see in this European gem of a city and its surroundings.

Oman Explorer

All the insider info you'll ever need to make the most of this beautiful, beguiling country.

Explorer Photography Books

Where words fail, a picture speaks volumes. These award-winning photography books take you across landscapes and seascapes, through bold architecture, the past and the present, introducing a wonderland of diversity. They're an optical indulgence as well as stimulating additions to bookshelves and coffee tables everywhere.

Dubai: Tomorrow's City Today

A photography book showcasing the sheer splendour and architectural audacity of this stunning city.

Images of Geneva

From snow-capped mountains and azure waters to historic cobbled streets and contemporary architecture, the beauty of Geneva and its surroundings is captured in a stunning collection of photographs.

Sharjah's Architectural Splendour

Magnificent photographs show how modern-day Sharjah has remained true to its cultural heritage.

Images of Dubai & the UAE

Breathtaking images from this land of contrasts - from unspoilt desert, to the truly 21st century city of Dubai.

Images of Abu Dhabi & the UAE

Awe inspiring images of exquisite natural beauty and ancient cultures juxtaposed with the modern metropolis of Abu Dhabi.

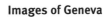

Explorer Activity Books

Why not visit stunning marine life and mysterious wrecks, or stand poised on the edge of a natural wadi or pool in the mountains? Get a tan and a life with our activity guidebooks.

Off-Road Explorer (UAE)

Let's go off-road! Over 20 adventurous routes covered in minute detail. Go off the beaten track and discover another side to the UAE.

Underwater Explorer

Dive dive dive! Detailed info on all the underwater action, from reefs to wrecks, all around the UAE.

Family Explorer (Dubai & Abu Dhabi)

The only family-friendly guide of its kind for the UAE – just add kids!

Trekking Guide (Oman)

A booklet and individual cards detailing amazing walks through spectacular scenery. The maps correspond to waypoints that are actually painted on the ground to aid navigation.

Street Map Explorer (Dubai)

Never get lost again. A first of its kind for Dubai, this handy map book lists every highway and byway in crystal clear detail.

Dubai Tourist Map

This detailed fold-out map means getting lost in Dubai is now a thing of the past. Compiled and published by Dubai Municipality it highlights landmarks and attractions throughout the city, making it a must for tourists and residents alike.

STREET MAP **EXPLORER**

Explorer Other Products

With such an incredible array of insider's guides and photography and activity books you'd think we wouldn't have the time or energy to produce anything else. Well think again! Here are some of our other products – no home should be without them.

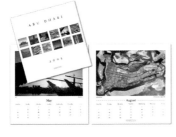

2005 Calendar (Abu Dhabi)

Spend a whole year in the company of stunning images of the capital of the Emirates.

2005 Calendar (Dubai)

A 12-month visual feast, featuring award-winning images of Dubai's finest sights.

Starter Kit (Dubai)

Three great books - the Dubai Explorer, Zappy Explorer and Street Map - everything you need to get started and sorted!

Images Collection (UAE)

A combination of award-winning excellence, containing both the Images of Dubai and Images of Abu Dhabi photography books (Limited Edition).

Zappy Explorer (Dubai)

Page after page of fuss-free advice on getting things done in Dubai. All the info you'll ever need to get yourself sorted.

STREET MAP EXPLORER

BUSINESS LOCATIONS

Banks

ABN Amro Bank	Mankhool	24-H6	351 2200
Abu Dhabi Commercial Bank	Ayal Nasir	25-B4	295 8888
Abu Dhabi National Bank	Riggat Al Buteen	25-A8	666 6800
Arab Bank for Investment & Foreign Trade	Riggat Al Buteen	25-A7	221 2100
Bank Banorab	Al Muraqqabat	25-B8	228 4655
Bank Melli Iran	Al Garhoud	41-A7	226 8207
Bank of Sharjah	Al Garhoud	41-A7	282 7278
Bank Pariba	Riggat Al Buteen	25-A6	222 5200
Bank Saderat Iran	Riggat Al Buteen	25-A5	222 1161
Banque Du Caire S.A.E.	Al Muteena	25-D7	271 5175
Banque Indosuez	Trade Centre 2	22-M9	331 4211
Banque Libannaise Pour Le Commerce	Al Muraqqabat	25-A7	222 2291
Barclays Bank Plc	Oud Metha	39-E3	335 1555
Citibank	Umm Hurair 2	39-F7	324 5000
Dubai Bank	Trade Centre 2	22-M9	800 5555
Dubai Commercial Bank	Mankhool	24-J5	352 3355
Emirates Bank International	Al Buteen	24-M4	225 6256
Habib Bank AG Zurich	Al Hamriya	24-K7	221 4535
HSBC Bank Middle East	Al Souk Al Kabeer	24-K3	353 5000
Lloyds TSB Bank Plc	Jumeira 2	20-H4	342 2000
Mashreq Bank	Al Muraqqabat	25-C7	222 9131
Middle East Bank	Al Buteen	24-M4	800 4644
National Bank of Dubai	Al Muraqqabat	25-A8	222 2111
National Bank of Ras Al Khaimah	Riggat Al Buteen	41-B1	222 6291
Standard Chartered	Mankhool	24-G5	800 4949
Union National Bank	Al Muraqqabat	25-B7	800 2600
United Arab Bank	Riggat Al Buteen	25-A8	222 0181

DEWA

Al Qusais	Al Twar 1	42-M8	261 3719
Al Rashidiya	Al Rashidiya	57-E2	285 0622
Al Satwa	Al Hudaiba	23-C3	398 5560
Ayal Nasser	Riggat Al Buteen	25-A6	271 7864
Burj Nahar	Al Muteena	25-D6	271 4777
HQ	Umm Hurair 2	40-G7	334 8888
Jebel Ali	Jebel Ali Free Zone	2-H8	883 6423
Jumeira	Al Wasl	21-D9	343 1666
Safia	Hor Al Anz	42-J1	266 2445
Steam Power Station	Jebel Ali	4-J1	884 6100

Embassy/Consulate

Australia	Al Wasl	20-L7	321 2444
Bangladesh	Al Muteena	25-C7	272 7553
Canada	Mankhool	24-J6	352 1717
China	Al Jafiliya	23-D7	398 4357
Denmark	Al Rigga	25-B7	222 7699
Egypt	Umm Hurair 1	24-K7	397 1122
Finland	Al Garhoud	41-C5	282 3338
France	Trade Centre 1	22-L8	332 9040

Germany	Mankhool	24-K8	397 2333
India	Umm Hurair 1	24-K8	397 1222
Iran	Umm Hurair 1	24-L7	344 4717
Italy	Trade Centre 2	22-M9	331 4167
Japan	Trade Centre 2	22-M9	331 9191
Jordan	Umm Hurair 1	24-K8	397 0500
Kuwait	Umm Hurair 1	24-L8	397 8000
Lebanon	Umm Hurair 1	24-L8	397 7450
Malaysia	Oud Metha	39-F2	335 5528
Netherlands	Mankhool	24-J6	352 8700
Norway	Al Souk Al Kabeer	24-J2	353 3833
Oman	Umm Hurair 1	24-K8	397 1000
Pakistan	Umm Hurair 1	24-K8	397 0412
Palestine	Hor Al Anz East	42-K2	397 2363
Qatar	Al Jafiliya	23-D7	398 2888
Romania	Jumeira 3	19-A4	394 0580
Saudi Arabia	Umm Hurair 1	24-L8	397 9777
South Africa	Al Karama	24-K7	397 5222
Sri Lanka	Al Hudaiba	23-C4	398 6535
Sweden	Al Mina	23-D2	345 7716
Switzerland	Trade Centre 2	23-A9	329 0999
Syria	Al Wuheida	26-L6	266 3354
Thailand	Jumeira 2	20-K3	349 2863
Turkey	Trade Centre 2	22-M8	331 4788
UK	Al Hamriya	24-L6	397 1070
USA	Trade Centre 2	22-M9	311 6000
Yemen	Al Hamriya	24-K7	397 0213

Emirates Post

Abu Hail	Abu Hail	26-H5	269 4301
Airport	Dubai International Airport	49-E2	216 4994
Airport Free Zone	Dubai International Airport	50-L2	299 6130
Al Mussalla	Al Souk Al Kabeer	24-K5	359 6699
Al Sanaweya	Al Rigga	25-A6	223 3656
Al Twar	Al Twar 2	51-A5	261 2687
Deira Main Office	Hor Al Anz East	42-L2	262 2222
DNATA	Al Khabaisi	41-C3	295 5949
Hor Al Anz	Hor Al Anz	26-G9	262 9334
HQ	Al Karama	24-J9	337 1500
Satwa	Jumeira 1	21-F5	344 0364
Trade Centre	Trade Centre 2	23-A9	331 3306

Etisalat

Al Khaleej	Al Raffa	24-J5	355 3333
Al Wasl	Trade Centre 2	37-E1	343 2000
HQ	Riggat Al Buteen	25-A8	101
Jebel Ali	Jebel Ali Free Zone	3-A4	881 6216

Free Zones

Dubai Airport Free Zone Authority	Dubai International Airport	50-L2	299 5555
Dubai Healthcare City	Umm Hurair 2	40-H6	324 5555
Dubai Internet City	Al Sufouh 1	14-H5	391 1111
Dubai Maritime City	Al Shindagha	24-G1	390 3820

Dubai Media City	Al Sufouh 1	14-G4	391 4615
Jebel Ali Free Zone	Jebel Ali Free Zone	2-J8	881 5000

Government

Department of Civil Aviation	Dubai International Airport	41-E7	224 5333
Department of Economic Development	Riggat Al Buteen	25-A8	222 9922
Department of Health & Medical Services	Al Jafiliya	23-D8	337 0031
Department of HH the Ruler's Affairs & Protocol Affairs	Al Mina	23-F2	353 1060
Department of Ports & Customs	Al Mina	23-D1	345 9575
Department of Tourism & Commerce Marketing	Riggat Al Buteen	25-A8	351 1600
Development Board	Riggat Al Buteen	25-A7	228 8866
Dubai Chamber of Commerce & Industry	Al Rigga	24-M8	228 0000
Dubai Courts	Umm Hurair 2	40-L2	334 7777
Dubai Development & Investment Authority	Trade Centre 2	22-J9	330 2222
Dubai Drydocks	Al Mina	23-C1	345 0626
Dubai Government Workshop	Al Jaddaf	47-E2	334 2999
Dubai Municipality - Advertising Section	Umm Ramool	49-E5	285 8661
Dubai Municipality - Emergency Office	Riggat Al Buteen	25-A7	223 2323
Dubai Municipality - Fees & Revenues Section	Riggat Al Buteen	25-A7	206 3274
Dubai Municipality - Garage Transport Department	Al Garhoud	49-D4	285 0700
Dubai Municipality - HQ	Riggat Al Buteen	25-A7	221 5555
Dubai Municipality - Legal Affairs Department	Riggat Al Buteen	25-A7	206 3331
Dubai Municipality - Public Relations Section	Riggat Al Buteen	25-A7	206 4678
Dubai Municipality - Public Transport (Inquiries)	Riggat Al Buteen	25-A7	286 1616
Dubai Municipality - Rent Committee	Riggat Al Buteen	25-A7	221 5555
Dubai Municipality - Store	Al Garhoud	49-D3	286 3999
Dubai Municipality - Umm Ramool Offices	Umm Ramool	49-E5	286 3366
Dubai Municipality - Used Car Exhibitions Complex	Ras Al Khor Industrial 3	55-B9	333 3800
Dubai Ports Authority	Al Mina	23-D1	881 5000
Economic Department	Al Muraqqabat	25-A8	222 9922
H.H. The Ruler's Court	Al Souk Al Kabeer	24-L4	353 3333
Lands Department	Riggat Al Buteen	25-A8	222 2253
Sheikh Mohammed Centre for Cultural Understanding	Jumeira 1	22-G3	344 7755
UAE Radio & TV - Dubai	Umm Hurair 2	40-K2	336 9999

Library

Al Rashidiya Public Library	Al Rashidiya	57-F4	226 2788
Archies Library	Al Karama	24-H8	396 7924
British Council Library	Umm Hurair 2	40-K2	337 1540
Dubai Lending Library	Jumeira 1	22-H3	334 6480
Hor Al Anz Public Library	Hor Al Anz East	42-M2	266 1788
Juma Al Majid Cultural Centre	Hor Al Anz	42-G1	262 4999
Public Library	Al Ras	24-K2	226 2788

Ministries

Ministry of Agriculture & Fisheries	Al Muraqqabat	41-B2	295 8161
Ministry of Communication	Al Khabaisi	41-D3	295 3330
Ministry of Defence	Al Souk Al Kabeer	24-K4	353 2330
Ministry of Economy & Commerce	Al Khabaisi	41-C2	295 4000
Ministry of Education & Youth	Al Twar 1	42-J4	299 4100
Ministry of Electricity & Water	Al Muteena	25-E9	262 2000
Ministry of Finance & Industry	Al Souk Al Kabeer	24-H2	393 9000
Ministry of Health	Al Karama	24-H7	396 6000

Ministry of Information & Culture	Al Qusais 1	42-M7	261 5500
Ministry of Labour & Social Affairs	Hor Al Anz East	42-L3	269 1666
Ministry of Planning	Al Muteena	25-C7	228 5219
Ministry of Public Works & Housing	Al Qusais 1	43-A8	269 3900
Ministry of Youth & Sports	Hor Al Anz East	42-K2	269 1680

EDUCATIONAL

Nursery

Butterflies & Busy Bees Nursery	Jumeira 1	21-B4	344 4394
Dubai Gem Private Nursery & School	Oud Metha	40-H4	337 0913
French Children's Nursery House	Jumeira 1	22-K3	349 6868
Gulf Montessori Nursery	Al Garhoud	41-C9	282 2402
Happy Home Nursery	Al Karama	24-J8	396 1995
Kid's Island Nursery	Jumeira 2	20-K4	394 2578
Kindergarten Nursery School	Port Saeed	41-A4	344 3878
Ladybird Nursery	Al Bada'a	21-D6	344 1011
Little Princess Nursery	Al Qusais 2	51-C3	263 4666
Little Star Nursery	Al Satwa	22-M7	398 2004
Nido Nursery	Al Quoz	19-D9	206 4854
Palm's Nursery School	Jumeira 3	20-G4	394 7017
Small World Nursery	Jumeira 1	22-K3	345 7774
Tiny Home Montessori Nursery	Jumeira 1	22-G5	349 3201

Schools

Aaesha Preparatory School for Girls	Al Karama	24-J8	396 1010
Ahmad Bin Sulaim Elementary School for Boys	Al Baraha	25-F6	296 7420
Al Aqsa Elementary School for Boys	Al Rashidiya	57-F5	285 1715
Al Emam Abu Hanifa Elementary School	Al Quoz	35-F1	338 2297
Al Emam Al Shafei Preparatory School for Boys	Al Wasl	20-L6	344 1883
Al Emarat Preparatory School for Boys	Al Rashidiya	57-F6	285 6965
Al Falah Model School	Mankhool	23-E6	398 7555
Al Farooq Pakistani Islamic School	Al Qusais 3	51-B6	264 3848
Al Hikma Kindergarten	Al Rashidiya	57-F2	285 9840
Al Hudaiba Elementary School for Girls	Al Twar 2	50-M4	263 0455
Al Ittihad Private School	Al Mamzar	27-C7	296 6314
Al Ittihad Secondary School	Hor Al Anz East	42-K1	262 2037
Al Jahiz Elementary School for Boys	Al Rashidiya	57-E1	285 9700
Al Karama Kindergarten	Al Karama	24-J8	396 1774
Al Khaleej National School	Al Garhoud	49-A4	282 2707
Al Kuwait Elementary School for Girls	Al Twar 1	42-M7	261 5749
Al Maarif Secondary School for Boys	Al Baraha	25-F6	286 2237
Al Maktoum Preparatory School for Boys	Al Wasl	20-J6	344 2194
Al Manara Secondary School for Boys	Al Manara	17-F7	348 6229
Al Manhal Kindergarten	Al Satwa	22-G7	349 6126
Al Mankhool School	Mankhool	23-E5	398 5440
Al Mawakeb School	Al Garhoud	49-B4	285 1415
Al Mazhar Primary School for Girls	Al Twar 3	59-A1	287 4894
Al Muhallab Preparatory School for Boys	Al Mamzar	27-B8	296 7393
Al Mustaqbal Elementary School for Girls	Umm Suqeim 2	17-E4	348 0704
Al Quoz Elementary School for Girls	Al Quoz	19-F9	338 6611

Al Rabee Kindergarten	Jumeira 1	21-C4	349 1373
Al Raya Secondary School for Girls	Al Wasl	20-M4	344 8260
Al Sadiq Islamic English School	Al Qusais 2	51-B4	263 4083
Al Saeediya Preparatory School for Boys	Al Karama	24-G8	337 2354
Al Safa Secondary School for Boys	Al Wasl	20-K6	349 1893
Al Salam Preparatory School	Al Qusais 3	51-C8	264 0585
Al Shorooq Kindergarten	Al Twar 3	59-A1	264 7419
Al Waheeda Secondary School for Boys	Al Wuheida	26-M6	269 1136
Al Wasl Elementary School for Girls	Al Satwa	22-H7	331 6427
Allama Iqbal Islamic School	Al Quoz	35-E2	339 0778
Alliance Francaise	Oud Metha	40-G5	335 8712
American School of Dubai, The	Jumeira 1	21-E5	344 0824
Amina Bint Wahab Secondary School for Girls	Al Baraha	25-F6	271 8693
Arab Unity School	Al Mizhar 1	59-C9	288 6226
Asma Bint Abu Baker Multi Level for Girls	Al Twar 3	50-M8	254 3188
Bader Preparatory School for Boys	Muhaisnah 1	59-A6	288 7734
Bilal Bin Rabah Elemetary School for Boys	Al Satwa	22-G7	349 6224
Cambridge High School, The	Al Garhoud	49-A2	282 4646
Dubai College	Al Sufouh 2	15-A4	399 9111
Dubai English Speaking School	Umm Hurair 2	40-H4	337 1457
Dubai First School	Al Quoz	36-G2	338 0333
Dubai Gem Private School	Oud Metha	40-G4	337 6661
Dubai Infants School	Oud Metha	40-H4	337 0913
Dubai National School	Al Barshaa 1	31-E1	347 4555
Emirates International School	Umm Al Sheif	17-B8	348 9804
English Speaking School, The	Umm Hurair 2	40-H4	337 1457
Fatima English School	Al Rashidiya	57-E4	285 1139
Gharnata Elementary School for Girls	Al Rashidiya	57-F2	285 7566
Grammar School	Al Garhoud	49-A4	282 4822
Gulf Montessori Centre	Mankhool	24-J6	335 2073
Hessa Preparatory School for Girls	Za'abeel 1	39-D4	398 8647
Iman Private School	Al Rashidiya	58-G2	285 1037
Indian High School	Oud Metha	40-H3	337 7475
International School of Choueifat	Umm Suqeim 1	18-M2	399 9444
Islamic Preparatory School	Al Mamzar	27-B8	296 7483
Islamic School for Education	Muhaisnah 1	59-D4	264 6001
Jamal Abdulnasir Elementary School for Boys	Al Satwa	22-M7	331 2308
Japanese School	Al Wasl	20-L6	344 9119
Jebel Ali Primary School	Jebel Ali Village	4-G3	884 6485
Jumeira College	Al Safa 1	19-A5	394 7985
Jumeira English Speaking School	Al Safa 1	19-E7	394 5515
Jumeira Primary School	Jumeira 1	19-A5	394 3500
Khalid Ibn Al Waleed School	Al Garhoud	49-A2	282 4964
Khawla Bint Al Azwar Elementary School for Girls	Al Satwa	21-E8	343 0257
Latifa Bin Hamdan Multi Level for Girls	Al Karama	24-H9	396 2075
Millenium School, The	Al Qusais Ind 1	43-E8	298 8567
Modern High School	Al Wasl	20-K6	344 4244
Mother to Mother Tykes	Trade Centre 2	22-M9	348 5896
National Charity School for Girls	Al Garhoud	49-A1	282 4499
New Indian Model School	Al Garhoud	49-A3	282 4313
Omer Al Mukhtar School for Boys	Al Bada'a	22-H6	344 0212
Our Own English High School	Oud Metha	40-G4	337 4112
Oxford School, The	Al Bada'a	22-K5	394 1222

Qortuba Preparatory School for Girls	Al Satwa	21-D8	343 4359
Regent School	Jumeira 3	19-F3	344 8049
Salma Al Ansariya Elementary School for Girls	Al Satwa	21-E8	343 0252
School of Research Science	Al Qusais Ind 1	43-E8	298 8772
Second of December Secondary School for Girls	Al Twar 1	42-M7	261 6261
Shurahbeel Elementary School	Al Qusais 2	51-C4	261 2073
St. Mary's Catholic High School	Umm Hurair 2	40-H4	337 0252
Tariq Bin Ziad Preparatory School for Boys	Al Baraha	25-E5	272 8439
Um Hani Preparatory School for Girls	Al Rashidiya	57-F5	285 7384
Umm Suqeim Preparatory School for Girls	Al Safa 2	18-J7	394 4672
Za'abeel Secondary School for Girls	Za'abeel 1	39-D4	337 4821

Colleges/Universities

American University in Dubai	Al Sufouh 1	14-G5	399 9000
Centre for American Education	Al Garhoud	49-A2	282 9992
Champlain College	Al Garhoud	41-B6	286 9786
Dubai Aviation College	Al Garhoud	41-A8	282 4000
Dubai English College	Al Safa 1	19-F6	394 3465
Dubai University College	Riggat Al Buteen	25-A8	224 2472
Higher Colleges of Technology (Men's)	Al Nahda 2	44-H7	269 0029
Higher Colleges of Technology (Women's)	Al Nahda 2	44-E7	267 2929
University of Wollongong	Jumeira 3	19-A2	395 4422
Zayed University	Al Twar 3	50-K9	264 8899

EMERGENCY

Hospital

Al Amal Hospital	Al Wasl	21-B7	344 4010
Al Baraha Hospital	Al Baraha	25-F5	271 0000
Al Maktoum Hospital	Naif	25-C6	222 1211
Al Wasl Hospital	Al Jaddaf	39-E7	324 1111
American Hospital	Oud Metha	40-G3	336 7777
Belhoul International Hospital Centre	Al Satwa	23-A7	345 4000
Dubai Hospital	Al Baraha	26-G5	271 4444
International Private Hospital	Al Rigga	25-A5	221 2484
Iranian Hospital	Al Bada'a	22-K4	344 0250
Rashid Hospital	Umm Hurair 2	40-J5	337 4000
Welcare Hospital	Al Garhoud	41-B7	282 7788

Police

Dubai Police - Air Wing	Dubai International Airport	41-D5	282 1111
Dubai Police - Airport	Dubai International Airport	41-E9	224 5555
Dubai Police - Al Muraqqabat	Al Muraqqabat	25-E9	266 0555
Dubai Police - Al Rafaa	Al Souk Al Kabeer	24-H3	393 7777
Dubai Police - Al Rashidiya	Ras Al Khor Industrial 3	55-B9	285 3000
Dubai Police - Bur Dubai	Al Jafiliya	23-B8	398 1111
Dubai Police - Criminal Investigation Department (CID)	Al Twar 1	42-L4	229 2222
Dubai Police - General Ports & Airport Department	Dubai International Airport	41-E9	206 6599
Dubai Police - Naif Rd	Naif	25-B4	228 6999
Dubai Police - Rashidiya	Al Rashidiya	57-F2	285 3000
Dubai Traffic Police - HQ	Al Quoz Industrial 3	16-L9	347 2222
Dubai Traffic Police - Qusais	Al Twar 1	42-K5	269 2222

ENTERTAINMENT

Beach

Al Mamzar Beach	Al Mamzar	27-D7
Jebel Ali Beach	Jebel Ali	1-D2
Jumeria Beach	Jumeira 1	22-H2
Mina Al Seyahi Beach	Al Mina Al Siyahi	13-D3
Umm Suqeim Beach	Umm Suqeim 3	17-B2

Cinema

Al Bustan Cinema	Al Qusais 1	43-A7	263 3444
Al Nasr Cinema	Oud Metha	40-G2	337 4353
Century Cinemas	Jumeira 1	21-B4	349 9773
Cine Club	Oud Metha	40-G5	335 8712
Cinestar	Port Saeed	41-B4	294 0222
Deira Cinema	Al Muraqqabat	25-B7	222 3551
Deira City Centre Cinema	Al Garhoud	41-B4	295 4545
Dubai Cinema	Hor Al Anz	25-F9	266 0632
Galleria Cinema	Al Shindagha	25-C3	209 6470
Grand Cinecity	Al Muraqqabat	25-C7	223 2333
Grand Cineplex	Umm Hurair 2	40-G8	324 2000
Lamcy Cinema	Oud Metha	39-E3	336 8808
Metroplex Cinema	Trade Centre 2	20-H8	343 8383
Plaza Cinema	Al Souk Al Kabeer	24-J2	393 9966
Rex Drive-in Cinema	Muhaisnah 1	59-B8	288 6447
Strand Cinema	Al Karama	24-K8	337 0304

Golf Course

Dubai Creek Golf & Yacht Club	Umm Hurair 2	40-M7	295 6000
Emirates Golf Club	Al Sufouh 1	14-G8	347 3222
Jebel Ali Golf Resort	Jebel Ali	1-E3	883 6000
Montgomerie, The	Al Barshaa 3	13-C8	399 9955
Nadd Al Shiba Golf Course	Nadd Al Shiba 1	45-B8	336 3666

Museum / Heritage

Al Ahmadiyyah School & Heritage House	Hor Al Anz	42-J2	226 0286
Dubai Museum	Al Raffa	24-K4	353 1862
Godolphin Gallery	Nadd Al Shiba 1	45-A5	336 3031
Heritage & Diving Village	Al Shindagha	24-L1	393 7151
Sheikh Saeed Al Maktoum's House	Al Shindagha	24-L1	393 7139

Park

Al Rashidiya Park	Al Rashidiya	58-G3
Al Wasl Park	Al Bada'a	22-H5
Dubai Creek Park	Umm Hurair 2	40-K6
Jumeriah Beach Park	Jumeira 2	20-J1
Mushrif National Park	Mushrif Park	67-E8
Naif Park	Naif	25-B4
Safa Park	Al Wasl	20-H6

ESSENTIAL INFO

Airport

| Terminal 1 | Dubai International Airport | 41-E9 | 224 5555 |
| Terminal 2 | Dubai International Airport | 42-J7 | 224 5555 |

Area Name

Area Name		Area Name	
Abu Hail	26-H6	Al Rigga	25-B6
Al Bada'a	22-J5	Al Safa 1	19-C6
Al Baraha	26-G6	Al Safa 2	18-L6
Al Barshaa 1	31-F1	Al Satwa	22-L6
Al Barshaa 2	32-G7	Al Shindagha	24-H1
Al Barshaa 3	31-B4	Al Souk Al Kabeer	24-J3
Al Buteen	24-M3	Al Sufouh 1	14-J4
Al Daghaya	25-A3	Al Sufouh 2	15-D6
Al Garhoud	49-B1	Al Twar 1	42-M9
Al Hamriya	24-K5	Al Twar 2	51-A4
Al Hamriya Port	27-A3	Al Twar 3	50-M8
Al Hudaiba	23-B4	Al Warqaa 1	64-M5
Al Jaddaf	48-G2	Al Warqaa 2	65-D1
Al Jafiliya	23-C6	Al Warqaa 3	65-C6
Al Karama	23-F8	Al Wasl	19-L4
Al Khabaisi	41-E2	Al Wuheida	26-L6
Al Kifaf	23-D9	Ayal Nasir	25-B3
Al Mamzar	27-A8	Bukadra	46-H9
Al Manara	17-E7	Corniche Deira	25-E3
Al Mankhool	23-E6	Dubai International Airport	50-H2
Al Marqadh	45-B3	Dubai Investment Park 1	7-E3
Al Mina	23-F2	Emirates Hills 1	13-C7
Al Mizhar 1	60-H9	Emirates Hills 2	14-H7
Al Mizhar 2	68-K5	Emirates Hills 3	29-E3
Al Muraqqabat	25-D9	Hor Al Anz	26-H9
Al Murar	25-C4	Hor Al Anz East	42-L2
Al Muteena	25-D6	Jebel Ali Village	4-G4
Al Nahda 1	43-D4	Jumeira 1	21-E4
Al Nahda 2	43-F6	Jumeira 2	20-K2
Al Quoz	35-D1	Jumeira 3	19-D3
Al Quoz Industrial 1	34-H2	Mankhool	23-E6
Al Quoz Industrial 2	34-H6	Marsa Dubai	13-C5
Al Quoz Industrial 3	33-B2	Mirdif	66-L2
Al Quoz Industrial 4	33-B6	Muhaisnah 1	59-C5
Al Qusais 1	43-B9	Muhaisnah 2	60-G3
Al Qusais 2	51-B3	Muhaisnah 3	52-G6
Al Qusais 3	51-C7	Muhaisnah 4	52-J3
Al Qusais Industrial 1	43-F9	Mushrif Park	66-M8
Al Qusais Industrial 2	51-F2	Nadd Al Hamar	56-J7
Al Qusais Industrial 3	44-K8	Nadd Al Shiba 1	53-A2
Al Qusais Industrial 4	52-L1	Nadd Al Shiba 2	54-G5
Al Qusais Industrial 5	52-L4	Nadd Al Shiba 3	62-K4
Al Raffa	23-F4	Nadd Al Shiba 4	61-E4
Al Ras	24-K3	Nadd Shamma	57-C4
Al Rashidiya	57-E3	Naif	25-C5

Oud Al Muteena	60-M8	Umm Al Sheif	16-M8
Oud Metha	39-F2	Umm Hurair 1	24-K8
Port Saeed	41-B3	Umm Hurair 2	40-G7
Ras Al Khor	48-K9	Umm Ramool	49-C6
Ras Al Khor Industrial 1	55-A2	Umm Suqeim 1	18-J4
Ras Al Khor Industrial 2	55-A5	Umm Suqeim 2	17-D4
Ras Al Khor Industrial 3	63-D1	Umm Suqeim 3	17-A4
Riggat Al Buteen	25-A6	Warsan 1	64-G7
Trade Centre 1	21-F9	Za'abeel 1	39-D5
Trade Centre 2	37-E1	Za'abeel 2	38-G6

LANDMARKS

Hotel

Admiral Plaza	Al Souk Al Kabeer	24-J3	393 5333
Airport Hotel	Al Garhoud	41-C7	282 3464
Al Bustan Rotana	Al Garhoud	41-C8	282 0000
Al Jawhara Hotel	Al Rigga	25-B6	222 3141
Al Khaleej Holiday Hotel	Riggat Al Buteen	24-M4	227 6565
Al Khaleej Palace Hotel	Riggat Al Buteen	25-A8	223 1000
Ambassador Hotel	Al Souk Al Kabeer	24-H2	393 9444
Arif Castle Hotel	Al Raffa	24-G2	393 3777
Ascot Hotel	Al Raffa	24-H3	352 0900
Astoria Hotel	Al Souk Al Kabeer	24-J3	353 4300
Avari Dubai International	Al Muraqqabat	41-C1	295 6666
Blue Diamond Hotel	Al Daghaya	25-A3	226 2121
Burj Al Arab	Umm Suqeim 3	16-L2	301 7777
Capitol Hotel	Al Mina	23-B3	346 0111
Carlton Tower	Al Rigga	25-B6	222 7111
Casablanca Hotel	Naif	25-B5	228 9111
Claridge Hotel	Al Muteena	25-C7	271 6666
Comfort Inn	Al Muraqqabat	25-B7	222 7393
Crowne Plaza	Trade Centre 1	22-J8	331 1111
Dallas	Al Souk Al Kabeer	24-H4	351 1223
Deira Park Hotel	Naif	25-B5	223 9922
Dubai Grand Hotel	Al Qusais 1	51-C1	263 2555
Dubai Marine Beach Resort & Spa	Jumeira 1	22-K2	346 1111
Dubai Palm Hotel	Al Muteena	25-D7	271 0021
Dusit Dubai	Trade Centre 2	37-E1	343 3333
Embassy Suites	Al Muteena	25-E8	269 8070
Emirates Towers	Trade Centre 2	38-J1	330 0000
Fairmont Dubai	Trade Centre 1	22-M8	332 5555
Four Points Sheraton	Al Hamriya	24-K6	397 7444
Grand Hyatt Dubai	Umm Hurair 2	40-H8	209 6993
Gulf Inn Hotel	Al Muraqqabat	25-B8	224 3433
Heritage International Hotel	Mankhool	24-J5	359 0111
Hilton Dubai Creek	Riggat Al Buteen	25-A9	227 1111
Hilton Dubai Jumeira	Al Mina Al Siyahi	13-A3	399 1111
Holiday Inn Bur Dubai	Oud Metha	39-F4	336 6000
Holiday Inn Downtown	Al Muraqqabat	41-C1	228 8889
Howard Johnson Hotel	Al Muraqqabat	25-B8	272 9748

Hyatt Regency	Al Shindagha	25-C3	209 1234
Ibis	Trade Centre 2	38-L1	332 4444
Imperial Suites Hotel	Al Raffa	24-H4	351 5100
InterContinental Dubai	Al Rigga	25-A6	222 7171
J.W. Marriott	Al Muraqqabat	41-E1	262 4444
Jebel Ali Hotel	Jebel Ali	1-E3	883 6000
Jumeira Beach Club, The	Jumeira 2	20-L1	344 5333
Jumeira Beach Hotel	Umm Suqeim 3	16-M3	348 0000
Jumeira Rotana Hotel	Al Bada'a	22-M4	345 5888
Le Meridien Hotel	Al Garhoud	41-D8	282 4040
Le Meridien Mina Seyahi	Al Mina Al Siyahi	13-F3	399 3333
Le Royal Meridien Beach Resort & Spa	Al Mina Al Siyahi	13-B3	399 5555
London Crown Hotel	Mankhool	24-J6	351 8888
Lords Hotel	Al Muraqqabat	25-B8	228 9977
Lotus Hotel	Al Muraqqabat	25-B8	227 8888
Marco Polo Hotel	Al Muteena	25-D6	272 0000
Marriott Executive Apartments	Riggat Al Buteen	41-B1	213 1000
Mayfair Hotel	Al Muraqqabat	41-B1	228 4444
Metropolitan Deira	Al Khabaisi	41-C2	295 9171
Metropolitan Hotel	Trade Centre 2	20-J8	343 0000
Metropolitan Palace Hotel	Al Muraqqabat	25-B9	227 0000
Metropolitan Resort & Beach Club Hotel	Al Mina Al Siyahi	13-C3	399 5000
Middle East Hotel	Ayal Nasir	25-A4	222 6688
Mina A'Salam	Al Sufouh 2	16-K3	366 8888
Nihal Rotana Inn	Al Muraqqabat	41-B1	295 7666
Novotel	Trade Centre 2	38-L2	344 7100
Oasis Beach Hotel	Al Mina Al Siyahi	13-A3	399 4444
One&Only Royal Mirage, The	Al Sufouh 1	14-G3	399 9999
Palm Beach Rotana Inn	Al Raffa	24-H3	393 1999
Palm Hotel, The	Al Sufouh 1	13-F5	399 2222
Panorama Hotel	Al Raffa	24-G5	351 8518
Phoenicia Hotel	Naif	25-A5	222 7191
President Hotel	Al Karama	24-J7	334 6565
Princeton Hotel	Al Garhoud	41-B6	282 7777
Quality Inn	Al Muraqqabat	25-B9	227 1919
Ramada Continental Hotel	Hor Al Anz East	42-K3	266 2666
Ramada Hotel	Mankhool	24-H5	351 9999
Ramee International Hotel	Naif	25-A5	224 0222
Regal Plaza Hotel	Mankhool	24-J5	355 6633
Regent Palace Hotel	Al Karama	24-J7	396 3888
Renaissance Dubai	Al Muteena	25-E8	262 5555
Ritz-Carlton, Dubai, The	Al Mina Al Siyahi	13-B3	399 4000
Riviera Hotel	Al Rigga	25-A6	222 2131
Rydges Plaza Hotel	Al Jafiliya	23-A6	398 2222
San Marco Hotel	Al Murar	25-D4	272 2333
Sea Rock Hotel	Naif	25-C6	228 1000
Sea Shell Inn	Al Raffa	24-H4	393 4777
Sea View Hotel	Al Raffa	23-F3	355 8080
Shangri-La Hotel	Trade Centre 1	21-F9	343 8888
Sheraton Deira	Al Muteena	25-F8	268 8888
Sheraton Dubai Creek Hotel & Towers	Al Rigga	25-A7	228 1111
Sheraton Jumeira Beach Resort & Towers	Al Mina Al Siyahi	4-M1	399 5533
Sofitel City Centre Hotel & Residence	Al Garhoud	41-B5	294 1222

St. George Hotel	Al Ras	24-K3	225 1122
Sun & Sand Hotel	Al Muraqqabat	41-B1	223 9000
Sun Rock Hotel	Mankhool	23-D5	351 4222
Swiss Plaza Hotel	Al Souk Al Kabeer	24-J3	393 9373
Taj Palace Hotel	Al Muraqqabat	25-B9	223 2222
Towers Rotana Hotel	Trade Centre 1	21-F9	343 8000
Vasantam Hotel	Al Souk Al Kabeer	24-J3	393 8006
Vendome Plaza Hotel	Al Muraqqabat	41-B1	222 2333
West Hotel	Al Murar	25-B4	271 7001
Western Hotel	Al Raffa	24-G5	351 8518
World Trade Centre Hotel	Trade Centre 2	22-M9	331 4000
York International Hotel	Al Raffa	24-J5	355 5500

Major Developments

Al Murooj Complex	Trade Centre 2	37-E2	-
Arabian Ranches	-	10-J7	800 4887
Autodrome	-	10-G6	294 9490
Burj Dubai	Trade Centre 2	37-C2	399 2299
Cargo Mega Terminal	Dubai International Airport	41-D5	-
Dubai Auto Parts City	Warsan 1	64-H6	-
Dubai Festival City	Ras Al Khor	48-K7	213 6213
Dubai Flower Centre	Dubai International Airport	41-E4	
Dubai Marina	Al Mina Al Siyahi	13-D4	399 2299
Dubai Metals & Commodities Centre	Emirates Hills 1	13-B6	390 3899
Dubai Pearl	Al Sufouh 1	14-J3	324 6664
Dubai Textile City	Warsan 1	63-D7	-
Dubailand	-	10-K9	330 2222
Emirates Hills	Emirates Hills 3	29-E3	380 1888
Gardens Mall	Jebel Ali	4-H3	884 5555
Gardens, The	Jebel Ali	4-J4	884 5555
Gate, The	Trade Centre 2	38-J1	330 0100
Green Community	Dubai Investment Park 1	7-E5	294 9490
Greens, The	Emirates Hills 2	14-K7	399 3366
Hydropolis	Marsa Dubai	13-C1	330 2222
Jumeira Beach Residence	Al Mina Al Siyahi	13-A3	391 1114
Jumeirah Islands	Al Sufouh 1	13-A8	390 3401
Jumeirah Lake Towers	Emirates Hills 1	13-A6	-
Lakes, The	Emirates Hills 2	30-G1	380 1111
Mall of the Emirates	Al Barshaa 1	32-J1	213 6213
Meadows, The	Emirates Hills	13-B8	399 3366
Palm Jebel Ali, The	Jebel Ali	1-A1	390 3333
Palm Jumeirah, The	Al Sufouh 1	14-J1	390 3333
Springs, The	Emirates Hills 3	29-D7	399 3366
Za'abeel Park	Za'abeel 1	39-C1	-

SHOPPING

Malls

Al Ain Centre	Mankhool	24-J5	352 1099
Al Bustan Centre	Al Twar 1	43-A7	263 0000
Al Ghurair City	Al Muraqqabat	25-C7	223 2333

Al Hamriya Shopping Complex	Hor Al Anz East	26-K9	-
Al Hana Centre	Al Satwa	23-A5	398 2229
Al Karama Shopping Complex	Al Karama	39-F1	-
Al Khaleej Centre	Al Souk Al Kabeer	24-H5	355 8590
Al Mamzar Centre	Al Mamzar	43-A3	295 6699
Al Manal Centre	Naif	25-A4	227 7701
Al Mulla Plaza	Al Qusais 1	43-A4	298 8999
Al Qusais Shopping Complex	Al Qusais 1	51-A1	-
Al Rais Centre	Mankhool	24-H5	352 7755
Beach Centre, The	Jumeira 1	22-G3	344 9045
Bin Sougat Centre	Al Rashidiya	57-F1	286 3000
Bur Juman Centre	Mankhool	24-J7	352 0222
Center, The	Al Muteena	25-E9	269 3155
Century Plaza	Jumeira 1	22-G3	349 8062
Deira City Centre Mall	Al Garhoud	41-B4	295 4545
Dune Centre	Al Bada'a	22-M5	345 5042
Emirates Towers Boulevard	Trade Centre 2	31-J1	330 0000
Galleria Shopping Mall	Al Shindagha	25-C3	209 6000
Gold & Diamond Park	Al Quoz Industrial 3	17-A9	347 7788
Hamarain Centre	Al Muraqqabat	41-E1	262 1110
Holiday Centre Shopping Mall	Trade Centre 1	22-K8	331 7755
Jumeira Centre	Jumeira 1	22-J3	349 9702
Jumeira Plaza Mall	Jumeira 1	22-H3	349 7111
Lamcy Plaza	Oud Metha	39-F3	335 9999
Magrudy Shopping Mall	Jumeira 1	22-J3	344 4192
Mazaya Centre	Trade Centre 1	21-D9	343 8333
Mercato	Jumeira 1	21-D4	344 4161
Oasis Centre	Al Quoz	19-C8	339 5459
Spinneys Centre	Al Safa 2	19-A5	321 2225
Town Centre	Jumeira 1	21-C4	344 0111
Twin Towers	Al Rigga	25-A6	221 8833
Wafi City	Umm Hurair 2	39-F6	324 4555
Warba Centre	Al Muraqqabat	41-E1	266 6376

Market

Abattoir & Cattle Market	Al Qusais Ind 2	52-H2
Al Shindagha Market	Al Shindagha	24-J2
Deira Old Souq	Al Buteen	24-M3
Fish, Meat & Vegetable Market – Deira	Al Shindagha	25-A2
Wholesale Fruit & Vegetable Market – Ras Al Khor	Ras Al Khor Industrial 3	63-E4

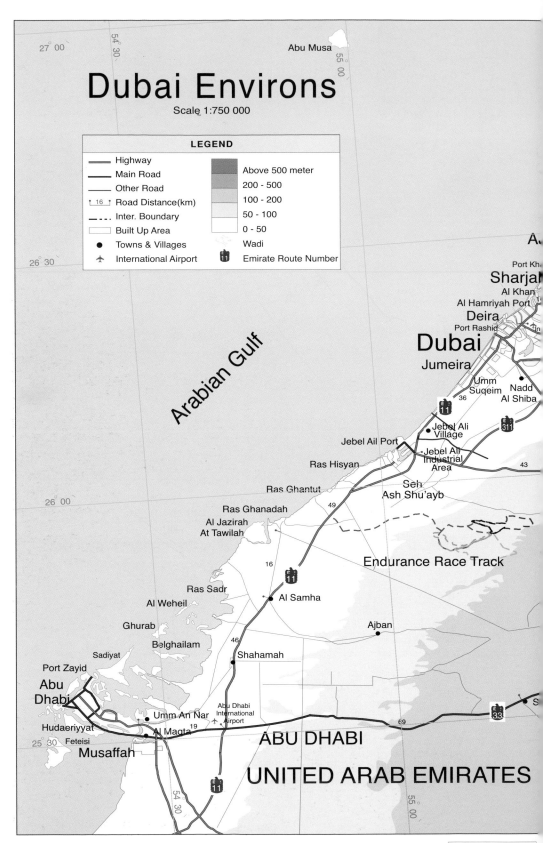

Dubai Environs

Scale 1:750 000

LEGEND

——	Highway		Above 500 meter
——	Main Road		200 - 500
—	Other Road		100 - 200
↑ 16 ↑	Road Distance(km)		50 - 100
— · — ·	Inter. Boundary		0 - 50
▢	Built Up Area		
●	Towns & Villages		Wadi
✈	International Airport	🏛	Emirate Route Number

Abu Musa

Arabian Gulf

Port Kh.
Sharja
Al Khan
Al Hamriyah Port
Deira
Port Rashid
Dubai
Jumeira
Umm
Suqeim   Nadd
Al Shiba
36
Jebel Ali
Village
Jebel Ail Port
Jebel Ali
Industrial
Area
Ras Hisyan
43
Seh
Ash Shu'ayb
Ras Ghantut
49
Ras Ghanadah
Al Jazirah
At Tawilah
16
Endurance Race Track
Ras Sadr
Al Weheil
Al Samha
Ghurab
Ajban
Belghailam
46
Sadiyat   Shahamah
Port Zayid
**Abu
Dhabi**
Umm An Nar
Hudaeriyyat
Abu Dhabi
International
Airport
25 30 Feteisi
Al Magta 19
Musaffah
ABU DHABI
33   S

UNITED ARAB EMIRATES

27 00
54 30
55 00
26 30
26 00
54 30
55 00

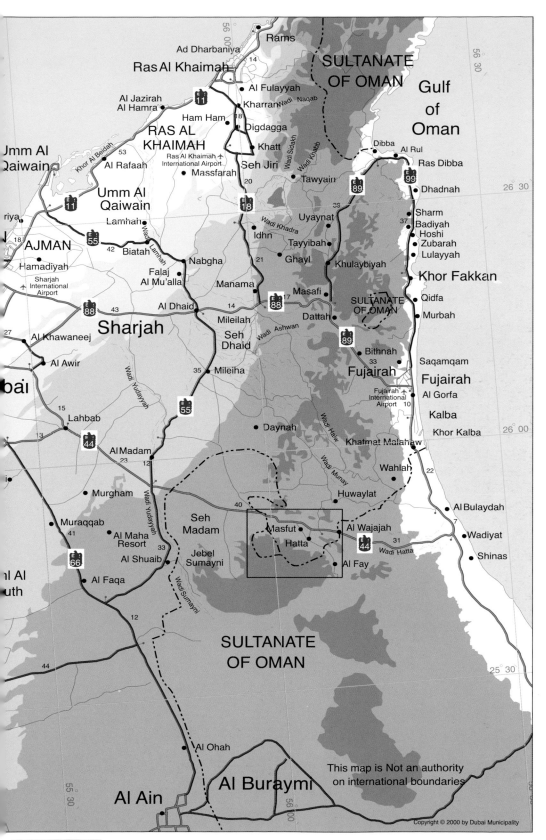

Rams

Ad Dharbaniya

Ras Al Khaimah

SULTANATE
OF OMAN

Gulf
of
Oman

Al Fulayyah

14

Al Jazirah
Al Hamra

Kharran   Wadi Naqab

Ham Ham

RAS AL
KHAIMAH

18

Digdagga

Dibba   Al Rul

Ras Dibba

Khatt

26 30

Dhadnah

Umm Al
Qaiwain

53

Khor Al Beidah

Al Rafaah

Ras Al Khaimah ✈
International Airport

Seh Jiri

Massfarah

20

Tawyain

89

E
99

Sharm

Badiyah
Hoshi

Zubarah

Lulayyah

E
11

Umm Al
Qaiwain

Lamhah

Idhn

Uyaynat

18

Wadi Khadra

Tayyibah

33

37

riya

18

E
55

AJMAN

42   Biatah

Nabgha

21

Ghayl

Khulaybiyah

Khor Fakkan

Hamadiyah

Sharjah ✈
International
Airport

Falaj
Al Mu'alla

Wadi Lamhah

Manama

Masafi

88

17

SULTANATE
OF OMAN

Qidfa

Murbah

27

E
88

43

Al Dhaid

14

Sharjah

Mileilah

Dattah

89

Bithnah

Al Khawaneej

Seh
Dhaid

Wadi Ashwan

33

Saqamqam

Al Awir

35

Mileiha

Fujairah

Fujairah

bai

E
55

Lahbab

15

Daynah

Wadi Halw

Fujairah ✈
International
Airport 10

Al Gorfa

Kalba

Khor Kalba

26 00

13

44

Al Madam

23   12

Wadi Yudayyah

Khatmat Malahaw

Wadi Munay

Wahlah

22

Murgham

40

Huwaylat

Al Bulaydah

7

Muraqqab

41

Seh
Madam

Masfut

Al Wajajah

Wadiyat

Al Maha
Resort

33

Jebel
Sumayni

Hatta

44

31   Wadi Hatta

Shinas

E
66

Al Shuaib

Al Fay

Al Faqa

Wadi Sumayni

12

SULTANATE
OF OMAN

44

l Al
uth

Al Ohah

This map is Not an authority
on international boundaries

Al Buraymi

Al Ain

25 30

55 30

56 00

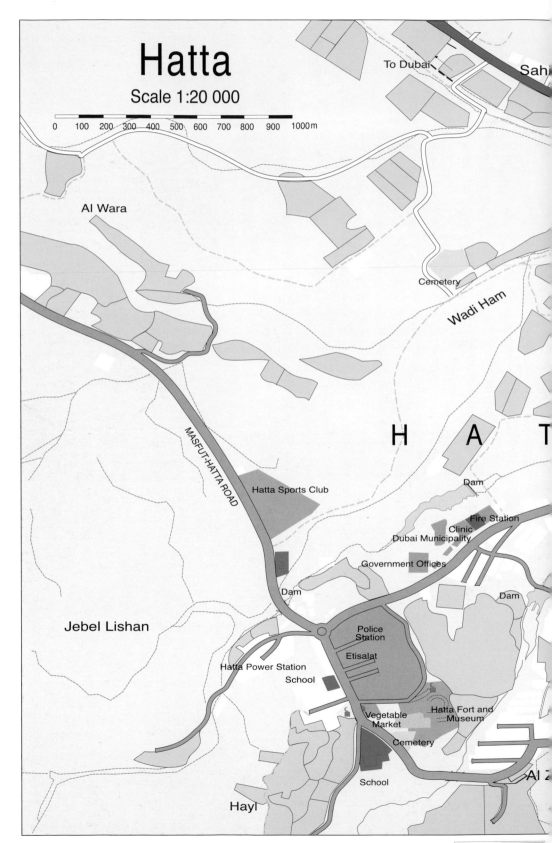

Hatta

Scale 1:20 000

0 100 200 300 400 500 600 700 800 900 1000m

To Dubai

Sah

Al Wara

Cemetery

Wadi Ham

H A T

MASFUT-HATTA ROAD

Hatta Sports Club

Dam

Fire Station

Clinic

Dubai Municipality

Government Offices

Dam

Dam

Jebel Lishan

Police Station

Etisalat

Hatta Power Station

School

Vegetable Market

Hatta Fort and Museum

Cemetery

School

Al Z

Hayl

To Huwaylat

Hatta Fort Hotel

To Sultanate
of Oman

Dam

Al Harawa

T   A

Wadi Hatta

Dam

Wadi Abu Suh

Camp Site

Wadi Jeemah

a

Jeemah

To Jeemah

STREET MAP EXPLORER

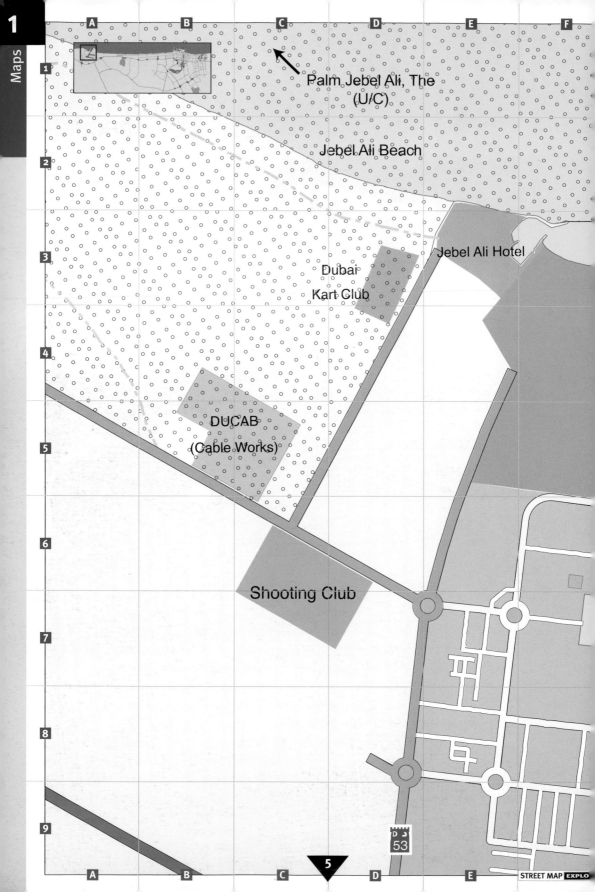

Palm Jebel Ali, The
(U/C)

Jebel Ali Beach

Jebel Ali Hotel

Dubai
Kart Club

DUCAB
(Cable Works)

Shooting Club

53

1

2

JEBEL ALI HARBOUR

3

4

5

Marine
Control
Tower

6

3

7

8

Jebel Ali
Free Zone

9

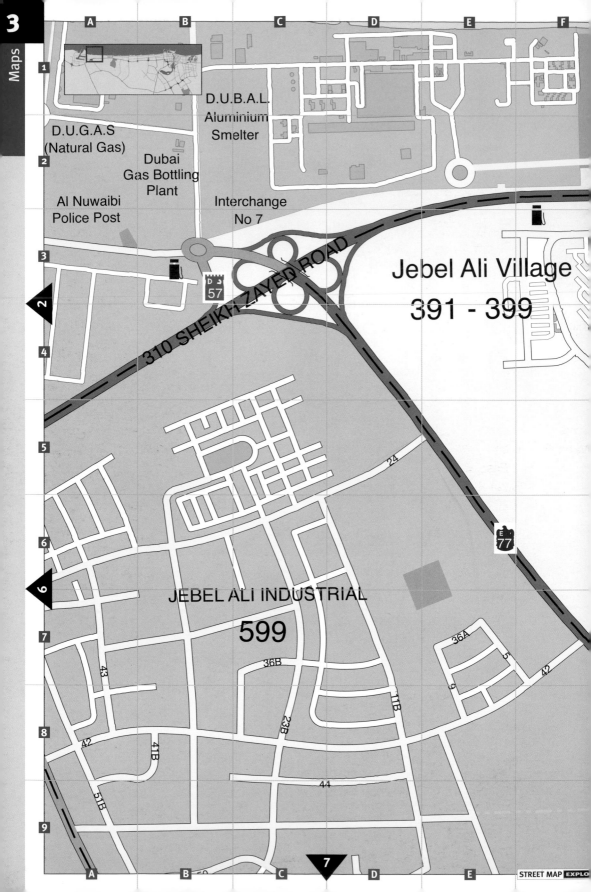

D.E.W.A Steam
Power Station

Sheraton
Jumeirah Beach

Jebel Ali
Interchange
No 6

310 SHEIKH ZAYED ROAD 11

Gardens Mall
(U/C)

Jebel Ali
School

The Gardens

59

Clinic

Jumeirah
Islands
(U/C)

Jebel Ali
Water Reservoir

Etisalat
Earth Station

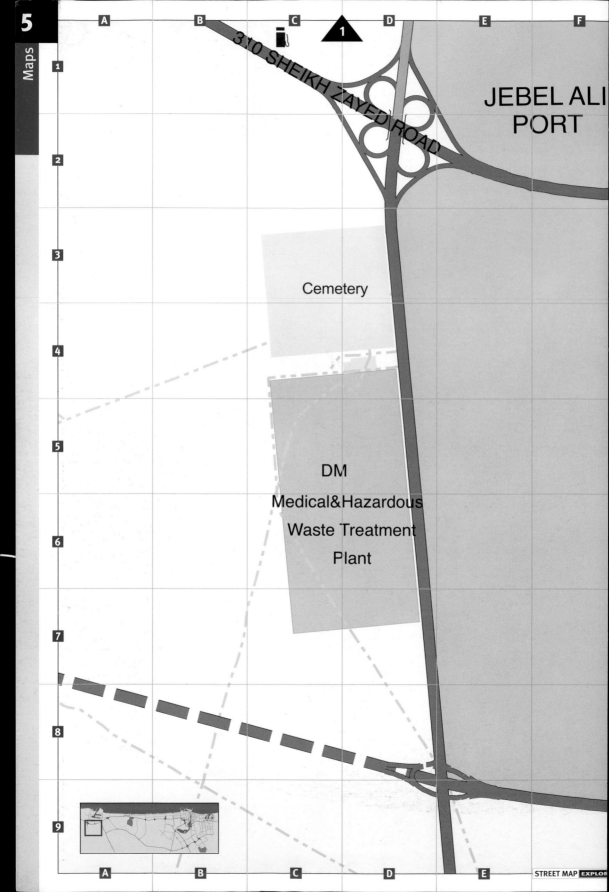

310 SHEIKH ZAYED ROAD

JEBEL ALI
PORT

Cemetery

DM

Medical&Hazardous

Waste Treatment

Plant

JEBEL ALI

511 - 519

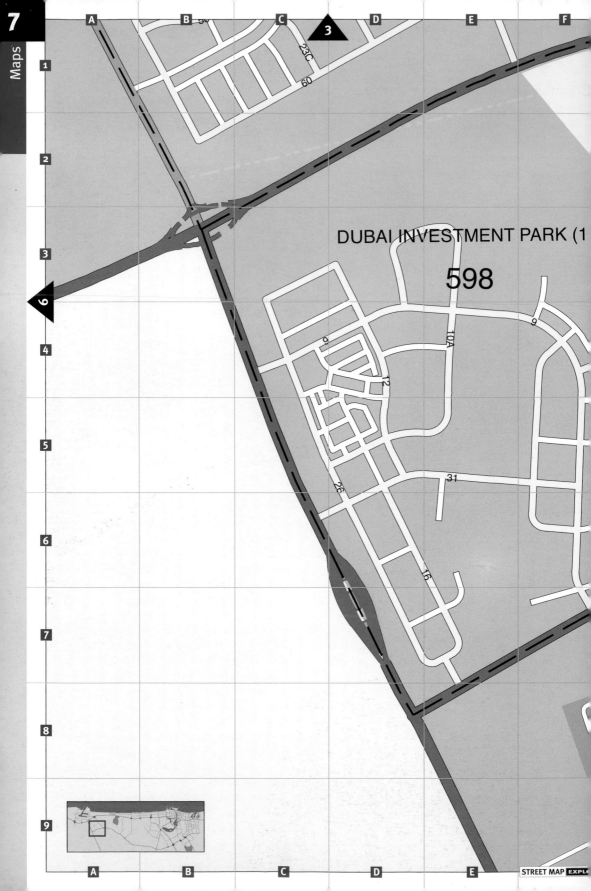

DUBAI INVESTMENT PARK (1

598

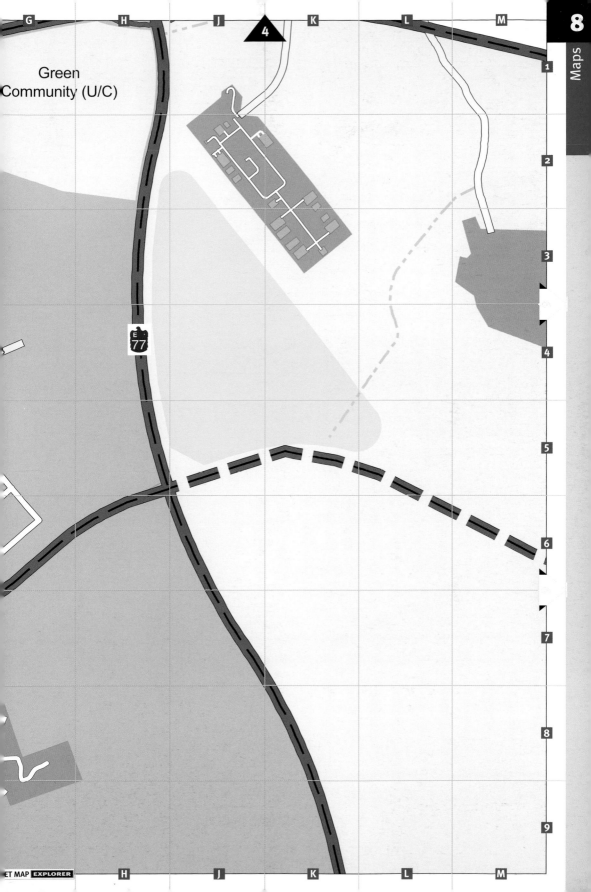

Green
Community (U/C)

E 77

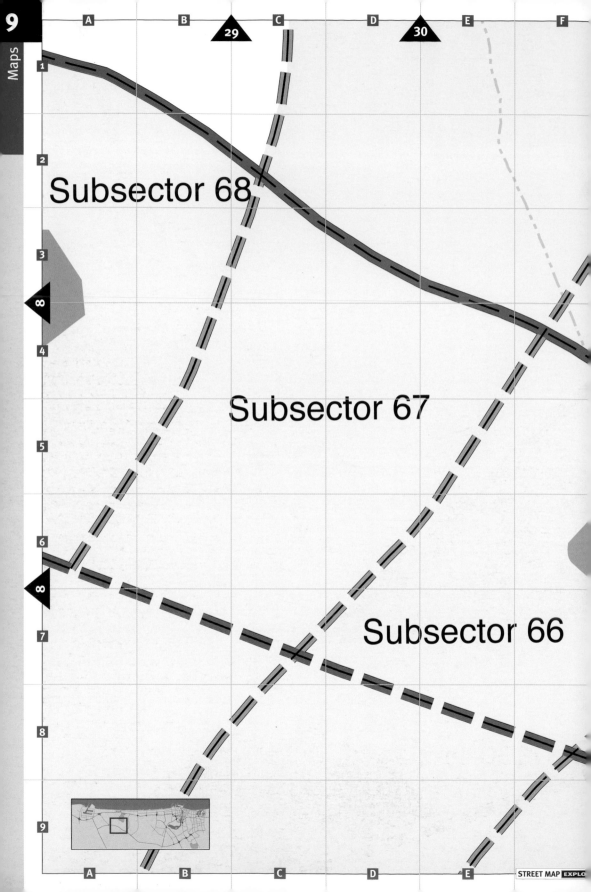

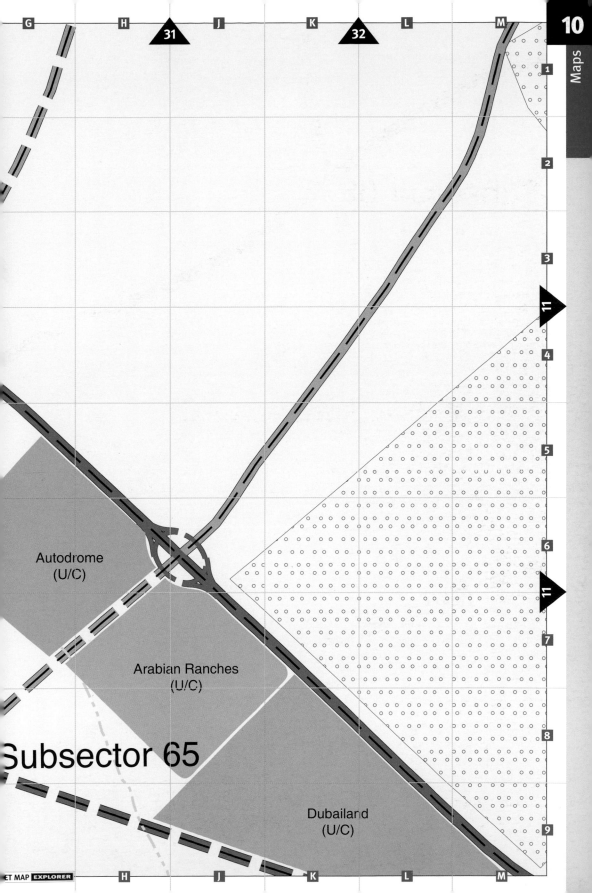

Autodrome
(U/C)

Arabian Ranches
(U/C)

Subsector 65

Dubailand
(U/C)

CONSERVATION AREA

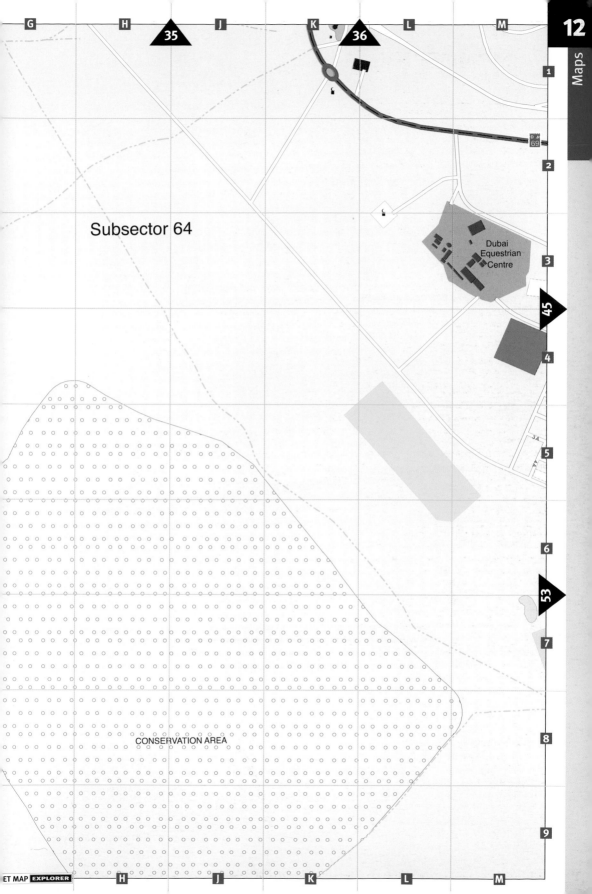

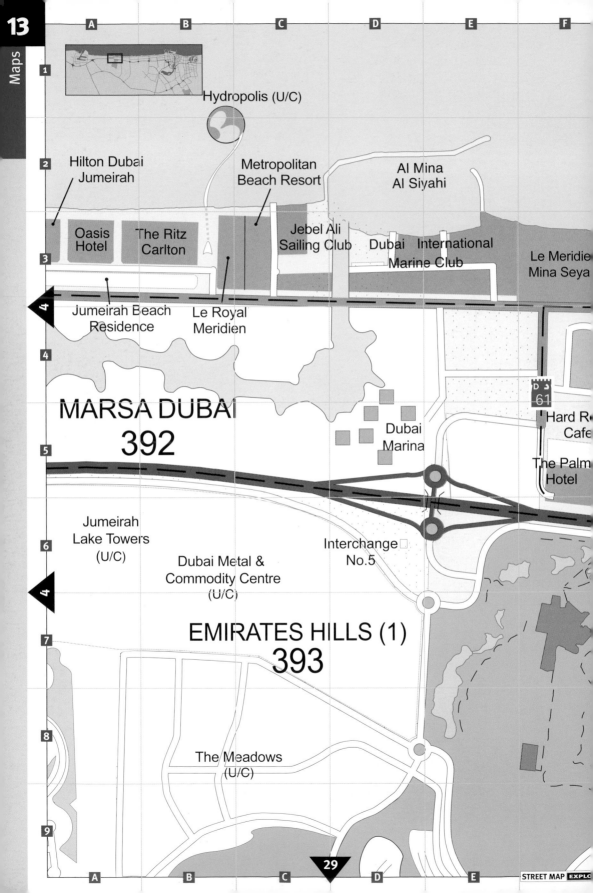

Hydropolis (U/C)

Hilton Dubai
Jumeirah

Metropolitan
Beach Resort

Al Mina
Al Siyahi

Oasis
Hotel

The Ritz
Carlton

Jebel Ali
Sailing Club

Dubai   International
Marine Club

Le Meridie
Mina Seya

Jumeirah Beach
Residence

Le Royal
Meridien

MARSA DUBAI
392

Dubai
Marina

Hard R
Cafe

The Palm
Hotel

Jumeirah
Lake Towers
(U/C)

Dubai Metal &
Commodity Centre
(U/C)

Interchange
No.5

EMIRATES HILLS (1)
393

The Meadows
(U/C)

61

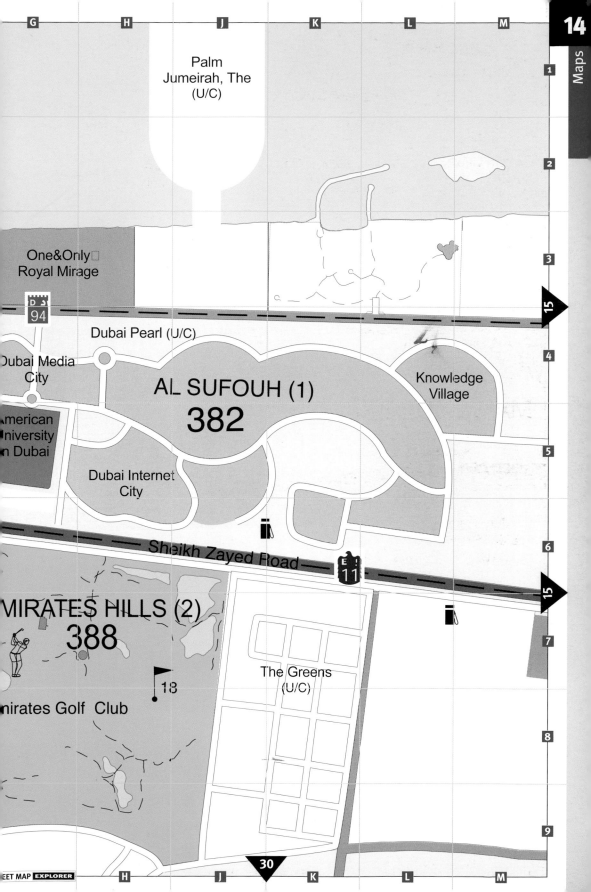

G H J K L M

1

2

3

4

5

6

7

8

9

15

15

Palm
Jumeirah, The
(U/C)

One&Only
Royal Mirage

D 3
94

Dubai Pearl (U/C)

Dubai Media
City

AL SUFOUH (1)
382

Knowledge
Village

American
University
n Dubai

Dubai Internet
City

Sheikh Zayed Road

E
11

MIRATES HILLS (2)
388

The Greens
(U/C)

18

mirates Golf Club

30

H J K L M

A B C D E F

1

2

3

14

302

D 94

4

Dubai College

2B
41
4B
37
43
35
33A
6D
39
6C
8

19

5

33B

AL SUFOUH (2)

372

331

23

6

14

7

Desert Spring Village

15

13

8

45A
45B
2C
37A
43A
37B
8D
35A
33A
47
41
39A
39A
2B
4C
27A
8C
6 B
31

9

14C
43B
22D
39B
35B
33A
12D
14B
31
12C
10B
29A
8B
25A

A B C D E

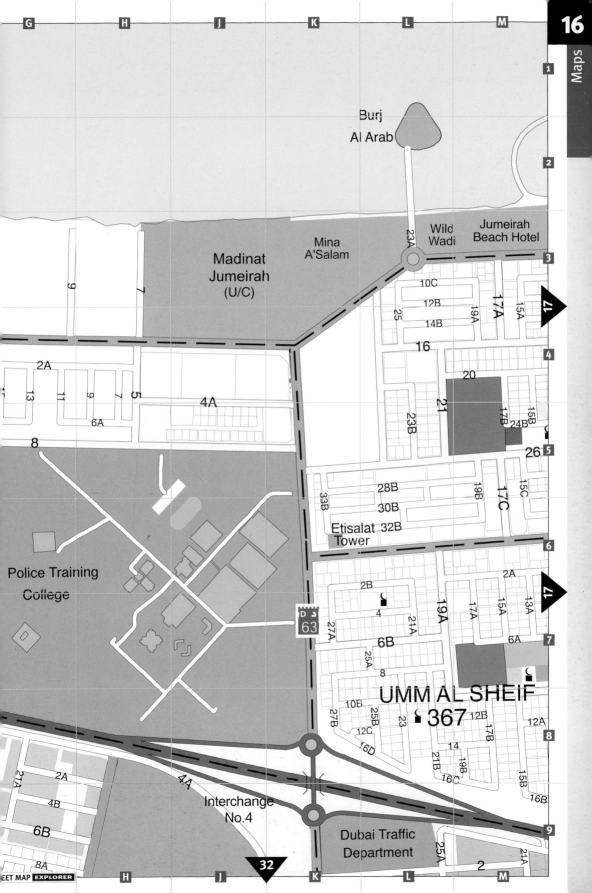

Burj
Al Arab

Mina
A'Salam

Madinat
Jumeirah
(U/C)

Wild
Wadi

Jumeirah
Beach Hotel

23A

3

10C

12B

14B

25

17A

19A

15A

17C

16

20

21

23B

17B

15B

24B

2A

13

11

9

7

5

6A

4A

8

26

5

28B

30B

32B

33B

Etisalat
Tower

17C

15C

19B

6

Police Training
College

2B

4

6B

8

21A

19A

27A

25A

17A

15A

13A

6A

2A

17

7

DJ
63

UMM AL SHEIF
367

10B

27B

12C

25B

23

16D

12B

17B

12A

8

Interchange
No.4

4A

14

21B

19B

16C

15B

16B

2A

4B

6B

8A

21A

Dubai Traffic
Department

25A

2

21A

9

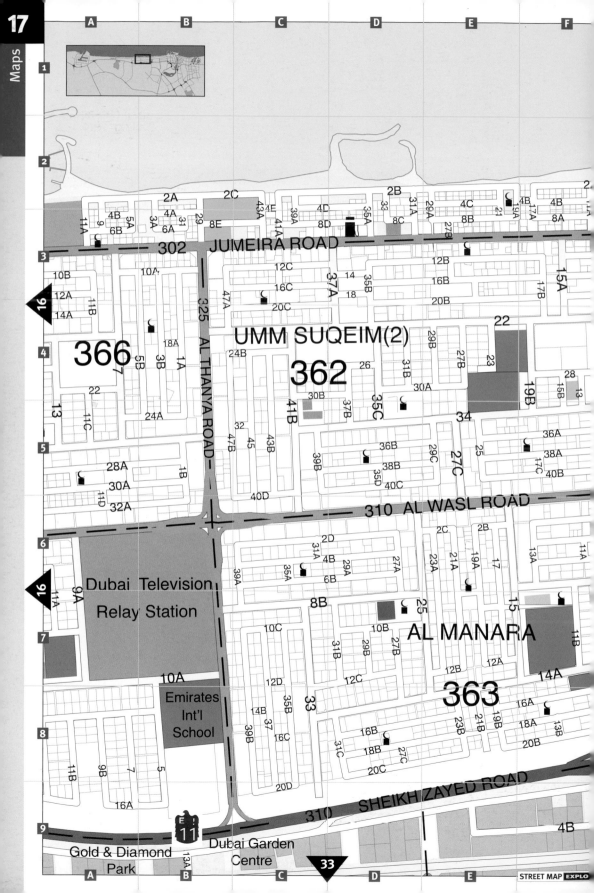

Dubai Offshore
Sailing Club

JUMEIRA ROAD

UMM SUQEIM(1)

356

Cemetery

310 AL WASL ROAD

Cemetery

AL SAFA(2)

357

SHEIKH ZAYED ROAD

INTERCHANGE
No.3

34

A B C D E F

JUMEIRA ROAD

JUMEIRA(3)

352

317 UMM AL SHEIF STREET

Cemetery

Romania
Consulate

310 AL WASL ROAD

Park N Shop

Spinneys
Centre

AL SAFA(1)

353

Jumeira
English
Speaking
School

Tyre Express

SHEIKH ZAYED ROAD

Ace
Hardware

Oasis
Centre

Khaleej
Times

Al Futtaim Motors
Showroom

Cemetery

Cemetery

STREET MAP EXPLO

35

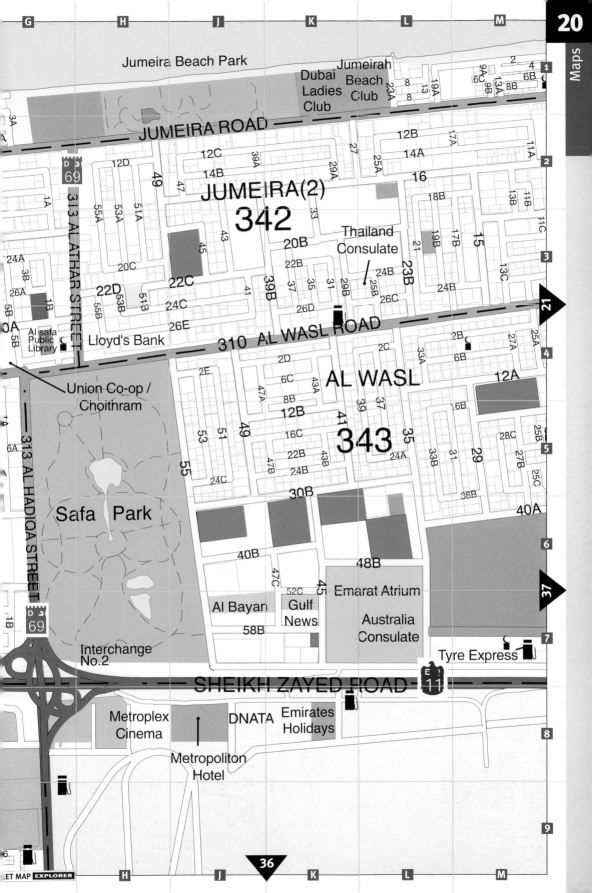

Jumeira Beach Park

Dubai Ladies Club

Jumeirah Beach Club

JUMEIRA ROAD

JUMEIRA(2) 342

Thailand Consulate

310 AL WASL ROAD

Lloyd's Bank

Al Safa Public Library

Union Co-op / Choithram

AL WASL 343

Safa Park

313 AL ATHAR STREET

313 AL HADIQA STREET

Interchange No.2

40B

Al Bayan

Gulf News

Emarat Atrium

Australia Consulate

Tyre Express

SHEIKH ZAYED ROAD

E 11

Metroplex Cinema

DNATA

Emirates Holidays

Metropoliton Hotel

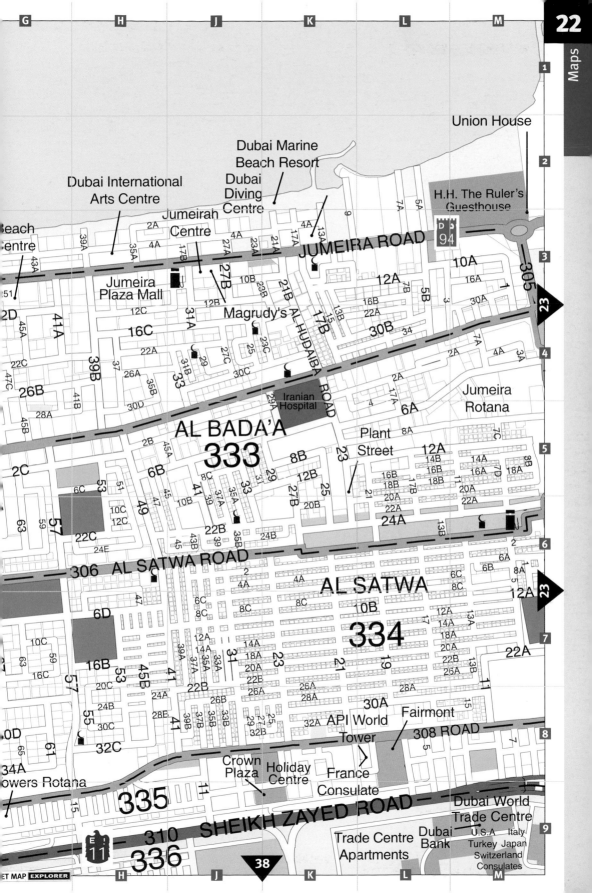

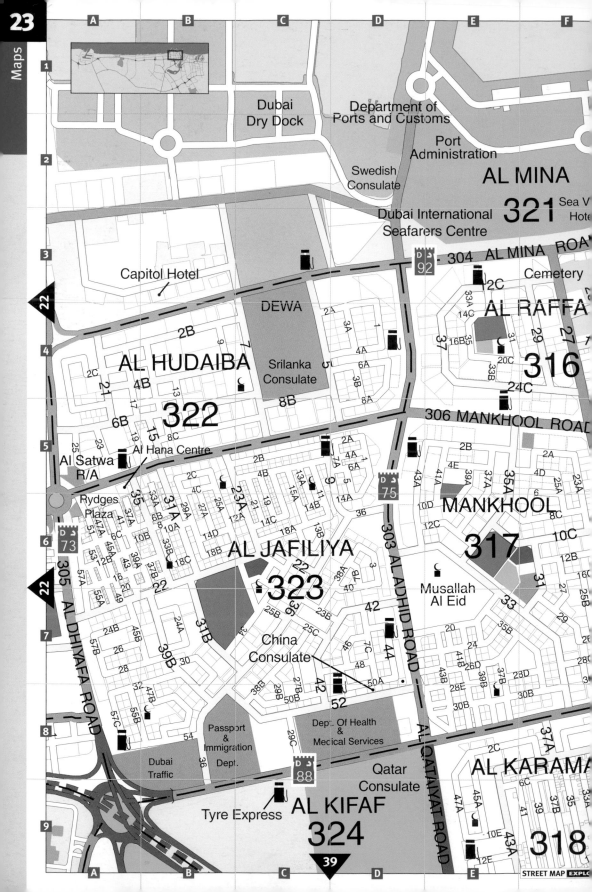

Dubai ↑
Maritime City
(U/C)

Coaster
Berth

AL SHINDAGHA

304 AL KHALEEJ ROAD

24 AL GHUBAIBA ST

Al Shindagha
Market

Al Shindagha
Tunnel

Sheikh Saeed
Al Maktoum House

311

Highland
Hotel

Palm Beach
Rotana Hotel

Sea Shell
Inn

10A

**AL SOUK
AL KABEER**

Vasantam Hotel

Norway
Consulate

HSBC
Bank

10 AL KHOR ST

**AL
RAS**

112

106 SIKKAT AL KHAIL ST

Deira Old
Souk

Cemetery

Dallas
Hotel

Ascot
Hotel

Imperial
Suites

24B

312

44B

Dubai
Museum

Ministry of
Defence

AL BUTEEN

114

115

AL
SABKHA

Middle East
Bank

Emirates Bank
International

Heritage
International Hotel

Al Khaleej
Centre

Al Rais
Centre

Al Fahidi
R/A

90

Ramada
Hotel

Spinneys

Al Ain Centre

Golden
Sands

Commercial
Bank of Dubai

ABN Amro
Bank

Regal
Plaza

Al Mussala
Towers

AL HAMRIYA

Four Points
Sheraton

313

Cemetery

British
Embassy

DUBAI CREEK

AL SEEF ROAD

12A

Netherland
Consulate

Canadian
Consulate

Habib
Bank Ltd

**Bur Juman
Centre**

Spinneys

88

ADE CENTRE ROAD

Regent Palace
Hotel

79 **UMM HURAIR (1)** 4

84

Dept. Of
Health

Jordanian
Consulate

German
Consulate

Egyptian
Consulate

Oman
Consulate

Saudi
Consulate

Indian
Consulate

Kuwaiti
Consulate

Lebanan
Consulate

314

Strand
Cinema

Dubai Municipality

Dhow Wharfage

40

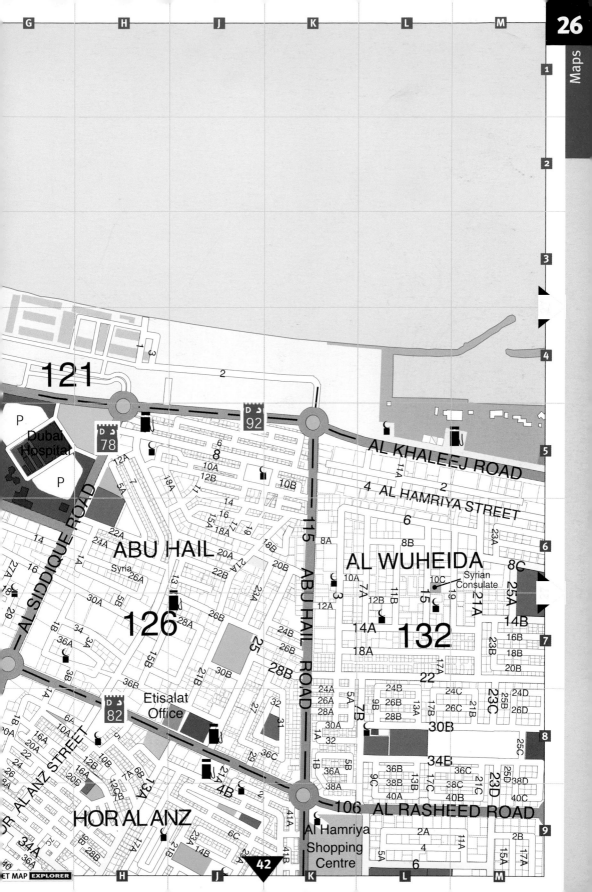

G H J K L M

1

2

3

4

5

6

7

8

9

121

Dubai
Hospital

P

P

D 78

D 92

ABU HAIL

126

AL SIDDIQUE ROAD

AL KHALEEJ ROAD

4 AL HAMRIYA STREET

AL WUHEIDA

Syrian
Consulate

132

115 ABU HAIL ROAD

Etisalat
Office

D 82

HOR AL ANZ

AL ANZ STREET

106 AL RASHEED ROAD

Al Hamriya
Shopping
Centre

42

Syria

8

8C

25A

14B

16B

18B

20B

25C

25D

23D

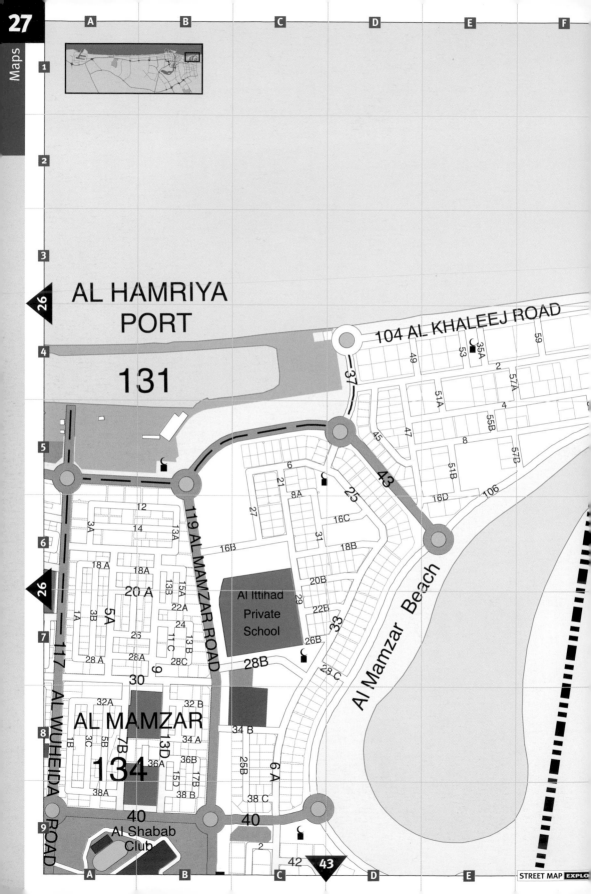

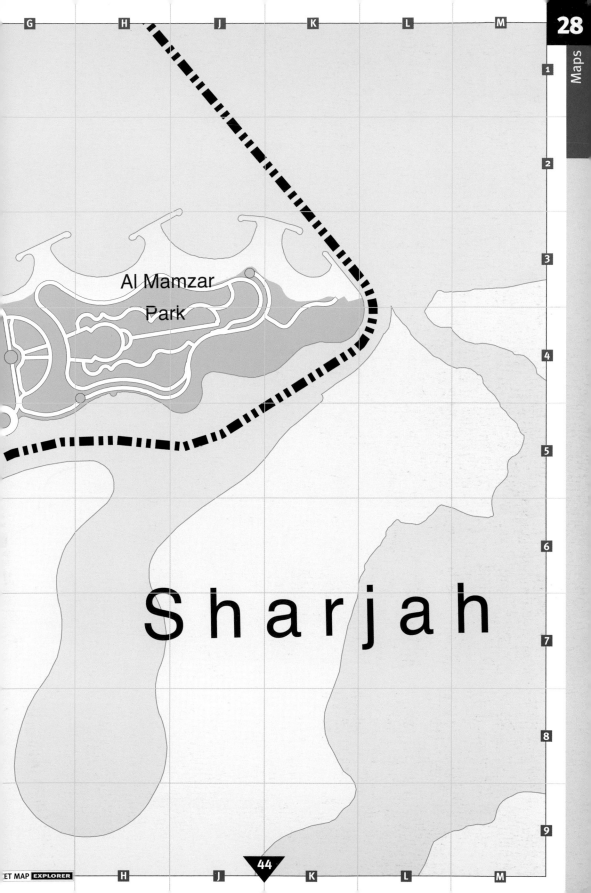

Al Mamzar
Park

S h a r j a h

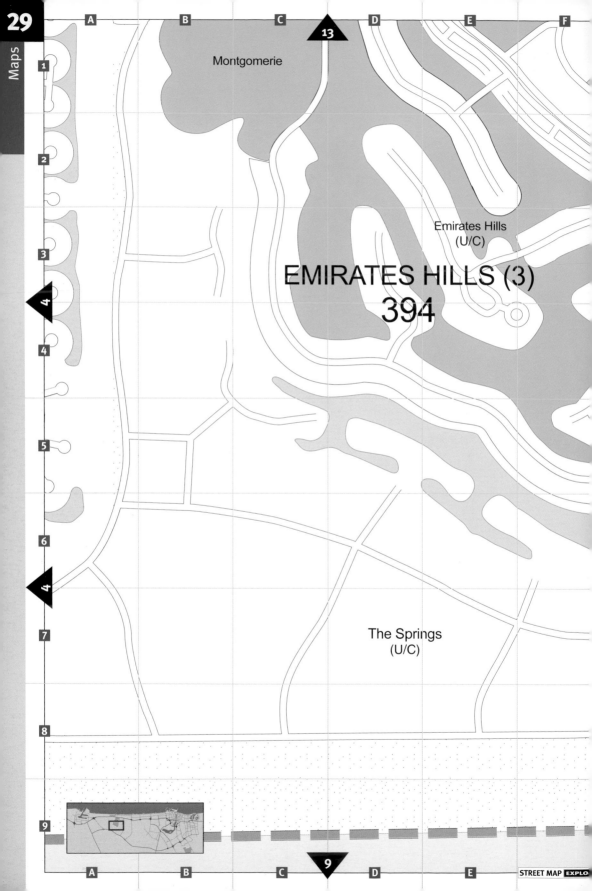

Montgomerie

Emirates Hills
(U/C)

EMIRATES HILLS (3)
394

13

The Springs
(U/C)

9

The Lakes
(U/C)

Jebel Ali Horse
Racecourse

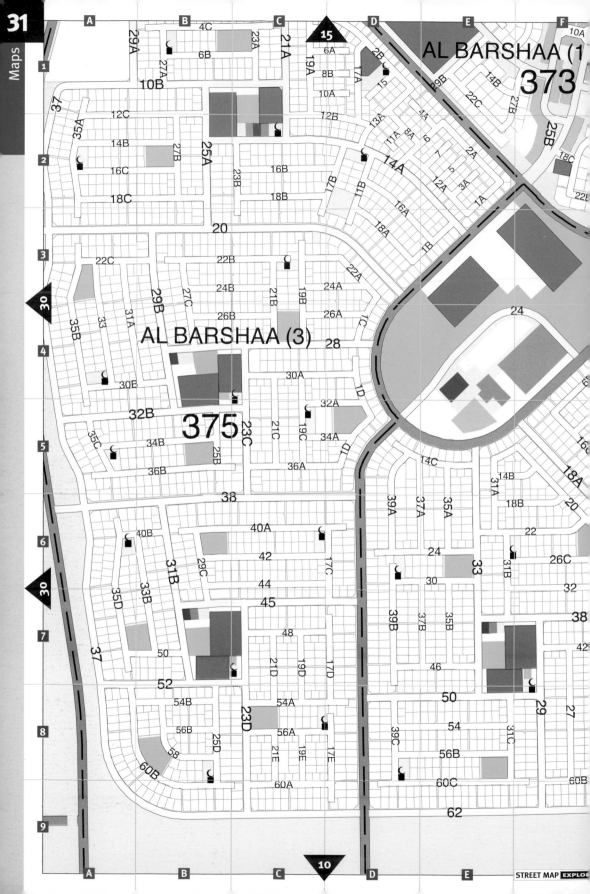

Mall of the
Emirates (U/C)

AL BARSHAA (2)

376

UMM SUQEIM ROAD

327

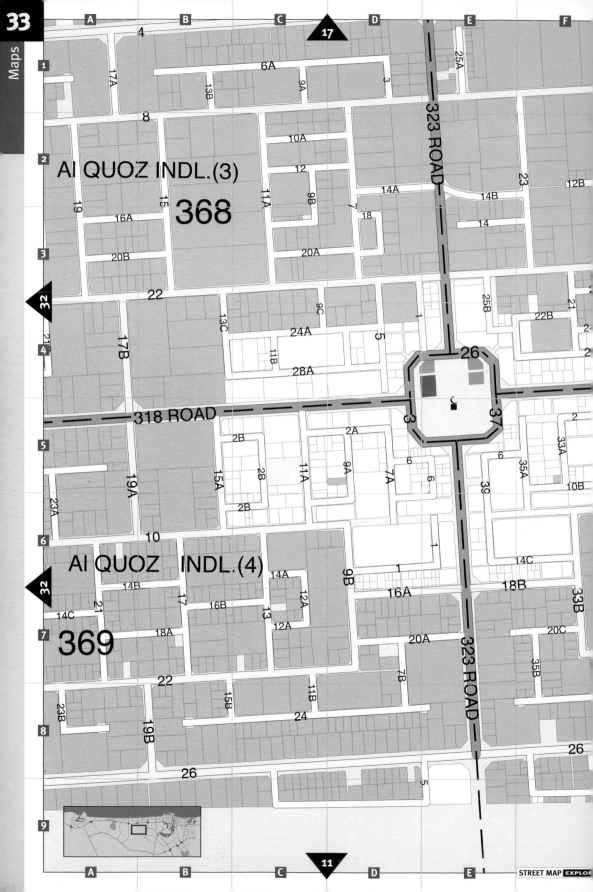

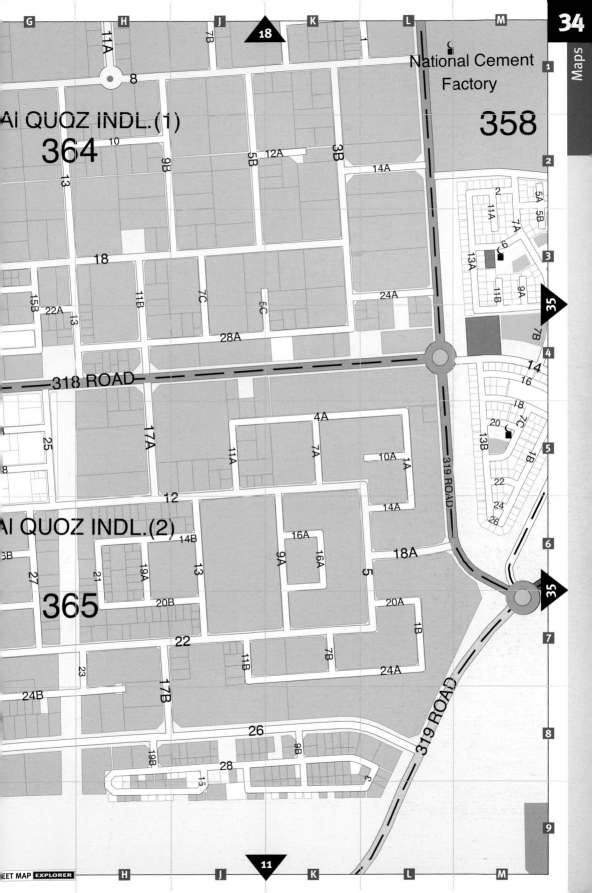

G H J K L M

11A

8

7B

18

1

National Cement
Factory

358

AI QUOZ INDL.(1)

364

10

9B

13

5B 12A 3B

14A

2
5A
11A 7A 5B

13A 6

9A

11B

7B

18

2

3

35

4

14
16

18
7C

13B 20

1B

5

22

24

26

35

6

18

11B 22A 13

15B

7C

5C

28A

318 ROAD

25

17A

11A

4A

7A

12

AI QUOZ INDL.(2)

14B

19A

20B

21

13

9A

16A

16A

10A 1A

14A

18A

319 ROAD

5

20A

1B

365

27

22

23

11B 7B 24A

24B

17B

26

19B

9B

28

15

3

319 ROAD

7

8

9

H J K L M

11

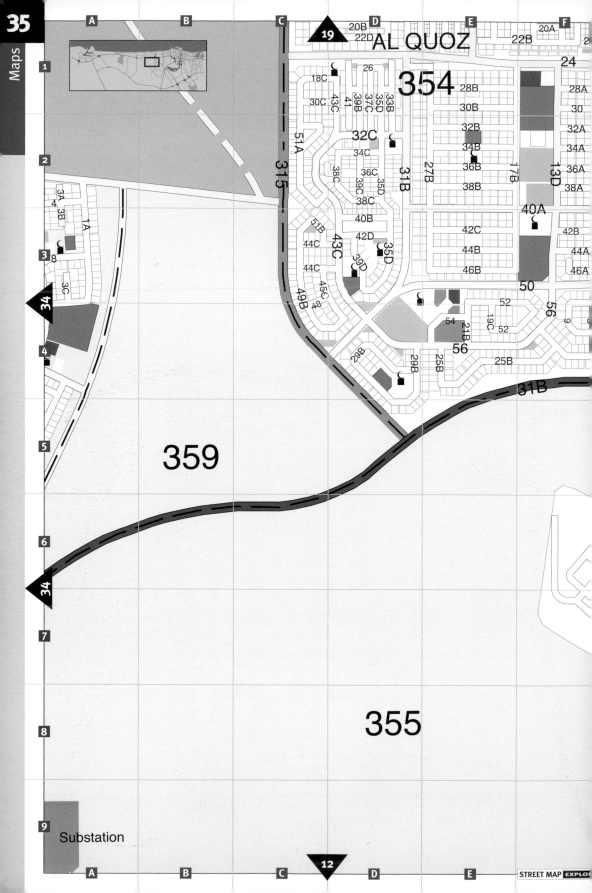

AL QUOZ

354

359

355

Substation

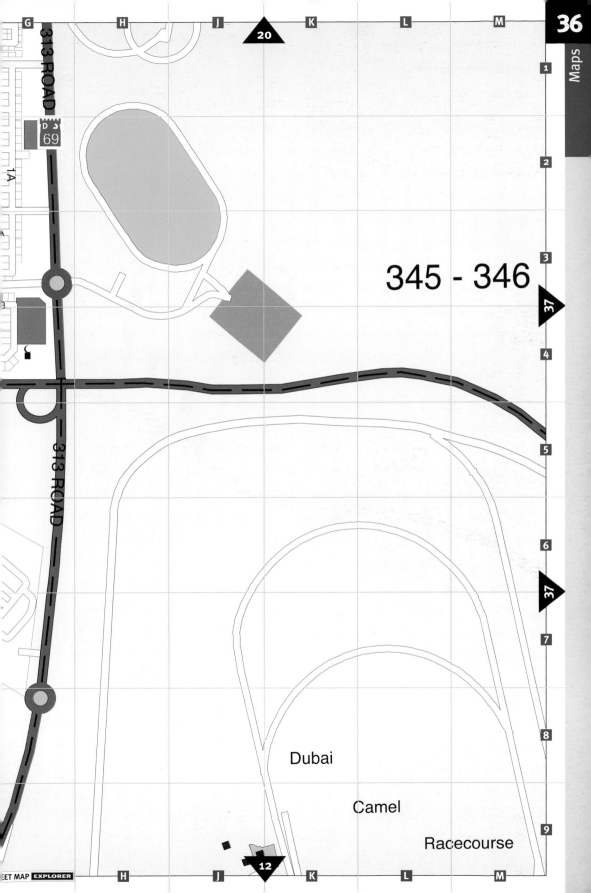

345 - 346

Dubai

Camel

Racecourse

313 ROAD

313 ROAD

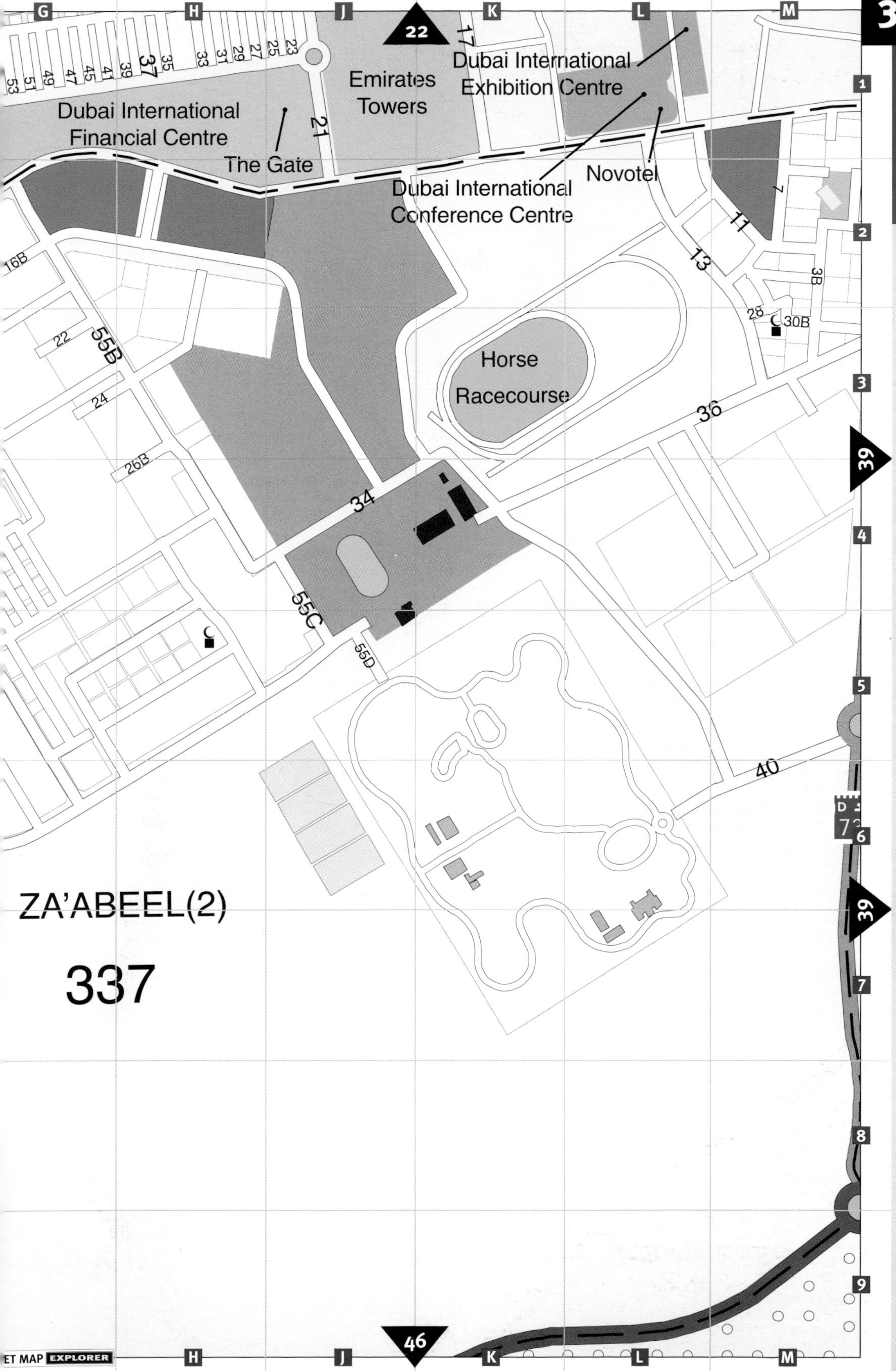

G H J K L M

53 51 49 47 45 43 41 39 37 35 33 31 29 27 25 23

22

17

1

Emirates
Towers

Dubai International
Exhibition Centre

Dubai International
Financial Centre

21

The Gate

Novotel

2

Dubai International
Conference Centre

7

11

16B

3B

13

28

30B

3

22

55B

24

Horse
Racecourse

36

39

26B

4

34

55C

36

55D

40

5

D
73

6

ZA'ABEEL(2)

39

337

7

8

9

46

H J K L M

A B C D 23 E F

1

Za'abeel Park
(U/C)

Al Karama
Shopping
Centre

47B
45B
4D
18B

47C

43B

2

Malaysi
Consula

Za'abeel
Roundabout

4A

8B

319

Larncy
Plaza

4

6

3

19A

3U5 2ND ZA'ABEEL ROAD

10

18

14 A

EPPCO

10

17A

38

20

Mövenp
Hotel

4

5

24

12B

Barcleys
Bank

303

28A

12B

ZA'ABEEL(1)

325

49

41

34A

5

17

38

158

6

Wafi
Shoppi
Mall

38

Al Wasl
Hospital

Citibank

7

E
66

9

Tyre Express

8

13

Al Wasl
Club

4

Dubai
Police Clu

5

9

A B C 47 D E

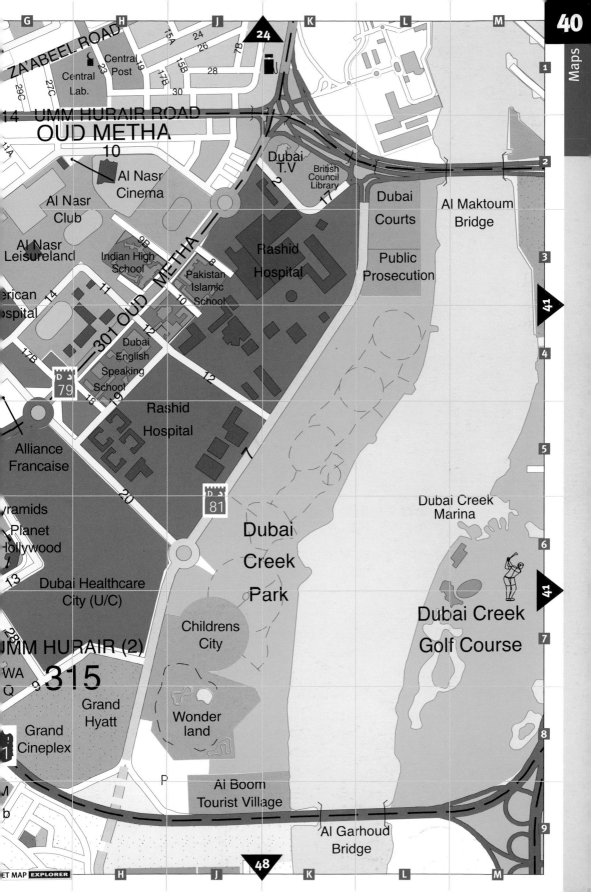

ZA'ABEEL ROAD

Central Post
Central Lab.

UMM HURAIR ROAD

OUD METHA

10

Al Nasr Cinema

Al Nasr Club

Al Nasr Leisureland

Indian High School

OUD METHA

301 OUD METHA

Pakistan Islamic School

Dubai English Speaking School

Rashid Hospital

Dubai T.V

British Council Library

Dubai Courts

Public Prosecution

Rashid Hospital

Al Maktoum Bridge

erican ospital

D 79

Alliance Francaise

D 81

ramids Planet ollywood

Dubai Healthcare City (U/C)

Dubai Creek Park

Childrens City

Dubai Creek Marina

Dubai Creek Golf Course

UMM HURAIR (2)

315

WA Q

Grand Hyatt

Wonder land

Grand Cineplex

Ai Boom Tourist Village

Al Garhoud Bridge

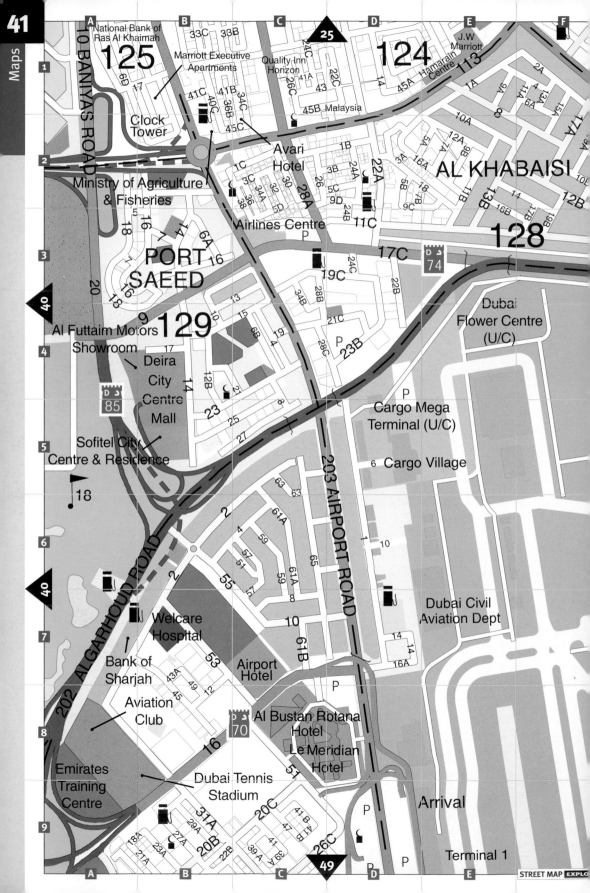

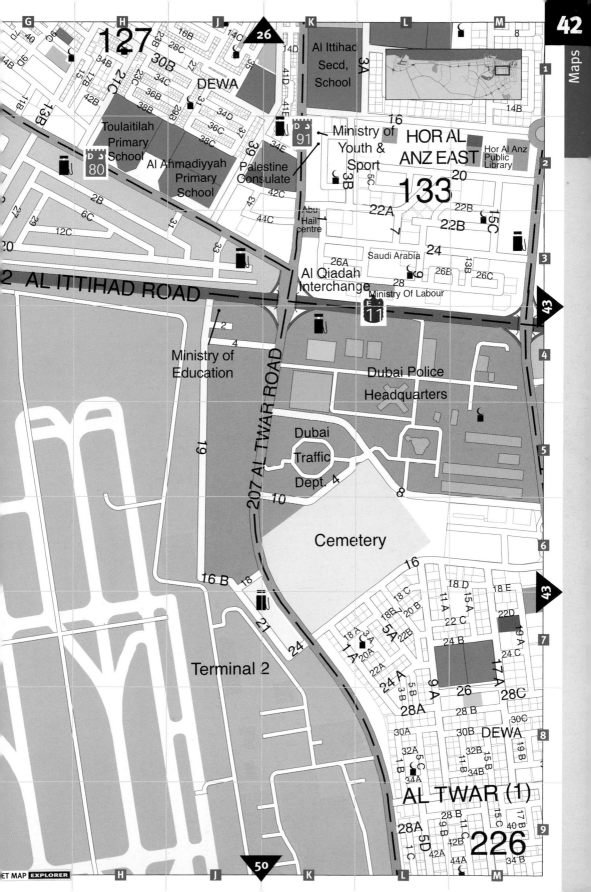

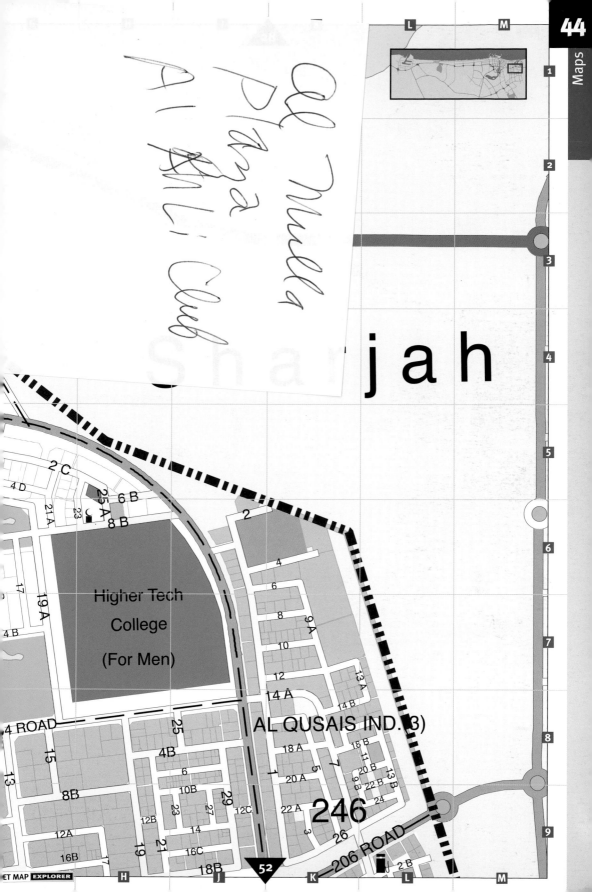

al Mulla
Plaza
Al Ahli Club

j a h

Sharjah

2 C

4 D

21 A

23

25 A

6 B

8 B

2

4

6

8

9 A

10

12

13 A

14 B

Higher Tech
College
(For Men)

17

19 A

4 B

14 A

4 ROAD

25

AL QUSAIS IND. 3)

15

4B

6

18 A

18 B

11 B

13 B

13

8B

10B

1

20 A

5

20 B

9 B

22 B

24

246

12A

12B

23

29

27

14

12C

22 A

3

26

16B

19

21

16C

18B

206 ROAD

2 B

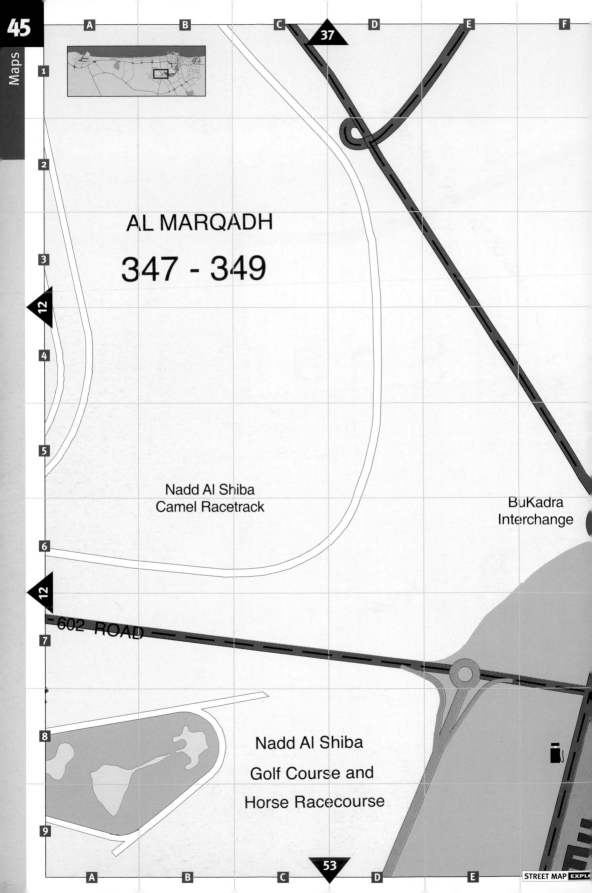

AL MARQADH

347 - 349

Nadd Al Shiba
Camel Racetrack

BuKadra
Interchange

602 ROAD

Nadd Al Shiba

Golf Course and

Horse Racecourse

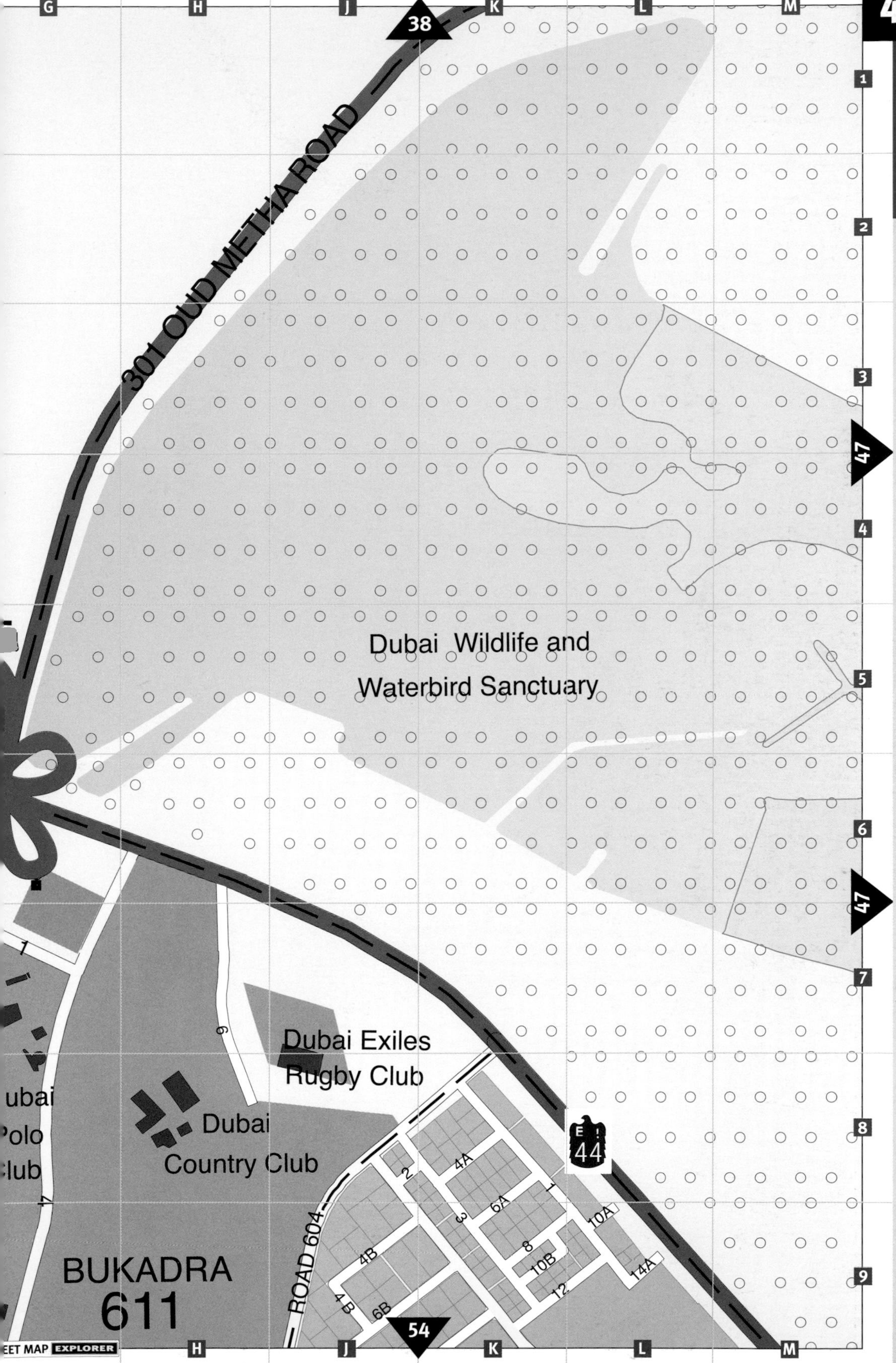
G
H
J
K
L
M
38
301 OUD METHA ROAD
1
2
3
4
5
6
7
8
9
47
47
Dubai Wildlife and
Waterbird Sanctuary
Dubai Exiles
Rugby Club
Dubai
Country Club
ubai
Polo
Club
BUKADRA
611
ROAD 604
E 44
2
4A
1
6A
3
10A
8
10B
14A
4B
12
4 B
6B
9
54

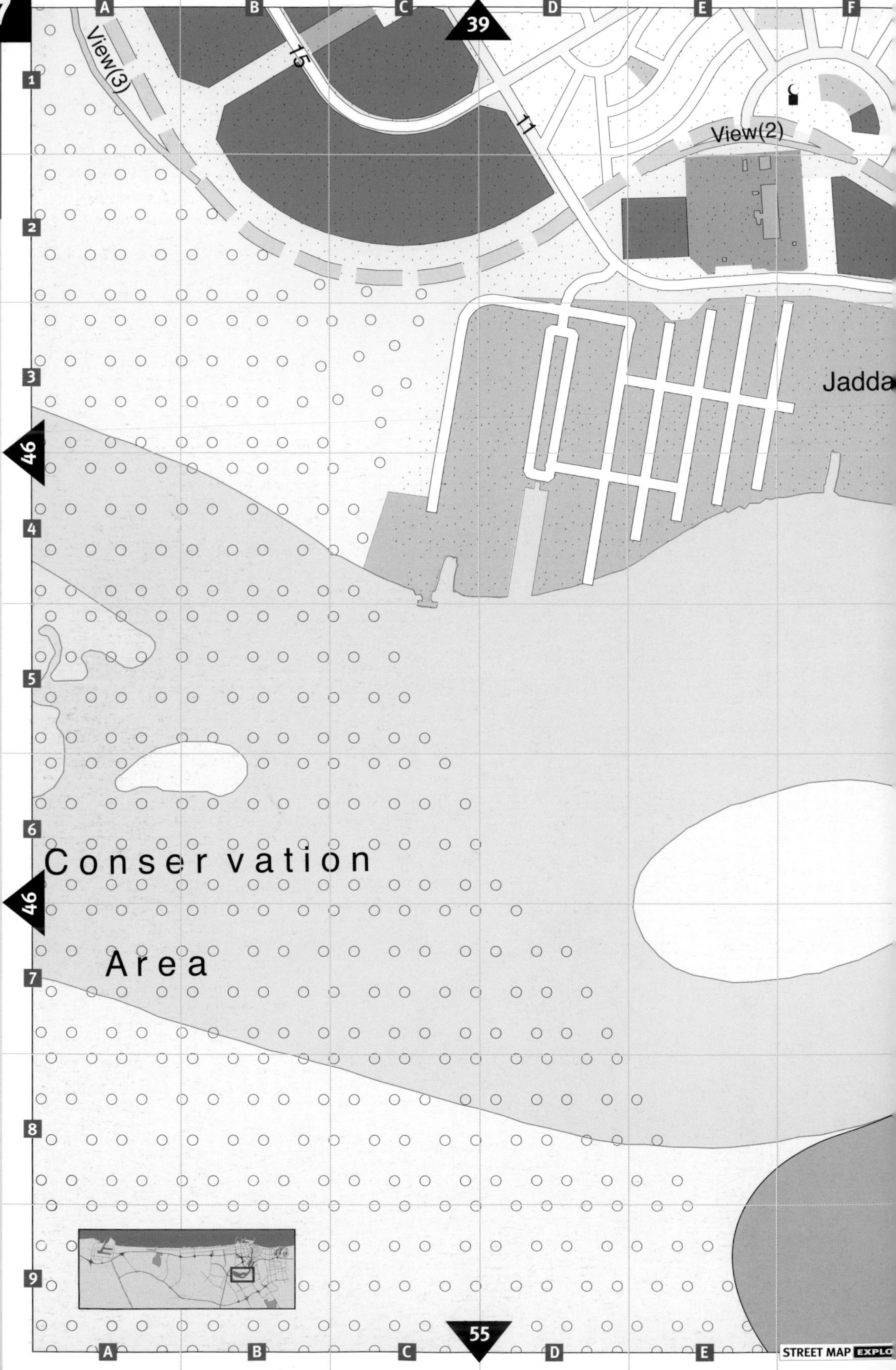

A B C D E F

1

39

View(3)

15

11

View(2)

2

3

Jadda

46

4

5

Conservation

46

7 Area

8

9

55

A B C D E

L JADDAF

26 - 329

40

49

49

Dubai Festival City
(U/C)

56

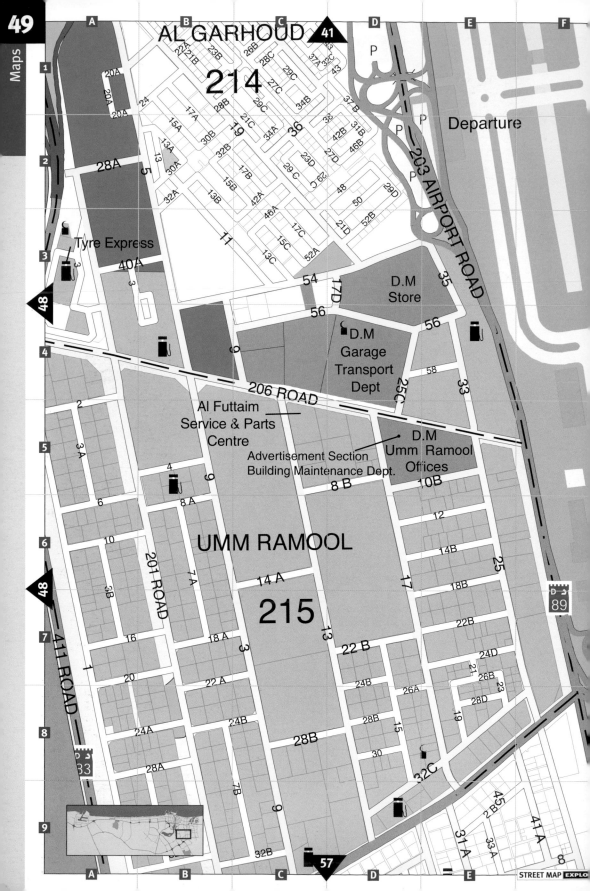

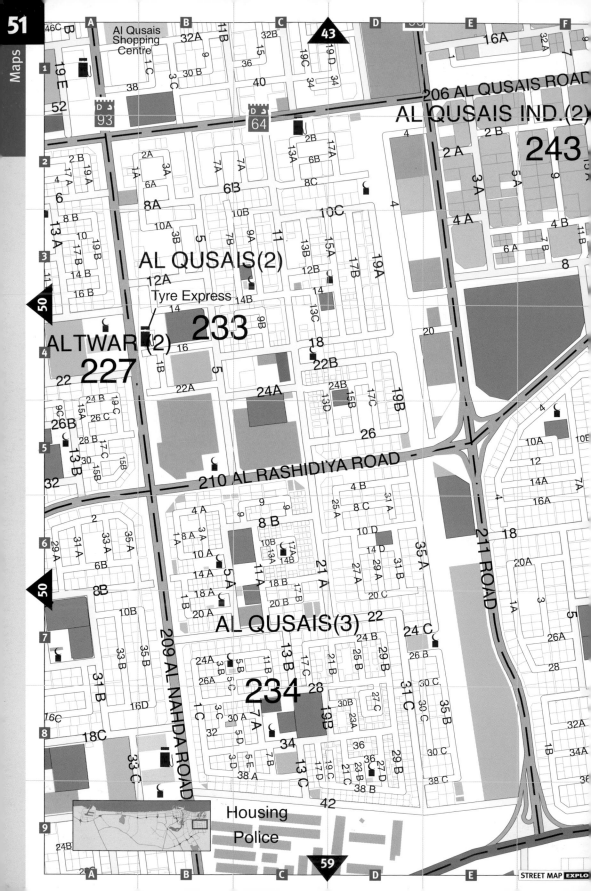

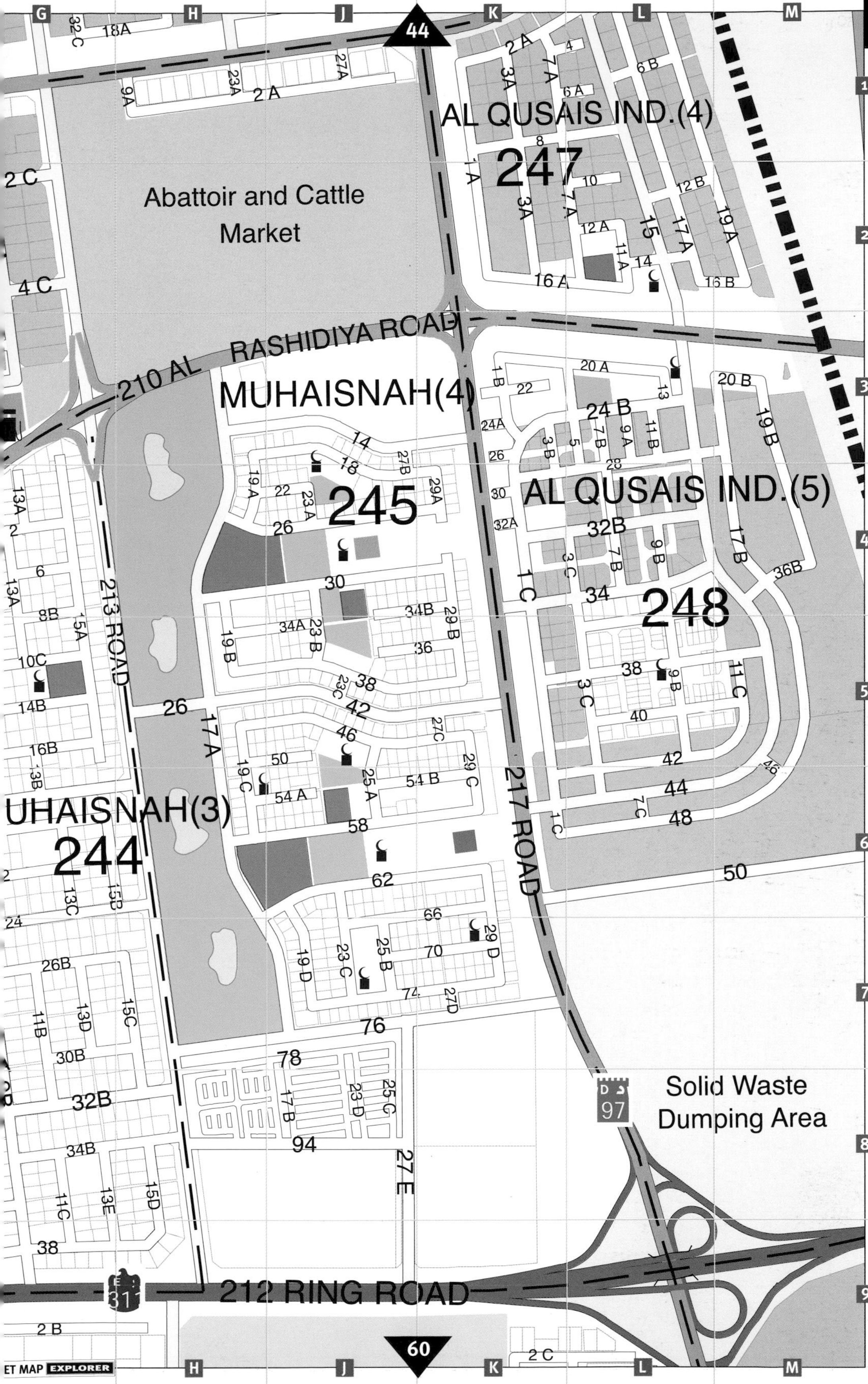

44

AL QUSAIS IND.(4)
247

G
H
J
K
L
M

32 C
18A
9A
23A
2 A
27A

2 A
3A
7 A
6 A
4
6 B

1 A
10
12 B
19 A

3A
7 A
12 A
15
17 A

16 A
11 A
14
16 B

1

2

2 C

4 C

RASHIDIYA ROAD

210 AL

MUHAISNAH(4)

1 B
22
20 A
13
20 B

24A
24 B
11 B
19 B

26
9A

30
3 B
28

32A
7 B
9 B

AL QUSAIS IND.(5)

3

14
18
27B
29A

19 A
22
23 A
245
29A

26

30
32B
34

34B
29-B

34A
23-B
36
248

13A
2

6
245

13A
8B
15A
19 B

10C
14B
38
9 B
11 C

16B
38

26
17 A
42
40

UHAISNAH(3)
244

50
46
25 A
54 B
29 C
42

19 C
54 A
44

58
48

62
50

2

24
66
70
29 D

26B
19 D
23-C
25 B
74
27 D

11B
13D
15C
76

30B

32B
78

34B
17 B
23 D
25 C
27 E

11C
13E
15D
94

38

E 31

212 RING ROAD

2 B

60

2 C

1
2
3
4
5
6
7
8
9

97

Solid Waste Dumping Area

213 ROAD
217 ROAD

NADD AL SHIBA (1)

NADD AL SHIBA (

615

Nadd Al Shiba Palace

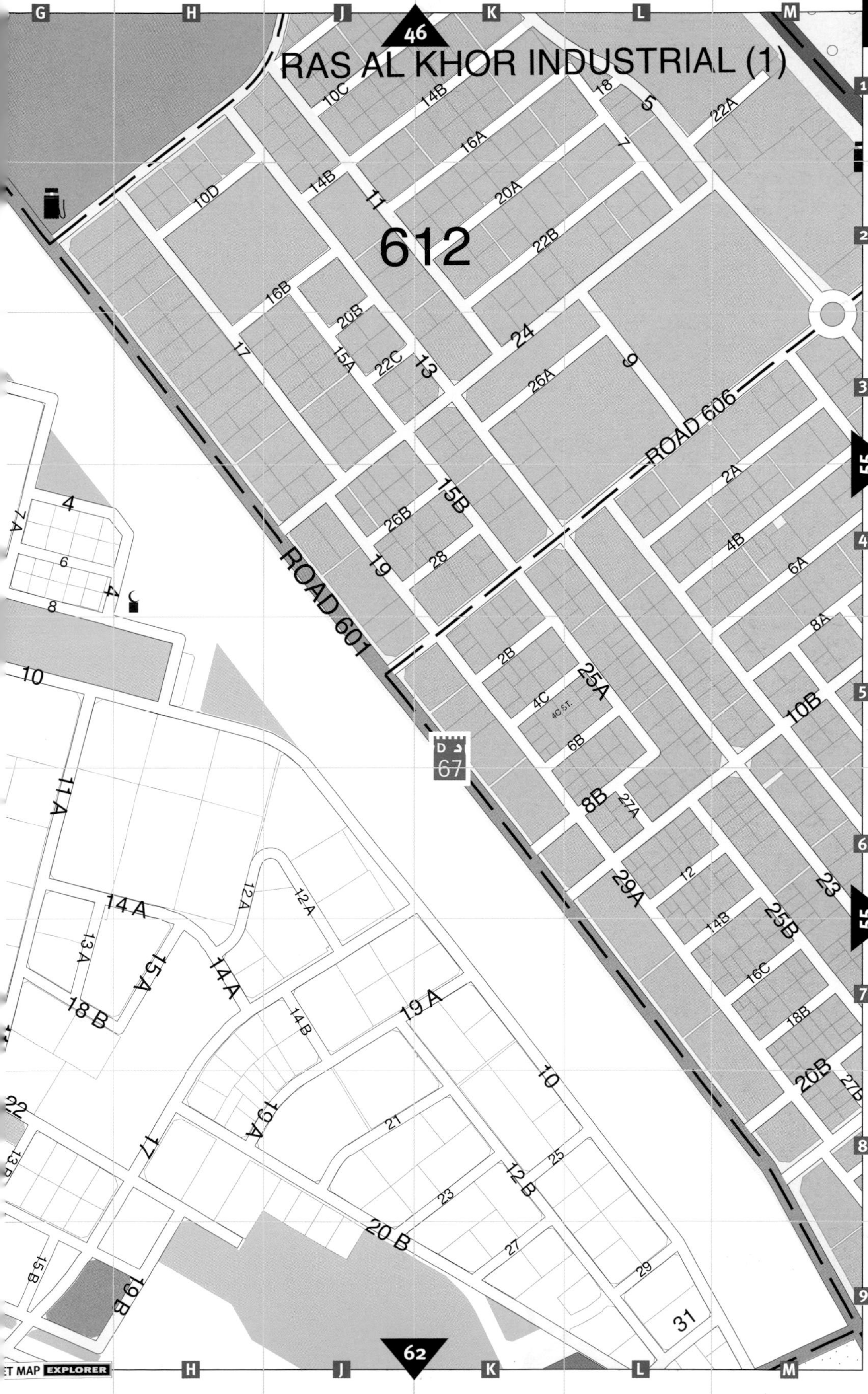

RAS AL KHOR INDUSTRIAL (1)

46

612

G H J K L M

10C
14B
18
5
22A
16A
7
14B
20A
10D
22B
11
16B
24
20B
9
17
15A 22C 13
26A
26B 15B
19 28
2B
25A
4C
46 ST.
6B
8B 27A
29A 12
14B 25B
16C
19 A
18B
10
20B 27B
12B
25
23
27
20 B
29
31

ROAD 601
ROAD 606
2A
4B
6A
8A
10B
23

4
6
7A
8
4

10
11A
12A 12A
14 A
13A
15A
18 B
14 A 14B
19 A 16 A
17
19 A
13B
22
15B 19 B

D 3
67

1
2
3
55
4
5
6
55
7
8
9

62

ET MAP EXPLORER

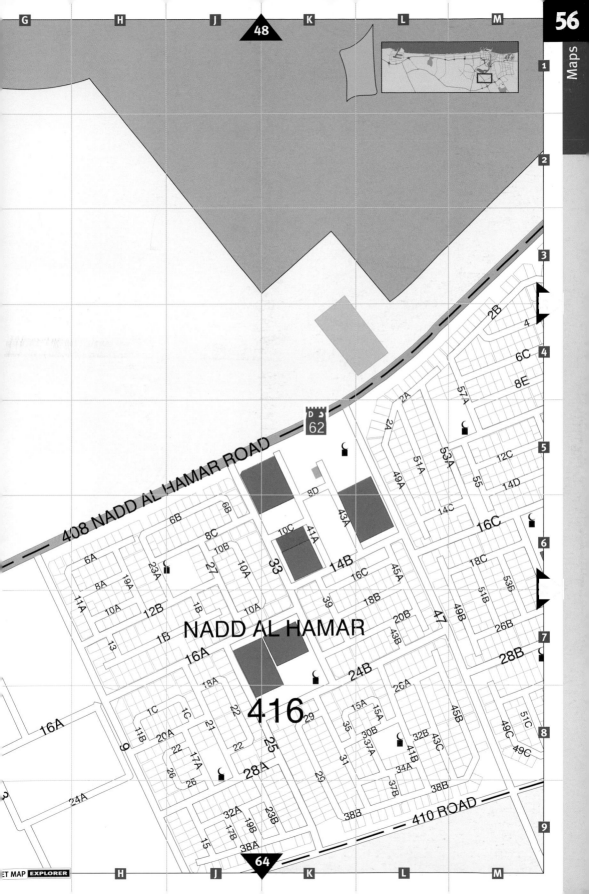

G   H   J   K   L   M

48

1

2

3

2B
4

6C
4

8E

57A

12C
5

53A

55

14D

51A

49A

16C

16C

D
62

8D

43A

14C

6B
6B

33

41A
10C

14B

18C
6

8C

10B

27

10A

16C

45A

18C

6A

23A

39

18B

53B

51B

26B

NADD AL HAMAR

8A
19A

47

49B

11A
10A

12B

1B

10A

1B

18B

20B

43B

28B
7

16A

24B

45B

416

18A

29

26A

28A

16A

1C

15A
15A

32C
43C

41B

51C

49C
8

11B
20A

35

30B

49C

1C
21

22

17A

31

37A

34A

34A

22
26

26

28A

25

29

37B

38B

16A

24A

32A
23B

38B

410 ROAD
9

17B
19B

15
38A

64

H   J   K   L   M

408 NADD AL HAMAR ROAD

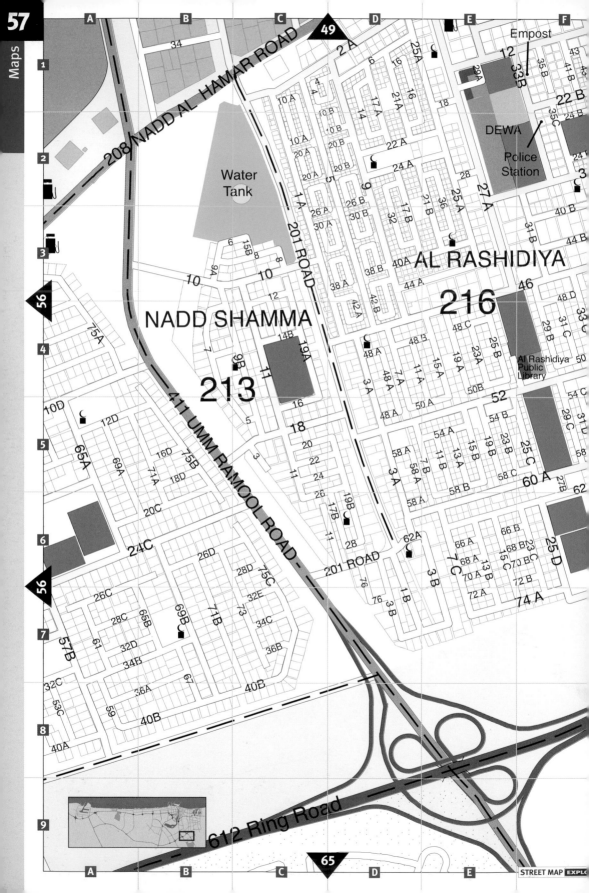

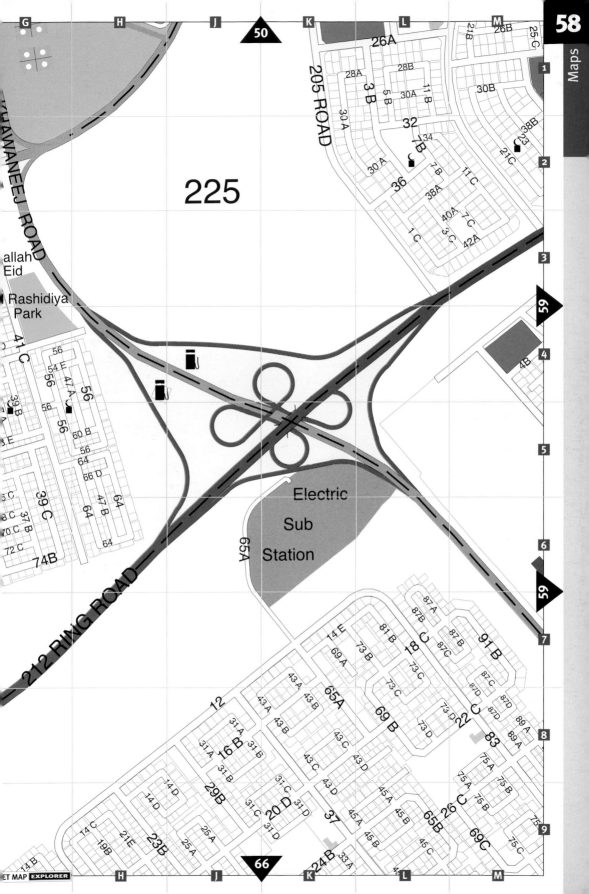

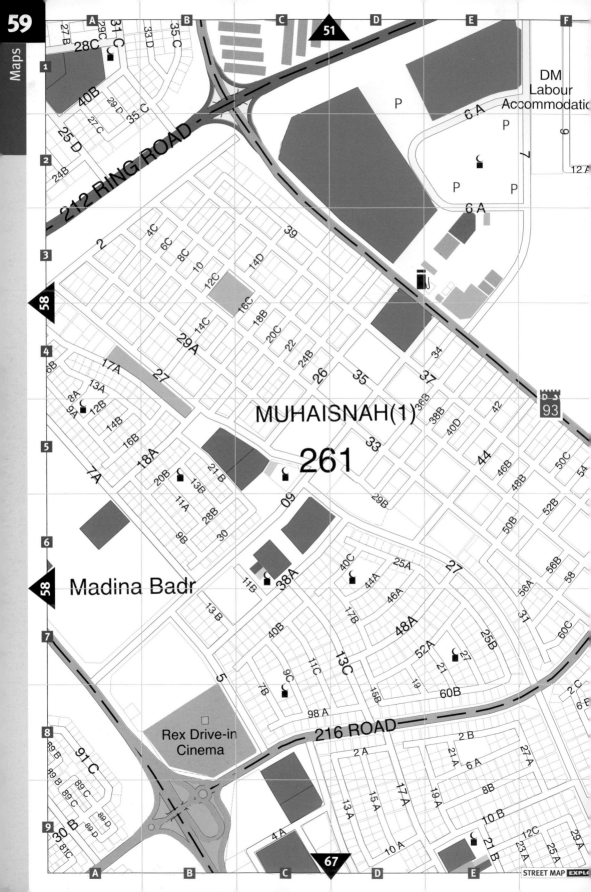

MUHAISNAH(1)

261

Madina Badr

212 RING ROAD

DM Labour Accommodatio

Rex Drive-in Cinema

216 ROAD

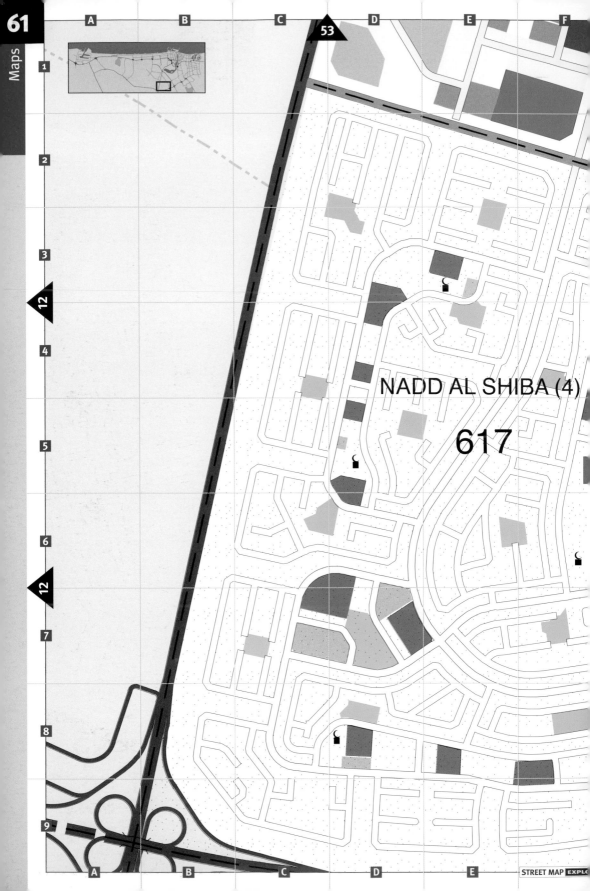

NADD AL SHIBA (4)

617

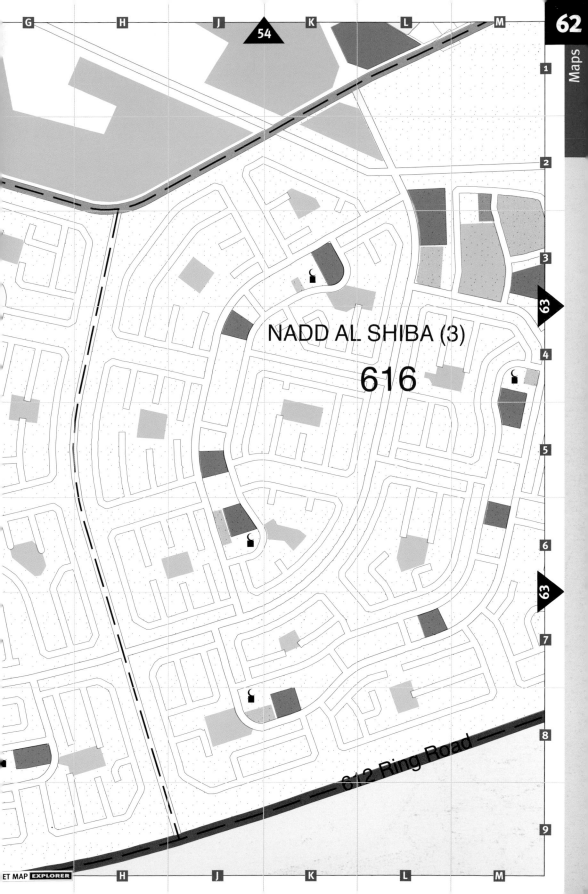

54

63

63

1
2
3
4
5
6
7
8
9

G H J K L M

NADD AL SHIBA (3)

616

612 Ring Road

H J K L M

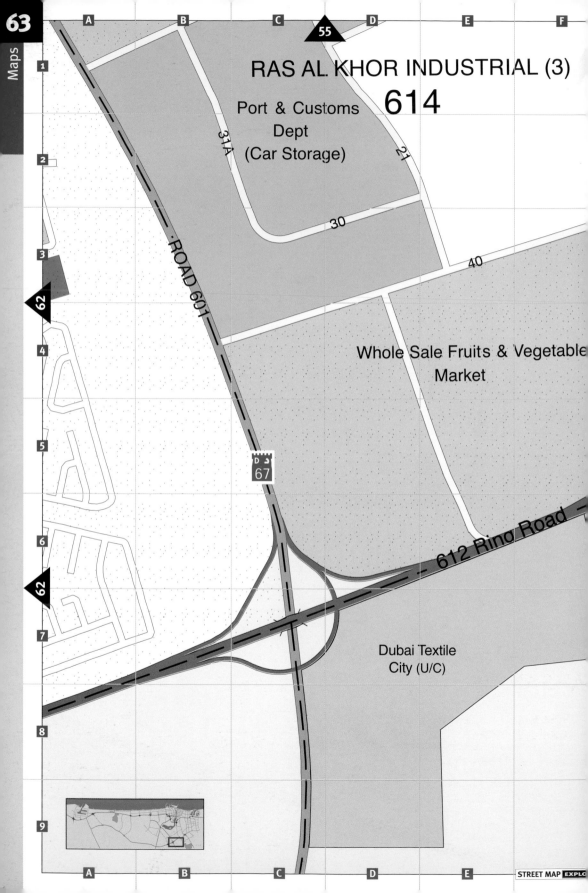

RAS AL. KHOR INDUSTRIAL (3)
614

Port & Customs
Dept
(Car Storage)

31A

21

30

40

Whole Sale Fruits & Vegetable
Market

ROAD 601

D 5
67

612 Ring Road

Dubai Textile
City (U/C)

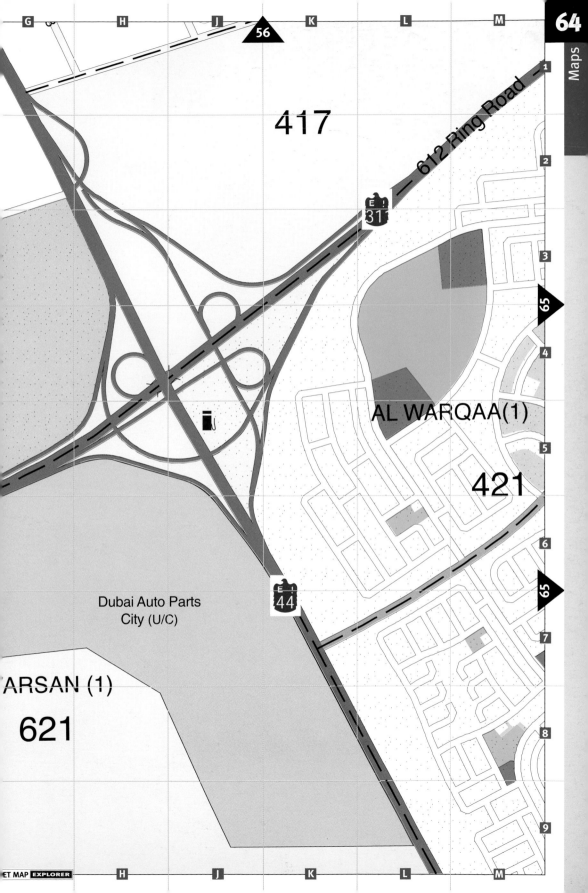

G H J K L M

56

417

612 Ring Road

1

2

E
31

3

65

4

AL WARQAA(1)

421

5

6

65

7

E
44

Dubai Auto Parts
City (U/C)

ARSAN (1)

621

8

9

H J K L M

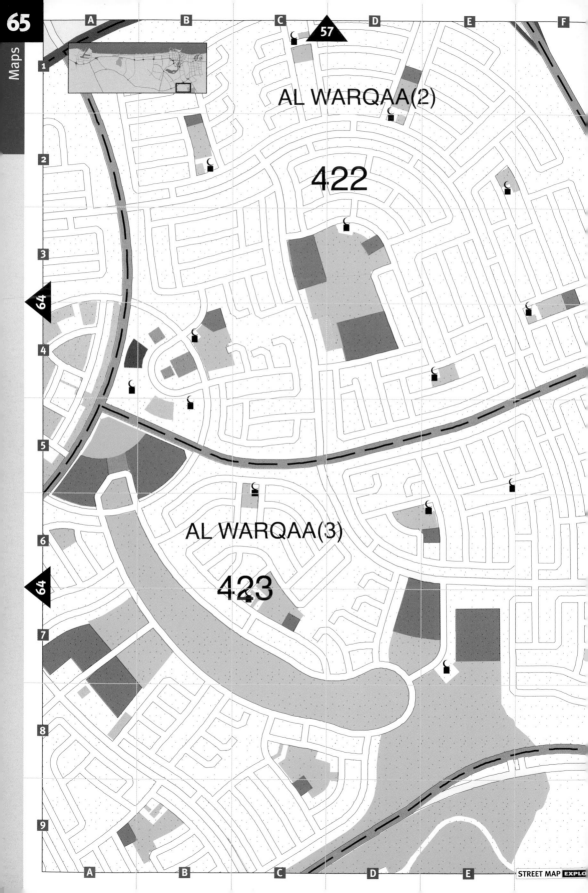

AL WARQAA(2)

422

AL WARQAA(3)

423

57

64

64

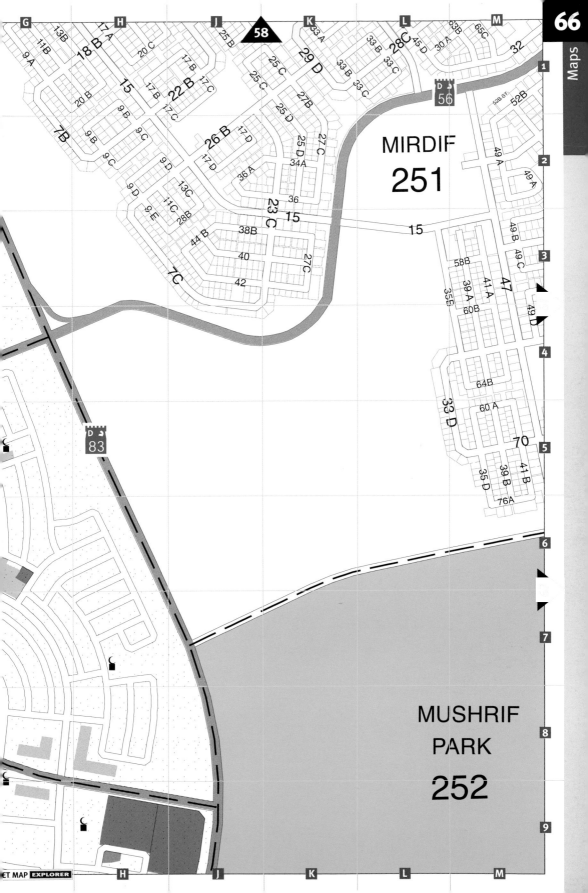

MIRDIF

251

MUSHRIF
PARK

252

58

D
56

52B ST.

52B

D
83

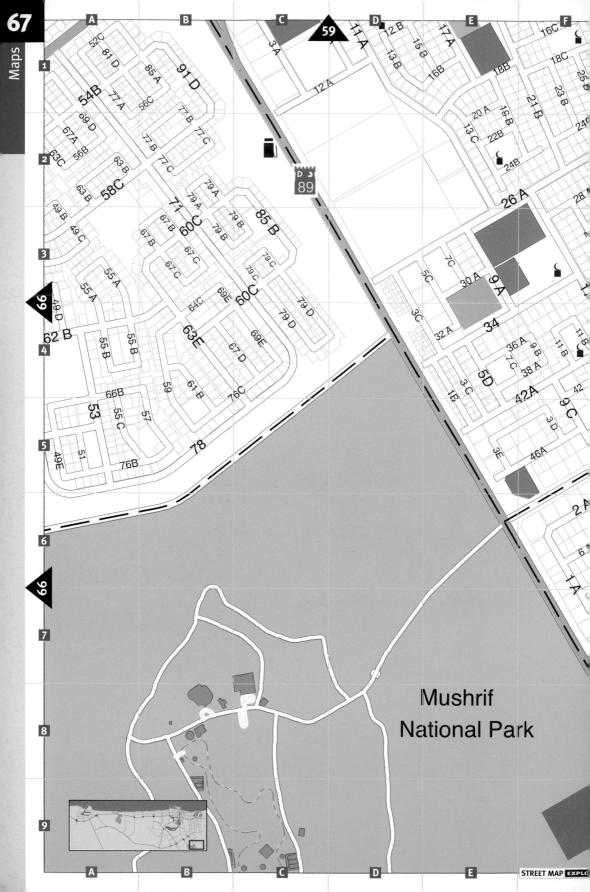

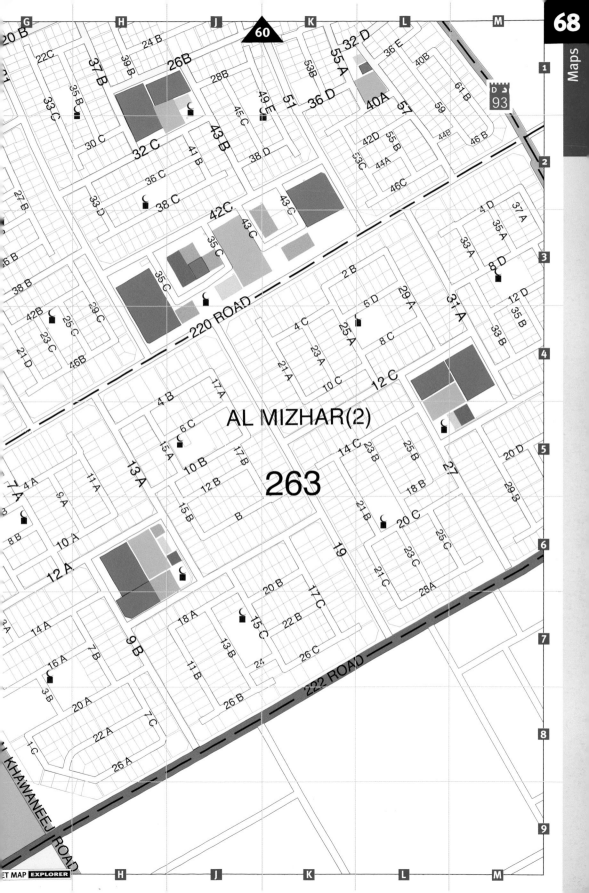

AL MIZHAR(2)

263

93

60

220 ROAD

222 ROAD

AL KHAWANEEJ ROAD

A B C D E F

1

304 AL KHALEEJ ROAD

Sheikh Saeed
Al Maktoum House

pedestrian

AL SHINDAGHA

311

2

P

P

P

Al Shindagha
Market

P

National
Flour Mills

304 AL GHUBAIBA ROAD

Emirates
Science Club

P

3

Al Rifa'a
Clinic

Al Ghubaiba
Bus Station

Plaza
Cinema

Ministry of Finance
and Industry

HSBC Bank
Middle East

P

AL

Public
Library

13A

Dubai
Taxi Station

3A

Norway

22A

23

Abra'

106 AL RA

St. George
Hotel

4

Hyde Park
Hotel

21A

Penninsula
Hotel

13C

Ambassador
Hotel

5A AL SUQ ST.

11B

P

26

11A

18 AL RAFFA ST

**AL SOUK
AL KABEER**

Abra'

D

5

301 KHALID BIN AL WALEED ROAD

35A

35B

20

37C

Astoria
Hotel

21D

34

Textile Souk

3B

Dubai
Old Souk

5B

54A

Grand
Mosque

13E

45B

AL NAHDHA STREET

29A

29B

21B

AL FAHIDI STREET

Souk Area

13D

AL ALI BIN ABI TALEB STREET

13E

312

P

30 AL ESBIJ STREET

32

25C

38B

40A

44A

46

50A

54B

6

Ascot Hotel

22A

5C

7C

3C

32

29B

38C

40B

42

44A

50A

13E

Dubai
Museum

23

11B

20A

7C

37D

38C

40C

28C

33A

44B AL HISN SREET

Canada

50B

52

7

AL ROLLA STREET

9B

24A

7D

5D

3D

5E

33B

27D

25D

60A

62B

21D 76A

21D

Al Muss

8

Imperial Suites
Hotel

22B

13

11C

30

9B

7E

32

34A

9B

50C

41

60B

33C

27E

76B

25E

Al Rais
Centre

Al Khaleej
Centre

11D

34B

38

43D

64

68

MUSSALLAH ROAD

2A

11A

P

306

MANKHOOL ROAD

P

2C

15A

6

9

Ramada
Hotel

Germany

Al Saeediya
Interchange

40

Commercial Bank
of Dubai

4A

A B C D E

G H J K L M

1

Al Shindagha
Tunnel

2

Pedestrian
Tunnel

Deira Fish, Meat
& Vegetable
Market

P

P

P

P

Deira
Bus
Station

P

P

AL RAS

10 AL KHOR STREET

10 AL KHOR STREET

3

112

10 AL
KHOR STREET

OLD BALADIYA ST

ST.

17A

19

25A

27

33

37A

16A

47AC

43

45

41

14B
16B
18D

47B

New 14C
Gold
Souk

1A
28

32

103

1A

51

12

9A

11A

13A

15A

26A

15B

105
24B

12

12 AL DAGHAYA ST

25A

16A

16B
37

39A

AL DAGHAYA

AL SOR STREET

24

27A

22

35B

37

20

8

25

4

madiya
ool

25A

27

18

25B

29B

24 25C

23B

27C

SIKKAT AL KHAIL ROAD

33

35

2A

2B Gold
Souk

36B

38A

42A

11B

13A

13B

40
42B
46A
48A

36B
36CB

27B

29B

29A

34B

28C

44
46B
48C

34B

37

18

3

16

12A

14

DOha
Palace
Hotel

4

34

Deira
Old Souk

32A

16A

12B

10

7C

4A

7B

11A

17A

19B

21

4B

25A

16B

17B

AL BUTEEN

23A

29B

6B

5

Abra

P

24 BANIYAS ROAD

22

AL SOUK AL KABEER STREET

20

11B

17B

16C

25B

23

27A

33A

2

Deira
Covered
Souk

107 AL SABKHA ROAD

4A

3A

22

20

Deira
Old Souk

A L   C R E E K

Ruler Court

ASTAKIA

Al Fahidi
Roundabout

1 SCENIC ROAD

Pedestrian

Cemetery

16C

18A

28B

114

16B

18A

18B

69

115

AL SABKHA

18

20

22

24

National Bank
of Dubai

Emirates
Bank Int'l.

Abra'

Deira Post
Office

P

Netherlands

P

P

16

12

10A DEIRA STREET

34A AL BURJ STREET

Hotel
Florida Intl.

5B

8A

26A

36A

Habib Bank
AG Zurich

HSBC

18

3

P

Flora Hotel
Apts.

Baniyas
Square

P

Deira
Tower

Carlton
Hotel

Dubai Tower

5

Safari Palace
Hotel

Naif
Souk

Al Manal
Centre

24A

30

Phoenicia
Hotel

6

7

8

9

40

H J K L M

25

25

...Al Manara 18-G7
...Al Nahda 1 43-A4, 43-E4
...Al Quoz 20-G9
...Al Quoz Industrial 2 34-L8
...Al Quoz Industrial 3 33-D1
...Al Qusais Ind 1 43-E9
...Al Qusais Ind 3 44-K9
...Al Safa 1 20-G5
...Al Twar 2 50-M3
...Al Wasl 21-D9
...Al Wuheida 26-K7
...Corniche Deira 26-H4
...Dividing Road 33-D5
...Jumeira 1 21-A4, 22-L3
...Muhaisnah 3 51-F7
...Nadd Al Hamar 56-A9
...Nadd Al Shiba 2 53-E7
...Nadd Shamma 57-C5
...Ras Al Khor Industrial 1 46-K9
...Riggat Al Buteen 25-A8
...Umm Hurair 1 24-L7
...Umm Ramool 49-C7
...Umm Suqeim 1 18-M3

3A
...Abu Hail 26-H7
...Al Bada'a 22-M4
...Al Barshaa 2 32-K4
...Al Barshaa 3 12-M5, 31-E2
...Al Hudaiba 23-D4
...Al Karama 24-J9
...Al Khabaisi 41-D2
...Al Mamzar 27-A6
...Al Mizhar 1 67-C1
...Al Mizhar 2 68-G7
...Al Muraqqabat 25-C7
...Al Nahda 2 43-E5
...Al Quoz 35-A2
...Al Quoz Industrial 1 18-K8
...Al Qusais 1 43-B8
...Al Qusais 2 51-B2
...Al Qusais 3 51-B6
...Al Qusais Ind 2 51-E2
...Al Qusais Ind 4 52-K1, 52-K2
...Al Rashidiya 57-D4, 57-D5
...Al Safa 2 19-A5
...Al Souk Al Kabeer 24-K3
...Al Twar 1 42-L7
...Al Twar 3 50-K8
...Hor Al Anz East 42-L1
...Jumeira 3 20-G2
...Mankhool 24-J6
...Ras Al Khor Industrial 2 55-B4
...Umm Ramool 49-A5
...Umm Suqeim 2 18-G3
...Umm Suqeim 3 17-B3

3B
...Abu Hail 26-G7
...Al Bada'a 22-M5
...Al Barshaa 2 32-K5
...Al Hudaiba 23-D4
...Al Karama 24-J9, 40-J1
...Al Khabaisi 41-D2
...Al Mamzar 27-A7
...Al Mizhar 2 68-G8
...Al Nahda 2 43-E5
...Al Quoz 35-A3
...Al Quoz Industrial 1 34-K2
...Al Qusais 1 43-B9
...Al Qusais 2 51-B3
...Al Qusais 3 51-B7
...Al Qusais Ind 5 52-K3
...Al Rashidiya 57-E6
...Al Safa 2 19-A6
...Al Twar 1 42-L8
...Al Twar 3 58-L1
...Hor Al Anz East 42-K2
...Jumeira 3 20-G3
...Mankhool 24-J6
...Nadd Shamma 57-D7
...Umm Al Sheif 999-C3

...Umm Ramool 49-A7
...Umm Suqeim 1 18-G4, 18-M6
...Umm Suqeim 3 17-B4
...Za'abeel 2 38-M2

3C
...Al Khabaisi 41-C2
...Al Mamzar 27-A8
...Al Mizhar 1 67-D4, 67-E4
...Al Quoz 35-A3
...Al Qusais 1 51-B1
...Al Qusais 3 51-B8
...Al Qusais Ind 5 52-L4, 52-L5
...Al Raffa 24-H4
...Al Twar 3 58-M3

3D
...Al Mamzar 43-A3
...Al Mizhar 1 67-F5
...Al Qusais 3 51-C8
...Umm Ramool 49-B9

3E
...Al Mizhar 1 67-E5

4

4
...Al Bada'a 22-L5
...Al Baraha 25-E4
...Al Bukadra 46-G8
...Al Garhoud 41-C6
...Al Jaddaf 39-F8, 48-J1
...Al Khabaisi 41-F1
...Al Mamzar 27-E5
...Al Nahda 1 43-C4, 43-E2
...Al Quoz 20-G8, 35-A2
...Al Quoz Industrial 3 33-B1
...Al Quoz Industrial 4 32-M5
...Al Qusais 1 43-B6
...Al Qusais 2 51-D2
...Al Qusais Ind 3 44-K6
...Al Qusais Ind 4 52-K1
...Al Rashidiya 57-C1
...Al Twar 1 42-K5
...Al Twar 2 51-A2
...Al Twar 3 50-M6
...Al Wuheida 26-L5
...Dubai International Airport 42-J4
...Hor Al Anz East 26-L9
...Jumeira 2 20-M1
...Jumeira 3 19-E8
...Muhaisnah 3 51-F5
...Nadd Al Hamar 56-M4
...Nadd Al Shiba 2 54-G4, 54-H4
...Oud Metha 39-F2
...Port Saeed 41-C4
...Riggat Al Buteen 25-A9
...Umm Al Sheif 16-L7
...Umm Hurair 1 24-L7
...Umm Ramool 49-B5

4A
...Al Bada'a 22-M4
...Al Barshaa 1 16-J9
...Al Barshaa 2 32-H4
...Al Barshaa 3 31-E1
...Al Hudaiba 23-D4
...Al Jafiliya 23-D5
...Al Karama 24-J8
...Al Manara 17-F6
...Al Mizhar 1 59-C9
...Al Mizhar 2 68-G5
...Al Nahda 2 43-D5
...Al Quoz Industrial 2 34-K5
...Al Qusais 3 51-B6
...Al Qusais Ind 1 43-E9
...Al Qusais Ind 2 51-E3
...Al Safa 2 19-A6
...Al Satwa 22-J6, 22-K6
...Al Sufouh 1 16-J4

...Jumeira 1 21-D3, 21-E3, 22-H3, 22-J3, 22-K3
...Jumeira 3 19-E5, 20-G1
...Mankhool 24-H5
...Muhaisnah 2 60-G1
...Ras Al Khor Industrial 1 46-K8
...Ras Al Khor Industrial 2 55-A3
...Umm Suqeim 1 18-G6, 18-J9, 18-L2
...Umm Suqeim 2 18-G2
...Umm Suqeim 3 17-B3
...Za'abeel 1 39-C3

4B
...Al Barshaa 1 16-G9
...Al Barshaa 2 32-G4
...Al Barshaa 3 12-M5, 31-C1
...Al Hudaiba 23-B4
...Al Jafiliya 23-C5
...Al Karama 24-H8
...Al Manara 17-C6
...Al Mizhar 1 60-G7
...Al Mizhar 2 68-H4
...Al Nahda 2 43-E5, 44-J8
...Al Quoz Industrial 1 17-F9
...Al Quoz Industrial 2 34-G5
...Al Qusais 3 51-D5
...Al Qusais Ind 2 51-F3
...Al Safa 1 19-B5
...Al Safa 2 18-L6
...Al Satwa 21-E7
...Al Sufouh 2 15-B4
...Hor Al Anz 26-J9
...Jumeira 1 21-C3
...Jumeira 3 19-C2
...Mankhool 24-G5
...Muhaisnah 1 58-M4
...Muhaisnah 2 60-L1
...Ras Al Khor Industrial 1 46-J9
...Ras Al Khor Industrial 2 54-M4
...Umm Suqeim 1 18-G9, 18-K2
...Umm Suqeim 2 17-F2
...Umm Suqeim 3 17-A3

4C
...Al Barshaa 1 15-E8
...Al Barshaa 3 31-B1
...Al Jafiliya 23-B5
...Al Karama 24-G8
...Al Mizhar 2 68-K4
...Al Nahda 2 43-F5
...Al Qusais Ind 2 52-G2
...Al Safa 2 18-J6
...Al Satwa 21-E8
...Jumeira 1 21-B3, 21-C3
...Jumeira 3 19-B2
...Mankhool 24-G5
...Muhaisnah 1 59-B3
...Ras Al Khor Industrial 2 54-K5
...Umm Suqeim 1 18-J1
...Umm Suqeim 2 17-E2

4D
...Al Mizhar 2 68-M2
...Al Nahda 2 44-G5
...Jumeira 3 19-A2
...Mankhool 23-F5
...Umm Suqeim 1 18-H2
...Umm Suqeim 2 17-C3

4E
...Mankhool 23-E5
...Umm Suqeim 1 18-M2
...Umm Suqeim 2 17-C3

5

5
...Al Barshaa 1 32-H2
...Al Barshaa 3 31-E2
...Al Garhoud 49-B2
...Al Hudaiba 23-C4

...*Al Jaddaf* 39-F9, 48-J2
...*Al Jafiliya* 23-D5
...*Al Karama* 24-J8
...*Al Mizhar 2* 68-G6
...*Al Nahda 1* 43-C4, 43-D3
...*Al Quoz Industrial 2* 34-L6
...*Al Quoz Industrial 3* 33-D4
...*Al Quoz Industrial 4* 33-E9
...*Al Qusais 1* 43-B6
...*Al Qusais 2* 51-B3, 51-B4
...*Al Qusais Ind 1* 43-F9
...*Al Qusais Ind 3* 44-K8
...*Al Qusais Ind 5* 52-L3
...*Al Rashidiya* 57-D2
...*Al Safa 1* 19-F5
...*Al Safa 2* 18-M6
...*Al Satwa* 22-M6
...*Al Sufouh 1* 16-H4
...*Al Twar 1* 50-M1
...*Al Wasl* 21-C9
...*Hor Al Anz* 26-H8
...*Jebel Ali Industrial* 3-E7
...*Jumeira 1* 21-A4
...*Jumeira 3* 19-F9
...*Muhaisnah 1* 59-B7
...*Muhaisnah 3* 51-F7
...*Nadd Al Hamar* 56-G7
...*Nadd Al Shiba 1* 53-A4
...*Nadd Al Shiba 2* 53-E8
...*Nadd Shamma* 57-C5
...*Port Saeed* 41-A3
...*Ras Al Khor Industrial 1* 54-L1
...*Riggat Al Buteen* 25-A9
...*Trade Centre 1* 22-L8
...*Umm Al Sheif* 17-B8
...*Umm Hurair 1* 24-L7
...*Za'abeel 1* 39-D4

5A
...*Abu Hail* 26-H5
...*Al Barshaa 2* 32-J4
...*Al Khabaisi* 41-E2
...*Al Mamzar* 27-A7
...*Al Muraqqabat* 25-C7
...*Al Nahda 2* 43-E5
...*Al Quoz* 19-F9, 34-M2
...*Al Quoz Industrial 1* 18-J9
...*Al Qusais 3* 51-B6
...*Al Qusais Ind 2* 51-F2
...*Al Souk Al Kabeer* 24-J3
...*Al Twar 1* 42-L7
...*Al Twar 2* 50-M2
...*Al Twar 3* 50-L8
...*Al Wuheida* 26-K8
...*Hor Al Anz East* 26-L9
...*Jumeira 1* 22-L2
...*Jumeira 2* 21-A4
...*Jumeira 3* 19-A8, 19-F1, 20-G2
...*Mankhool* 24-H6
...*Ras Al Khor Industrial 2* 55-C6
...*Umm Suqeim 1* 18-G6, 18-M2
...*Umm Suqeim 2* 18-G3
...*Umm Suqeim 3* 17-A3

5B
...*Abu Hail* 26-H7
...*Al Barshaa 2* 32-K8
...*Al Khabaisi* 41-D2
...*Al Mamzar* 27-A8, 43-B3
...*Al Manara* 18-G7
...*Al Muraqqabat* 25-C8
...*Al Nahda 2* 43-E6
...*Al Quoz* 34-M3
...*Al Quoz Industrial 1* 34-J2
...*Al Qusais 3* 51-C7
...*Al Twar 1* 42-L8
...*Al Twar 2* 50-M3
...*Al Twar 3* 58-L1
...*Al Wuheida* 26-K8
...*Hor Al Anz East* 42-L1
...*Jumeira 1* 22-L3
...*Jumeira 2* 20-G4, 21-A5

...*Jumeira 3* 20-G4
...*Mankhool* 24-J7
...*Ras Al Khor Industrial 2* 55-D7
...*Umm Suqeim 1* 18-G4, 18-M3
...*Umm Suqeim 2* 18-G4
...*Umm Suqeim 3* 17-B4

5C
...*Al Khabaisi* 41-D2
...*Al Mizhar 1* 67-E3
...*Al Muraqqabat* 25-B8
...*Al Quoz Industrial 1* 34-J4
...*Al Qusais 3* 51-C7
...*Al Twar 1* 42-L8
...*Al Twar 2* 50-M5
...*Hor Al Anz East* 42-L2

5D
...*Al Khabaisi* 41-C2
...*Al Mizhar 1* 67-E4
...*Al Qusais 3* 51-C8
...*Al Twar 1* 42-L9

5E
...*Al Qusais 3* 51-C8
...*Al Twar 1* 50-M2

6

6
...*Abu Hail* 26-J5
...*Al Barshaa 3* 31-E2
...*Al Bukadra* 46-H7
...*Al Hamriya* 24-K5
...*Al Mamzar* 27-C5
...*Al Murar* 25-E4
...*Al Nahda 1* 43-C4
...*Al Nahda 2* 44-J8
...*Al Quoz Industrial 1* 18-H9, 18-M9
...*Al Quoz Industrial 2* 33-E5
...*Al Quoz Industrial 4* 33-D5
...*Al Qusais 1* 43-C6
...*Al Qusais Ind 2* 51-F3
...*Al Qusais Ind 3* 44-K6
...*Al Rashidiya* 57-D1
...*Al Twar 2* 51-A2
...*Al Wuheida* 26-L6
...*Dubai International Airport* 41-D5
...*Hor Al Anz East* 26-L9
...*Jumeira 1* 21-B4
...*Jumeira 3* 19-A9
...*Mankhool* 23-F5
...*Muhaisnah 3* 52-G4
...*Nadd Al Shiba 2* 54-G4
...*Nadd Shamma* 57-B3
...*Oud Metha* 39-F2
...*Umm Hurair 1* 24-K8
...*Umm Ramool* 49-A6
...*Umm Suqeim 2* 18-G2

6A
...*Al Bada'a* 22-L5
...*Al Barshaa 2* 32-H4
...*Al Barshaa 3* 12-M5, 31-D1
...*Al Hudaiba* 23-D4
...*Al Jafiliya* 23-D5
...*Al Karama* 24-H8
...*Al Khabaisi* 41-F1
...*Al Mamzar* 27-C8
...*Al Manara* 17-F6
...*Al Mizhar 1* 59-E8
...*Al Mizhar 2* 67-F6
...*Al Nahda 1* 43-D4
...*Al Nahda 2* 43-F5
...*Al Quoz Industrial 3* 33-C1
...*Al Qusais 2* 51-B2
...*Al Qusais Ind 2* 51-E3
...*Al Qusais Ind 4* 52-L1
...*Al Safa 2* 18-M6
...*Al Satwa* 22-M6
...*Al Sufouh 1* 16-H5

...*Al Twar 3* 50-M6
...*Al Wasl* 21-A6
...*Hor Al Anz* 26-G8
...*Jumeira 1* 21-A4
...*Jumeira 3* 19-F8
...*Muhaisnah 2* 59-E1, 59-E3
...*Nadd Al Hamar* 56-H6
...*Port Saeed* 41-B3
...*Ras Al Khor Industrial 1* 46-K9
...*Ras Al Khor Industrial 2* 54-M4
...*Umm Al Sheif* 16-M7
...*Umm Suqeim 1* 18-G6, 18-K2

6B
...*Al Bada'a* 22-H5
...*Al Barshaa 1* 15-F9, 16-G9
...*Al Barshaa 2* 31-F4
...*Al Barshaa 3* 31-B1
...*Al Hudaiba* 23-A5
...*Al Jafiliya* 23-B6
...*Al Manara* 17-C6
...*Al Mizhar 1* 59-F8
...*Al Mizhar 2* 68-G6
...*Al Nahda 1* 43-E3
...*Al Nahda 2* 44-H5
...*Al Quoz Industrial 3* 32-L1
...*Al Qusais 2* 51-C2
...*Al Qusais Ind 4* 52-L1
...*Al Safa 1* 19-F5
...*Al Safa 2* 18-L6
...*Al Satwa* 22-M6
...*Al Sufouh 1* 16-G5
...*Al Twar 3* 51-A6
...*Al Wasl* 20-M4
...*Hor Al Anz* 26-H8
...*Jumeira 2* 20-M1, 20-M4
...*Jumeira 3* 19-B2, 19-F8
...*Muhaisnah 1* 59-A4
...*Muhaisnah 2* 60-G1
...*Nadd Al Hamar* 56-J6
...*Nadd Al Shiba 1* 53-A2
...*Port Saeed* 41-C4
...*Ras Al Khor Industrial 1* 46-J9
...*Ras Al Khor Industrial 2* 54-L5
...*Riggat Al Buteen* 25-A9
...*Umm Al Sheif* 16-L7, 999-C3
...*Umm Suqeim 1* 18-J1, 18-K2
...*Umm Suqeim 3* 17-A3

6C
...*Al Bada'a* 22-H5
...*Al Jafiliya* 23-A6
...*Al Karama* 23-F9
...*Al Mizhar 1* 60-G7
...*Al Mizhar 2* 68-J5
...*Al Quoz* 19-D8
...*Al Safa 1* 19-E5
...*Al Safa 2* 18-J6
...*Al Satwa* 22-J7, 22-M6
...*Al Sufouh 2* 15-C5
...*Al Wasl* 20-K4
...*Hor Al Anz* 26-J9
...*Jumeira 2* 20-M1
...*Jumeira 3* 19-A2
...*Muhaisnah 1* 59-B3
...*Muhaisnah 2* 60-L1
...*Nadd Al Hamar* 56-M4
...*Riggat Al Buteen* 25-A9
...*Umm Suqeim 1* 18-H2

6D
...*Al Bada'a* 21-F6
...*Al Mizhar 2* 68-L3
...*Al Safa 1* 19-B6, 19-C5
...*Al Safa 2* 18-H6
...*Al Satwa* 21-F7, 22-H7
...*Al Sufouh 2* 15-B5
...*Riggat Al Buteen* 41-A1
...*Umm Suqeim 1* 18-H2

6E
...*Al Bada'a* 21-E6

7

...Abu Hail 26-H5
...Al Barshaa 1 32-H2
...Al Barshaa 3 31-E2
...Al Hudaiba 23-C4
...Al Manara 18-G7
...Al Nahda 1 43-D3, 43-E2
...Al Quoz 19-F9
...Al Quoz Industrial 3 33-D2
...Al Qusais 1 43-B8
...Al Qusais Ind 1 51-F1
...Al Qusais Ind 3 44-K8
...Al Safa 1 19-F5, 19-F6
...Al Sufouh 1 16-H3, 16-H4
...Al Wasl 37-B1
...Hor Al Anz East 42-L3
...Jumeira 3 19-F2
...Mankhool 24-H5
...Muhaisnah 2 59-F2
...Nadd Al Shiba 1 53-A3
...Nadd Shamma 57-B4
...Port Saeed 41-A3, 41-B3
...Ras Al Khor Industrial 2 55-B5
...Riggat Al Buteen 25-A9
...Trade Centre 1 22-M8
...Trade Centre 2 38-G1
...Umm Al Sheif 17-A8, 999-B8
...Umm Hurair 2 40-J5
...Umm Suqeim 3 17-A4
...Za'abeel 2 38-M2

7A
...Al Bada'a 22-M4
...Al Barshaa 2 32-J4
...Al Jafiliya 23-D5
...Al Karama 24-J9
...Al Khabaisi 41-E2
...Al Mizhar 1 67-D1
...Al Mizhar 2 68-G5
...Al Nahda 2 43-F7
...Al Quoz 34-M3
...Al Quoz Industrial 2 34-K5
...Al Quoz Industrial 4 33-D5
...Al Qusais 2 51-B2, 51-C2
...Al Qusais 3 51-C8
...Al Qusais Ind 1 43-F8
...Al Qusais Ind 4 52-K1, 52-L2
...Al Raffa 24-G3
...Al Rashidiya 57-D4
...Al Safa 2 18-M6
...Al Twar 2 50-M2
...Al Twar 3 50-L9
...Al Wuheida 26-L6
...Hor Al Anz 26-H8
...Jumeira 1 21-A3, 22-L2
...Muhaisnah 1 59-A5
...Muhaisnah 3 51-F5
...Nadd Al Shiba 2 54-G4
...Umm Hurair 1 24-K7
...Umm Ramool 49-B6
...Umm Suqeim 1 18-G2, 18-J7

7B
...Al Barshaa 2 32-J8
...Al Jafiliya 23-D6
...Al Karama 40-J1
...Al Khabaisi 41-D2
...Al Mamzar 27-A8
...Al Mizhar 2 68-H7
...Al Quoz 35-A4
...Al Quoz Industrial 1 34-J1
...Al Quoz Industrial 2 34-K7
...Al Quoz Industrial 4 33-D7
...Al Qusais 2 51-B3
...Al Qusais 3 51-C8
...Al Qusais Ind 2 51-F3
...Al Qusais Ind 5 52-L3, 52-L4
...Al Rashidiya 57-E5

...Al Safa 2 18-M7
...Al Twar 2 50-M5
...Al Twar 3 58-L2
...Al Wuheida 26-L8
...Hor Al Anz 26-H9
...Jumeira 1 22-L3
...Jumeira 2 21-A4
...Jumeira 3 19-F2, 19-F3
...Mirdif 66-G2
...Muhaisnah 1 59-C8
...Muhaisnah 3 51-F6
...Nadd Al Shiba 2 53-F6
...Umm Ramool 49-C9
...Umm Suqeim 1 18-M3
...Umm Suqeim 2 18-G4

7C
...Al Bada'a 22-M5
...Al Jafiliya 23-D7
...Al Mamzar 43-A2
...Al Mizhar 1 67-E3, 67-E4
...Al Mizhar 2 68-H8
...Al Quoz 34-M5
...Al Quoz Industrial 1 34-J3
...Al Qusais Ind 5 52-L6
...Al Rashidiya 57-E6
...Al Twar 3 58-M3
...Hor Al Anz 26-G9
...Jumeira 3 20-G3
...Mirdif 66-J3
...Nadd Al Shiba 2 53-E8
...Umm Suqeim 1 18-M5
...Umm Suqeim 2 18-G5

7D
...Al Bada'a 22-M5
...Al Mamzar 43-A3
...Hor Al Anz 42-G1

7E
...Hor Al Anz 42-G1

8

...Abu Hail 26-J5
...Al Barshaa 1 12-M5
...Al Garhoud 41-C7
...Al Jafiliya 23-B6
...Al Khabaisi 41-E1
...Al Mamzar 27-E5
...Al Mizhar 2 67-F6
...Al Nahda 1 43-F4
...Al Quoz 35-A3
...Al Quoz Industrial 1 34-H1
...Al Quoz Industrial 2 34-G5
...Al Quoz Industrial 3 33-B2
...Al Quoz Industrial 4 32-L6
...Al Qusais 1 43-A7
...Al Qusais Ind 2 51-F3
...Al Qusais Ind 3 44-K7
...Al Qusais Ind 4 52-K1
...Al Rashidiya 49-F9
...Al Sufouh 1 16-G5
...Al Sufouh 2 15-C5
...Al Twar 1 42-L5
...Hor Al Anz East 42-M1
...Jumeira 2 20-L1
...Nadd Al Shiba 2 53-F4, 54-G4
...Nadd Shamma 57-C3
...Oud Metha 39-F2
...Port Saeed 41-C5
...Ras Al Khor Industrial 1 46-K9
...Umm Al Sheif 16-L7
...Umm Hurair 1 24-K8
...Umm Hurair 2 40-J3

8A
...Al Bada'a 22-L5
...Al Barshaa 1 16-G9
...Al Barshaa 2 32-J4
...Al Barshaa 3 31-D2

...Al Hudaiba 23-D5
...Al Karama 24-J8
...Al Mamzar 27-C5
...Al Manara 17-F6, 18-G6
...Al Nahda 2 43-E6
...Al Quoz 19-F8
...Al Qusais 2 51-B2
...Al Qusais 3 51-B6
...Al Qusais Ind 1 43-E9
...Al Safa 1 19-F5
...Al Safa 2 18-K6
...Al Satwa 22-M6
...Al Twar 2 50-M3
...Al Twar 3 50-L7
...Al Wasl 21-A6
...Al Wuheida 26-K6
...Jumeira 1 21-A4, 21-E4
...Jumeira 3 19-B2, 20-G2
...Mankhool 24-H5
...Muhaisnah 1 59-A4
...Muhaisnah 2 60-G2
...Muhaisnah 3 51-F5
...Nadd Al Hamar 56-H6
...Ras Al Khor Industrial 2 54-M5
...Umm Ramool 49-B6
...Umm Suqeim 1 18-G3, 18-J6, 18-M2

8B
...Al Bada'a 22-K5
...Al Barshaa 1 15-F9
...Al Barshaa 2 32-H4
...Al Barshaa 3 31-C1
...Al Hudaiba 23-C5
...Al Karama 24-H8
...Al Manara 17-C7
...Al Mizhar 1 59-E9
...Al Mizhar 2 68-G6
...Al Nahda 2 44-G9, 44-H6
...Al Quoz 19-E8
...Al Qusais 3 51-C6
...Al Safa 1 19-E5, 19-E5
...Al Safa 2 18-H6
...Al Twar 2 51-A3
...Al Twar 3 51-A7
...Al Wasl 20-K4
...Al Wuheida 26-L6
...Jumeira 1 21-C4
...Jumeira 2 20-M1
...Jumeira 3 19-C2
...Mankhool 24-G6
...Muhaisnah 2 60-L2
...Muhaisnah 3 52-G4
...Ras Al Khor Industrial 2 54-L6
...Umm Ramool 49-D5
...Umm Suqeim 1 18-L2
...Umm Suqeim 2 17-E3
...Za'abeel 1 39-A3

8C
...Al Bada'a 22-J5
...Al Barshaa 1 15-E9
...Al Barshaa 2 31-F5
...Al Hudaiba 23-B5
...Al Karama 24-G9, 24-H8
...Al Mizhar 1 59-F8
...Al Mizhar 2 68-L4
...Al Muteena 25-E7
...Al Quoz 19-D9
...Al Qusais 2 51-C2
...Al Qusais 3 51-D6
...Al Safa 1 19-D6
...Al Satwa 22-J7, 22-K7, 22-M6
...Al Wuheida 26-M6
...Jumeira 1 21-C4, 21-C4
...Jumeira 3 19-B2
...Mankhool 23-F6
...Muhaisnah 1 59-B3
...Nadd Al Hamar 56-J6

8D
...Al Barshaa 1 15-D8
...Al Mizhar 1 60-H7

...Al Mizhar 2 68-M3
...Jumeira 3 19-A2
...Nadd Al Hamar 56-K5
...Umm Suqeim 2 17-C3

8E
...Al Bada'a 21-F6
...Nadd Al Hamar 56-M4
...Umm Suqeim 2 17-B3

9

9
...Al Bada'a 22-M5
...Al Barshaa 1 32-H2
...Al Garhoud 49-C4
...Al Hamriya 24-K6
...Al Hudaiba 23-B4
...Al Jafiliya 23-D5
...Al Mamzar 27-B7, 43-A3
...Al Muraqqabat 25-C8
...Al Muteena 25-D7
...Al Nahda 1 43-E3
...Al Quoz 34-M3, 35-F4
...Al Qusais 1 51-B1
...Al Qusais 3 51-C6
...Al Qusais Ind 1 51-F1
...Al Qusais Ind 2 51-F2
...Al Rashidiya 57-D2
...Al Safa 2 18-M6
...Al Satwa 22-M6
...Al Sufouh 1 16-G3, 16-H4
...Al Wasl 21-C7
...Dubai Investment Park 1 0-E9, 0-J8, 7-C4, 7-F4
...Hor Al Anz East 42-L3
...Jebel Ali Industrial 0-A3, 3-E8
...Jumeira 1 22-K3
...Muhaisnah 2 59-F2
...Nadd Al Hamar 56-H8
...Port Saeed 41-B4
...Ras Al Khor Industrial 1 54-L3
...Ras Al Khor Industrial 2 55-C6
...Riggat Al Buteen 25-A9
...Umm Hurair 2 39-D8, 40-G8
...Umm Ramool 49-B5, 49-C9
...Umm Suqeim 3 17-A3

9A
...Al Barshaa 2 32-J4
...Al Karama 24-J8
...Al Khabaisi 41-E1
...Al Manara 17-F6
...Al Mizhar 1 67-E3
...Al Mizhar 2 68-G6
...Al Nahda 2 43-F5
...Al Quoz 34-M3
...Al Quoz Industrial 1 18-H9
...Al Quoz Industrial 2 34-K6
...Al Quoz Industrial 3 33-C1
...Al Quoz Industrial 4 33-D5
...Al Qusais 2 51-C3
...Al Qusais Ind 2 52-H1
...Al Qusais Ind 3 44-K7
...Al Qusais Ind 5 52-L3
...Al Twar 1 42-L7
...Al Twar 2 50-M2
...Al Twar 3 50-L8
...Jumeira 2 20-M1, 21-A4
...Jumeira 3 19-F2, 19-F5
...Mankhool 24-H5, 24-H6
...Mirdif 66-G1
...Muhaisnah 1 59-A5
...Muhaisnah 3 51-F5
...Nadd Al Shiba 2 53-F8
...Nadd Shamma 57-B3
...Umm Al Sheif 17-A7
...Umm Suqeim 1 18-G6, 18-M2
...Umm Suqeim 2 17-F3

9B
...Al Barshaa 2 32-J7

...Al Barshaa 3 12-M5
...Al Karama 24-J9
...Al Khabaisi 41-E2
...Al Manara 17-F7
...Al Mizhar 1 67-F4
...Al Mizhar 2 68-H7
...Al Nahda 2 43-F7
...Al Quoz Industrial 1 34-H2
...Al Quoz Industrial 2 34-K8
...Al Quoz Industrial 3 33-C2
...Al Quoz Industrial 4 33-D6
...Al Qusais 2 51-C4
...Al Qusais Ind 3 44-L8
...Al Qusais Ind 5 52-L4, 52-L5
...Al Raffa 24-H4
...Al Safa 1 19-F7
...Al Twar 1 42-L9
...Al Twar 2 50-M3
...Al Wuheida 26-L8
...Hor Al Anz 26-H9
...Jumeira 2 20-M1, 21-A6
...Jumeira 3 19-F3
...Mirdif 66-H1, 66-H2
...Muhaisnah 1 59-B6
...Muhaisnah 3 52-G8
...Nadd Al Shiba 1 53-B3
...Nadd Al Shiba 2 53-F8
...Nadd Shamma 57-C4
...Oud Metha 40-H3
...Umm Suqeim 1 18-M3
...Umm Suqeim 2 18-G3

9C
...Al Khabaisi 41-D2
...Al Mizhar 1 67-F5
...Al Quoz Industrial 3 33-C4
...Al Twar 2 50-M5, 51-A5
...Al Wuheida 26-L8
...Hor Al Anz 42-G1
...Jumeira 3 19-F4
...Mankhool 24-H7
...Mirdif 66-H2
...Muhaisnah 1 59-C7
...Umm Suqeim 1 18-G4
...Umm Suqeim 2 18-G4

9D
...Al Khabaisi 41-D2
...Hor Al Anz 42-G1
...Mirdif 66-H2, 66-J2

9E
...Mirdif 66-H3

10

10
...Al Garhoud 41-C7
...Al Quoz Industrial 1 34-H2
...Al Quoz Industrial 4 33-B6
...Al Qusais 1 43-C7
...Al Qusais Ind 3 44-K7
...Al Qusais Ind 4 52-L2
...Al Twar 1 42-K6, 42-L5
...Al Twar 2 51-A3
...Dubai International Airport 41-D6
...Jumeira 3 19-F2
...Muhaisnah 1 59-B3
...Muhaisnah 2 60-L2, 60-M2
...Nadd Al Shiba 2 54-G5, 54-K8
...Nadd Shamma 57-B3, 57-C3
...Oud Metha 39-F3, 40-H2
...Port Saeed 41-B4
...Umm Hurair 1 24-L9
...Umm Hurair 2 40-J3
...Umm Ramool 49-A6
...Za'abeel 1 39-B3

10A
...Abu Hail 26-J5
...Al Barshaa 1 31-F1
...Al Barshaa 2 32-J5

...Al Barshaa 3 12-M6, 31-C1
...Al Jafilia 23-B6
...Al Karama 24-H8
...Al Khabaisi 41-E2
...Al Manara 18-G7
...Al Mizhar 1 59-D9
...Al Mizhar 2 68-G6
...Al Nahda 2 44-G9
...Al Quoz 19-F9
...Al Quoz Industrial 2 34-L5
...Al Quoz Industrial 3 33-C2
...Al Qusais 2 51-B3
...Al Qusais 3 51-B6
...Al Raffa 24-G3
...Al Rashidiya 57-C1, 57-C2
...Al Safa 1 20-G5
...Al Safa 2 18-M6
...Al Twar 3 50-M7
...Al Wuheida 26-K6
...Dubai Investment Park 1 0-G9, 7-E4
...Hor Al Anz 26-G8
...Hor Al Anz East 42-L1
...Jumeira 1 22-M3
...Mankhool 24-H6
...Muhaisnah 3 51-F5
...Nadd Al Hamar 56-H7, 56-J6, 56-J7
...Ras Al Khor Industrial 1 46-L9
...Ras Al Khor Industrial 2 55-B4
...Umm Al Sheif 17-B7
...Umm Suqeim 3 17-B3

10B
...Abu Hail 26-K5
...Al Bada'a 22-J6
...Al Barshaa 1 15-E9
...Al Barshaa 2 32-G5
...Al Barshaa 3 31-B1
...Al Jafiliya 23-B6
...Al Karama 24-H8
...Al Khabaisi 41-F2
...Al Manara 17-D7
...Al Mizhar 1 59-E9
...Al Mizhar 2 68-J5
...Al Muteena 25-E7
...Al Nahda 2 44-J9
...Al Quoz 19-D9
...Al Quoz Industrial 2 33-F5
...Al Quoz Industrial 3 32-L2
...Al Qusais 1 43-C8
...Al Qusais 2 51-C3
...Al Qusais 3 51-C6
...Al Raffa 24-G3
...Al Rashidiya 57-C2, 57-D2
...Al Safa 2 18-L6
...Al Satwa 22-L7
...Al Twar 3 51-A7
...Hor Al Anz 26-H8
...Jumeira 1 22-J3
...Jumeira 3 19-E6
...Mankhool 24-H6
...Muhaisnah 3 51-F5
...Nadd Al Hamar 56-J6
...Nadd Al Shiba 1 53-A3
...Ras Al Khor Industrial 1 46-K9
...Ras Al Khor Industrial 2 54-M5
...Umm Al Sheif 16-K8
...Umm Ramool 49-E5

10C
...Al Bada'a 22-H6
...Al Karama 24-H8
...Al Manara 17-C7
...Al Mizhar 1 59-F8
...Al Mizhar 2 68-K4
...Al Muteena 25-F8
...Al Qusais 2 51-D3
...Al Safa 1 19-D6
...Al Safa 2 18-K6
...Al Satwa 22-G7
...Al Wuheida 26-L6
...Jumeira 1 22-H3
...Mankhool 23-F6

...Muhaisnah 3 52-G5
...Nadd Al Hamar 56-K6
...Ras Al Khor Industrial 1 54-J1
...Umm Suqeim 3 16-L3

10D
...Al Karama 24-G9
...Al Mizhar 1 60-H7
...Al Qusais 3 51-D6
...Al Safa 1 19-B6
...Al Safa 2 18-H7
...Al Satwa 21-F7
...Mankhool 23-E6
...Nadd Al Hamar 56-M5
...Ras Al Khor Industrial 1 54-H2
...Umm Suqeim 3 16-K3

10E
...Al Karama 23-E9, 24-G9
...Al Satwa 21-E7
...Umm Suqeim 1 18-M2

10F
...Umm Suqeim 1 18-L2

11

11
...Abu Hail 26-J5
...Al Bada'a 22-M5
...Al Barshaa 1 32-G2
...Al Garhoud 49-B3
...Al Jafiliya 23-C5
...Al Karama 24-H8
...Al Nahda 1 43-E3
...Al Quoz 19-F9
...Al Qusais 2 51-C3
...Al Qusais Ind 1 43-F9
...Al Qusais Ind 3 44-L8
...Al Rigga 25-A6
...Al Safa 2 18-M7
...Al Satwa 22-M7
...Al Sufouh 1 16-G4
...Al Sufouh 2 15-F3
...Jumeira 1 22-K3
...Jumeira 3 19-E2
...Muhaisnah 2 59-F2
...Nadd Shamma 57-C4, 57-C5, 57-D6
...Oud Metha 40-H3
...Ras Al Khor 63-D1
...Ras Al Khor Industrial 1 54-J2
...Riggat Al Buteen 41-A1
...Trade Centre 1 22-J9
...Umm Hurair 1 24-K8
...Za'abeel 2 38-M2

11A
...Al Barshaa 2 32-H3
...Al Barshaa 3 12-M5, 31-D2
...Al Khabaisi 41-F1
...Al Manara 17-F6
...Al Mizhar 1 67-D1
...Al Mizhar 2 68-H5
...Al Nahda 2 43-F7
...Al Quoz 34-M3
...Al Quoz Industrial 1 18-H9, 34-H1
...Al Quoz Industrial 2 34-J5
...Al Quoz Industrial 3 33-C2
...Al Quoz Industrial 4 33-C5
...Al Qusais 1 43-B8
...Al Qusais 3 51-C6
...Al Qusais Ind 4 52-L2
...Al Rashidiya 57-D4
...Al Souk Al Kabeer 24-J3
...Al Twar 1 42-L7
...Al Twar 2 50-M2
...Al Twar 3 50-L8
...Al Wuheida 26-L5
...Hor Al Anz East 26-M9
...Jumeira 2 20-M2
...Jumeira 3 19-E5, 19-F2

...Mankhool 24-H5
...Muhaisnah 1 59-B6
...Muhaisnah 3 52-G4, 52-G5
...Nadd Al Hamar 56-H7
...Nadd Al Shiba 2 54-G6, 54-G7
...Oud Metha 40-G2
...Ras Al Khor Industrial 2 55-A5
...Umm Al Sheif 17-A7
...Umm Suqeim 1 18-L2
...Umm Suqeim 2 17-F2
...Umm Suqeim 3 17-A3

11B
...Al Barshaa 2 32-J6
...Al Barshaa 3 31-D2
...Al Hamriya 24-K6
...Al Khabaisi 41-E2
...Al Mamzar 43-B2, 43-B3
...Al Manara 17-F7
...Al Mizhar 1 67-F4
...Al Mizhar 2 68-J7
...Al Quoz 34-M3
...Al Quoz Industrial 1 34-H3
...Al Quoz Industrial 2 34-J7
...Al Quoz Industrial 3 33-C4
...Al Quoz Industrial 4 33-C8
...Al Qusais 1 43-B9
...Al Qusais 3 51-C7
...Al Qusais Ind 2 51-F3
...Al Qusais Ind 5 52-L3
...Al Rashidiya 57-E5
...Al Safa 1 19-E7
...Al Twar 1 42-M8
...Al Twar 3 58-L1
...Al Wuheida 26-L7
...Hor Al Anz 42-G1
...Hor Al Anz East 42-M1
...Jebel Ali Industrial 2-M4, 3-D8
...Jumeira 2 20-M2
...Jumeira 3 19-F3
...Mankhool 24-H7
...Mirdif 66-G1
...Muhaisnah 1 59-C6
...Muhaisnah 3 52-G7
...Nadd Al Hamar 56-H8
...Nadd Al Shiba 1 53-A3
...Nadd Al Shiba 2 53-F8
...Ras Al Khor Industrial 2 55-C7
...Umm Suqeim 1 18-M4
...Umm Suqeim 2 17-F5
...Umm Suqeim 3 17-A4

11C
...Al Barshaa 2 32-J8
...Al Khabaisi 41-D3
...Al Mamzar 27-B7, 43-B3
...Al Mizhar 1 68-G5
...Al Qusais Ind 5 52-M5
...Al Souk Al Kabeer 24-K4
...Al Twar 1 42-M9
...Al Twar 3 58-M2
...Jumeira 2 20-M3
...Jumeira 3 19-F4
...Mirdif 66-J2
...Muhaisnah 1 59-C7
...Muhaisnah 3 52-G8
...Umm Suqeim 3 17-A5

11D
...Al Raffa 24-H5
...Umm Suqeim 3 17-A6

12

12
...Al Barshaa 2 32-J5
...Al Garhoud 41-B8
...Al Mamzar 27-B6, 43-A3
...Al Quoz Industrial 2 34-H6
...Al Quoz Industrial 3 33-C2
...Al Quoz Industrial 4 32-L6

...Al Qusais Ind 3 44-K7
...Al Rashidiya 57-F1
...Al Souk Al Kabeer 24-H2
...Al Twar 2 50-M3
...Dubai Investment Park 1 0-F9, 7-D4
...Hor Al Anz East 42-L1
...Mirdif 58-J8
...Muhaisnah 3 51-F5
...Nadd Shamma 57-C3
...Ras Al Khor Industrial 1 46-K9
...Ras Al Khor Industrial 2 54-L6
...Ras Al Khor Industrial 3 55-B9
...Umm Hurair 2 40-H4, 40-J4
...Umm Ramool 49-E6

12A
...Abu Hail 26-H5
...Al Bada'a 22-M6
...Al Barshaa 1 32-H1
...Al Barshaa 3 31-E2
...Al Jafiliya 23-C6
...Al Karama 24-J8
...Al Khabaisi 41-E2
...Al Manara 17-E7
...Al Mizhar 1 67-C1
...Al Mizhar 2 68-G6
...Al Muraqqabat 25-C7
...Al Nahda 2 44-G9
...Al Quoz 19-E9
...Al Quoz Industrial 1 34-K2
...Al Quoz Industrial 4 33-C7
...Al Qusais 2 51-B3
...Al Qusais Ind 4 52-L2
...Al Safa 1 20-G6
...Al Safa 2 18-M6
...Al Satwa 22-J7, 22-L7, 22-M7
...Al Twar 3 50-L8
...Al Wasl 20-L4
...Al Wuheida 26-K7
...Jumeira 1 22-L3
...Jumeira 2 20-M4, 21-A4
...Jumeira 3 19-F6
...Mankhool 24-G6
...Muhaisnah 2 59-F2, 60-G2
...Nadd Al Shiba 1 53-A4
...Nadd Al Shiba 2 54-H6, 54-J6
...Umm Al Sheif 16-M8, 17-A8
...Umm Suqeim 1 18-M3
...Umm Suqeim 2 17-F3, 18-G3
...Umm Suqeim 3 17-A3

12B
...Abu Hail 26-J5
...Al Bada'a 22-K5
...Al Barshaa 1 32-G1
...Al Barshaa 3 31-D2
...Al Jafiliya 23-A6
...Al Karama 24-H9
...Al Khabaisi 41-F2
...Al Manara 17-E7
...Al Mizhar 1 67-D1
...Al Mizhar 2 68-J5
...Al Muraqqabat 25-D9
...Al Nahda 2 44-H9
...Al Quoz 19-D9
...Al Quoz Industrial 1 33-F2
...Al Qusais 1 43-C7
...Al Qusais 2 51-C3
...Al Qusais Ind 4 52-L2
...Al Raffa 24-G3
...Al Safa 2 18-H7
...Al Twar 3 50-M7
...Al Wasl 20-K5
...Al Wuheida 26-L7
...Hor Al Anz 26-H8
...Jumeira 1 22-J3
...Jumeira 2 20-L2
...Jumeira 3 19-E6
...Mankhool 23-F6
...Muhaisnah 1 59-A5
...Muhaisnah 2 60-L2
...Nadd Al Hamar 56-H7

...Nadd Al Shiba 1 53-B3
...Nadd Al Shiba 2 54-K8
...Oud Metha 39-F4
...Port Saeed 41-B4
...Umm Al Sheif 16-M8
...Umm Suqeim 1 18-L3
...Umm Suqeim 3 16-L3

12C
...Al Bada'a 22-H6
...Al Barshaa 1 15-E9
...Al Barshaa 3 31-A2
...Al Karama 24-H9
...Al Khabaisi 42-G3
...Al Manara 17-D7
...Al Mizhar 1 59-F9
...Al Mizhar 2 68-L4
...Al Nahda 2 44-J9
...Al Quoz 19-C9
...Al Raffa 23-E3
...Al Safa 1 19-C6
...Hor Al Anz 26-H9
...Jumeira 1 22-H4
...Jumeira 2 20-J2
...Mankhool 23-E6
...Muhaisnah 1 59-B3
...Nadd Al Hamar 56-M5
...Umm Al Sheif 16-L8
...Umm Suqeim 1 18-K3

12D
...Al Bada'a 21-F6
...Al Barshaa 1 15-D9
...Al Karama 24-G9
...Al Manara 17-C7
...Al Mizhar 1 60-G8
...Al Mizhar 2 68-M3
...Al Safa 1 19-B6
...Jumeira 1 22-G4
...Jumeira 2 20-H2
...Nadd Al Hamar 57-A5
...Umm Suqeim 1 18-J3

12E
...Al Bada'a 21-E6
...Al Karama 23-E9
...Al Mizhar 1 60-H8
...Umm Suqeim 1 18-H3

13

13
...Abu Hail 26-J6
...Al Barshaa 1 16-J9
...Al Garhoud 49-B2
...Al Hudaiba 23-B4
...Al Muraqqabat 25-D8
...Al Nahda 1 43-F3
...Al Nahda 2 44-G8
...Al Quoz Industrial 1 34-G2, 34-G4
...Al Quoz Industrial 2 34-J6
...Al Quoz Industrial 4 33-C7
...Al Qusais 1 43-B6, 43-B8
...Al Qusais Ind 5 52-L3
...Al Raffa 24-H4
...Al Safa 1 19-E6
...Al Sufouh 1 16-G4
...Al Sufouh 3 15-D3
...Al Twar 1 50-M1
...Al Twar 3 50-L7
...Al Wasl 21-B7
...Jumeira 2 20-L1
...Muhaisnah 2 60-G2
...Nadd Al Hamar 56-H7
...Oud Metha 39-F2
...Port Saeed 41-C3
...Ras Al Khor Industrial 1 54-K3
...Riggat Al Buteen 41-B1
...Umm Hurair 2 39-C8, 39-F7
...Umm Ramool 49-D7
...Za'abeel 2 38-L2

13A
...Al Barshaa 2 32-H3
...Al Barshaa 3 31-D2
...Al Garhoud 49-B2
...Al Hamriya 24-K6
...Al Jafiliya 23-C5
...Al Karama 24-H8
...Al Khabaisi 41-F1
...Al Mamzar 27-B6
...Al Manara 17-F6
...Al Mizhar 1 59-D9
...Al Mizhar 2 68-H5
...Al Nahda 2 43-F6
...Al Quoz 19-F8, 34-M3
...Al Quoz Industrial 3 17-B9
...Al Qusais 2 51-C2
...Al Qusais 3 51-C6
...Al Qusais Ind 3 44-L7
...Al Rashidiya 57-E5
...Al Safa 2 18-L6
...Al Satwa 22-M7
...Al Twar 2 51-A3
...Al Wuheida 26-L8
...Hor Al Anz 26-H9
...Hor Al Anz East 42-M1
...Jumeira 1 22-K3
...Jumeira 2 20-M1
...Jumeira 3 19-E2
...Mankhool 24-G5
...Muhaisnah 1 59-A4
...Muhaisnah 3 52-G4
...Nadd Al Shiba 2 54-G7
...Ras Al Khor Industrial 2 55-A5
...Umm Al Sheif 16-M7
...Umm Suqeim 1 18-L2

13B
...Al Bada'a 22-L6
...Al Barshaa 2 32-H5
...Al Garhoud 49-B2
...Al Hamriya 24-K7
...Al Jafiliya 23-C6
...Al Karama 24-H8
...Al Khabaisi 41-E2
...Al Mamzar 27-B6, 27-B7
...Al Manara 17-F8
...Al Mizhar 1 67-D1
...Al Mizhar 2 68-J7
...Al Quoz 19-F8, 34-M5
...Al Quoz Industrial 3 33-B1
...Al Qusais 2 51-C3
...Al Qusais 3 51-C7
...Al Qusais Ind 3 44-L8
...Al Rashidiya 57-E6
...Al Safa 2 18-L7
...Al Satwa 22-M7
...Al Souk Al Kabeer 24-H2
...Al Twar 2 51-A5
...Al Wuheida 26-L8
...Hor Al Anz 42-G1
...Hor Al Anz East 42-M3
...Jumeira 1 22-K4
...Jumeira 2 20-M2
...Jumeira 3 19-E3
...Mankhool 24-G6
...Mirdif 66-G1
...Muhaisnah 1 59-B5, 59-B7
...Muhaisnah 3 52-G6
...Nadd Al Shiba 2 54-G8
...Oud Metha 39-F2
...Ras Al Khor Industrial 2 55-C7
...Umm Suqeim 1 18-L4

13C
...Al Barshaa 2 32-H7
...Al Garhoud 49-C3
...Al Mizhar 1 67-E2
...Al Quoz Industrial 3 33-B4
...Al Qusais 2 51-C4
...Al Qusais 3 51-C8
...Al Souk Al Kabeer 24-J3
...Jumeira 2 20-M3

...Jumeira 3 19-E4, 19-F9
...Mankhool 24-H6
...Mirdif 66-J2
...Muhaisnah 1 59-D7
...Muhaisnah 3 52-G6

13D
...Al Mamzar 27-B8
...Al Quoz 35-F2
...Al Qusais 2 51-D4
...Muhaisnah 3 52-G7

13E
...Muhaisnah 3 52-G8

14

14
...Abu Hail 26-J6
...Al Baraha 26-G6
...Al Khabaisi 41-F2
...Al Mamzar 27-A6
...Al Muraqqabat 41-D1
...Al Muteena 25-E7
...Al Nahda 2 44-J9
...Al Quoz 34-M4
...Al Quoz Industrial 1 33-E3
...Al Qusais 2 51-B4, 51-C3
...Al Qusais Ind 4 52-L2
...Al Rashidiya 57-D2
...Dubai International Airport 41-D7
...Muhaisnah 4 52-J3
...Nadd Al Shiba 1 53-B4
...Oud Metha 40-G3
...Port Saeed 41-B3, 41-B4
...Umm Al Sheif 16-M8
...Umm Suqeim 2 17-D3

14A
...Al Bada'a 22-M5
...Al Barshaa 1 32-J2
...Al Barshaa 2 32-J5
...Al Barshaa 3 31-D2
...Al Jafiliya 23-D6
...Al Karama 24-K8
...Al Manara 17-F7
...Al Mizhar 1 60-G9
...Al Mizhar 2 68-G7
...Al Nahda 2 43-F7
...Al Quoz 19-F9
...Al Quoz Industrial 1 34-L2
...Al Quoz Industrial 2 34-L6
...Al Quoz Industrial 3 33-D2
...Al Quoz Industrial 4 33-C6
...Al Qusais 1 43-A8
...Al Qusais 3 51-B6
...Al Qusais Ind 3 44-K8
...Al Raffa 24-H3
...Al Safa 1 19-E6
...Al Safa 2 18-M7
...Al Satwa 22-J7, 22-L7
...Al Twar 2 50-M3
...Al Wuheida 26-L7
...Hor Al Anz East 42-L1
...Jumeira 1 21-F4
...Jumeira 2 20-L2
...Jumeira 3 19-F2
...Muhaisnah 2 60-G2
...Muhaisnah 3 51-F5
...Nadd Al Shiba 2 54-H6, 54-H7
...Ras Al Khor Industrial 1 46-L9
...Umm Ramool 49-C6
...Umm Suqeim 1 18-L3
...Umm Suqeim 3 17-A4
...Za'abeel 1 39-E3

14B
...Al Bada'a 22-L5
...Al Barshaa 1 15-B9, 31-E1
...Al Barshaa 2 31-E5

...Al Barshaa 3 31-A2
...Al Jafiliya 23-C6
...Al Karama 24-J9
...Al Manara 17-C8
...Al Mizhar 1 60-H8
...Al Mizhar 2 68-J6
...Al Nahda 2 44-G7
...Al Quoz 19-D9
...Al Quoz Industrial 1 33-E2
...Al Quoz Industrial 2 34-J6
...Al Quoz Industrial 3 32-L3
...Al Quoz Industrial 4 33-A6
...Al Qusais 2 51-C3
...Al Qusais 3 51-C6
...Al Qusais Ind 3 44-K8
...Al Raffa 24-G3
...Al Safa 1 19-D6
...Al Safa 2 18-K7
...Al Twar 2 51-A3
...Al Twar 3 50-L8, 50-L9
...Al Wuheida 26-M7
...Dividing Road 32-J3
...Hor Al Anz 26-J9
...Hor Al Anz East 42-M1
...Jumeira 1 21-E4
...Jumeira 2 20-J2
...Jumeira 3 19-E2
...Mirdif 58-G9
...Muhaisnah 1 59-A5
...Muhaisnah 2 60-L2
...Muhaisnah 3 52-G5
...Nadd Al Hamar 56-K6
...Nadd Al Shiba 2 54-J7
...Nadd Shamma 57-C4
...Ras Al Khor Industrial 1 54-J2, 54-K1
...Ras Al Khor Industrial 2 54-M7
...Umm Ramool 49-E6
...Umm Suqeim 1 18-J3
...Umm Suqeim 3 16-L4

14C
...Al Barshaa 1 15-B9
...Al Barshaa 2 31-E5
...Al Jafiliya 23-C6
...Al Karama 23-F9
...Al Mizhar 2 68-K5
...Al Quoz 19-C9
...Al Quoz Industrial 2 33-F6
...Al Quoz Industrial 4 32-M7, 33-A7
...Al Qusais 1 43-C8
...Al Raffa 23-E4
...Al Safa 1 19-B7
...Hor Al Anz 42-J1
...Jumeira 1 21-D4
...Jumeira 3 19-C2
...Mirdif 58-H9
...Muhaisnah 1 59-B4
...Muhaisnah 2 60-M3
...Nadd Al Hamar 56-L6
...Umm Suqeim 1 18-H7

14D
...Al Jafiliya 23-B6
...Al Karama 23-F9
...Al Qusais 3 51-D6
...Al Safa 1 19-A6
...Hor Al Anz 42-K1
...Jumeira 1 21-B4
...Jumeira 3 19-B3
...Mirdif 58-H9, 58-J9
...Muhaisnah 1 59-C3
...Nadd Al Hamar 56-M5

14E
...Mirdif 58-K7

15
...Al Baraha 25-E6, 25-F5
...Al Barshaa 1 32-H1
...Al Barshaa 3 31-D1
...Al Hudaiba 23-B5
...Al Mamzar 43-C2
...Al Manara 17-E7
...Al Muraqqabat 25-B9
...Al Nahda 2 44-G8
...Al Quoz Industrial 2 34-J8
...Al Quoz Industrial 3 33-B2
...Al Qusais 1 51-C1
...Al Qusais Ind 4 52-L2
...Al Raffa 24-G3
...Al Safa 2 18-L7
...Al Satwa 22-M8
...Al Sufouh 1 16-G4
...Al Sufouh 2 15-D3
...Al Wuheida 26-L6
...Dubai International Airport 50-L7
...Hor Al Anz 42-H1
...Jumeira 1 22-K4
...Jumeira 2 20-M3
...Jumeira 3 19-E2
...Mirdif 66-H1, 66-K3, 66-L3
...Muhaisnah 2 60-G3
...Nadd Al Hamar 56-J9
...Oud Metha 40-G3
...Port Saeed 41-C4
...Ras Al Khor 63-B1
...Trade Centre 1 22-H9
...Umm Hurair 2 40-G5
...Umm Ramool 49-D8

15A
...Abu Hail 26-J6
...Al Barshaa 2 32-H3
...Al Garhoud 49-B2
...Al Hamriya 24-K5
...Al Jafiliya 23-C5
...Al Karama 24-H9, 40-J1
...Al Khabaisi 41-F1
...Al Mamzar 27-B6
...Al Mizhar 1 59-D9
...Al Mizhar 2 68-J5
...Al Nahda 2 44-G5
...Al Quoz 19-F9
...Al Quoz Industrial 1 18-G9
...Al Quoz Industrial 4 33-B5
...Al Qusais 2 51-D3
...Al Qusais Ind 2 51-F2
...Al Rashidiya 57-E4
...Al Safa 1 19-E5
...Al Twar 1 42-M7
...Al Twar 2 51-A5
...Al Wasl 21-A6
...Hor Al Anz East 26-M9
...Mankhool 24-G5
...Muhaisnah 3 52-G5
...Nadd Al Hamar 56-L8
...Nadd Al Shiba 2 54-H7
...Ras Al Khor Industrial 1 54-J3
...Ras Al Khor Industrial 2 55-A5
...Umm Al Sheif 16-M7
...Umm Suqeim 1 18-L2
...Umm Suqeim 2 17-F3
...Umm Suqeim 3 16-M4, 17-A3

15B
...Abu Hail 26-H7
...Al Barshaa 2 32-H5
...Al Garhoud 49-B2
...Al Hamriya 24-K6
...Al Jafiliya 23-D8
...Al Karama 40-J1
...Al Mizhar 1 67-D1
...Al Mizhar 2 68-J6
...Al Nahda 2 44-G6

...Al Quoz 19-F9
...Al Quoz Industrial 1 34-G3
...Al Quoz Industrial 4 33-B8
...Al Qusais 2 51-D5
...Al Rashidiya 57-E5
...Al Twar 1 42-M8
...Al Twar 2 51-A5
...Al Wasl 21-A7
...Dubai Investment Park 1 0-L9
...Hor Al Anz East 42-M1
...Jumeira 3 19-E7, 19-F9
...Mankhool 24-G6
...Muhaisnah 1 59-D8
...Muhaisnah 3 52-G6
...Nadd Al Shiba 2 54-G9
...Nadd Shamma 57-C3
...Ras Al Khor Industrial 1 54-K4
...Ras Al Khor Industrial 2 55-B7
...Umm Al Sheif 16-M8
...Umm Suqeim 1 18-L3
...Umm Suqeim 3 16-M5

15C
...Al Barshaa 2 32-H7
...Al Garhoud 49-C3
...Al Mizhar 2 68-J7
...Al Qusais 1 43-C9
...Al Rashidiya 57-E6
...Al Twar 1 42-M9
...Al Wasl 21-B9
...Hor Al Anz East 42-M3
...Muhaisnah 2 60-G4
...Muhaisnah 3 52-H7
...Umm Suqeim 1 18-L4
...Umm Suqeim 3 16-M5, 16-M5

15D
...Al Mamzar 27-B8
...Al Twar 1 42-M9, 50-M1
...Muhaisnah 3 52-H8

15E
...Al Twar 1 50-M1

16
...Abu Hail 26-J6
...Al Baraha 26-G6
...Al Garhoud 41-B8
...Al Hamriya 24-L6
...Al Jafiliya 23-A6
...Al Karama 23-F9, 24-G9
...Al Muteena 25-F8
...Al Nahda 2 43-F7
...Al Quoz 20-G9, 34-M4
...Al Qusais 1 43-B8
...Al Qusais 2 51-B4
...Al Rashidiya 57-D1
...Al Rigga 25-B4
...Al Safa 1 19-F6
...Al Souk Al Kabeer 24-H3
...Al Twar 1 42-L6
...Dubai Investment Park 1 0-G4, 7-E6
...Hor Al Anz East 42-L2
...Jumeira 2 20-L2
...Muhaisnah 2 60-J3
...Nadd Al Shiba 2 53-F6
...Nadd Shamma 57-C5
...Port Saeed 41-A3, 41-B3
...Umm Ramool 49-A7
...Umm Suqeim 3 16-L4

16A
...Al Bada'a 22-M5
...Al Barshaa 1 32-H4
...Al Barshaa 2 32-J5
...Al Barshaa 3 31-D2
...Al Khabaisi 41-E2
...Al Manara 17-F8
...Al Mizhar 2 68-G7

...Al Quoz Industrial 2 34-K6
...Al Quoz Industrial 3 33-A3
...Al Quoz Industrial 4 33-D7
...Al Qusais Ind 1 51-E1
...Al Qusais Ind 4 52-K2
...Al Raffa 23-F4, 24-G4
...Al Safa 2 18-M7
...Al Twar 2 50-M3
...Al Twar 3 50-K8
...Al Wasl 21-A7
...Dubai International Airport 41-D7
...Hor Al Anz 26-G8, 26-H8
...Jumeira 1 22-M3
...Jumeira 3 19-F2
...Mankhool 24-J6
...Muhaisnah 3 51-F6
...Nadd Al Hamar 56-G8, 56-J7
...Ras Al Khor Industrial 1 54-K1
...Ras Al Khor Industrial 2 55-C4
...Umm Al Sheif 17-A9
...Umm Suqeim 1 18-L3
...Umm Suqeim 2 18-G3

16B
...Al Bada'a 22-L5
...Al Barshaa 1 32-G2
...Al Barshaa 2 32-H5
...Al Barshaa 3 31-C2
...Al Khabaisi 41-E3
...Al Mamzar 27-B6
...Al Manara 17-D8
...Al Mizhar 1 67-E1
...Al Mizhar 2 68-J6
...Al Nahda 2 44-G9
...Al Quoz Industrial 2 34-G6
...Al Quoz Industrial 3 32-L3
...Al Quoz Industrial 4 33-B7
...Al Qusais Ind 4 52-M2
...Al Raffa 23-E4
...Al Safa 2 18-K7
...Al Satwa 22-H7
...Al Twar 2 51-A3
...Al Twar 3 50-L8
...Al Wasl 20-M5
...Al Wuheida 26-M7
...Dubai International Airport 42-J6
...Hor Al Anz 26-J9
...Jumeira 1 22-L3
...Jumeira 3 19-D2
...Mankhool 24-G6
...Mirdif 58-J8
...Muhaisnah 1 59-A5
...Muhaisnah 3 52-G5
...Ras Al Khor Industrial 1 54-J2
...Ras Al Khor Industrial 2 55-A6
...Umm Al Sheif 16-M9, 17-A8
...Umm Suqeim 1 18-K3
...Umm Suqeim 2 17-E3
...Za'abeel 2 38-G2

16C
...Al Barshaa 1 32-G2
...Al Barshaa 2 31-F5
...Al Barshaa 3 31-A2
...Al Mamzar 27-D6
...Al Manara 17-C8
...Al Mizhar 1 67-F1
...Al Mizhar 2 68-M4, 999-A4
...Al Nahda 2 44-J9
...Al Safa 2 18-J7
...Al Satwa 22-G7
...Al Wasl 20-K5
...Jumeira 1 22-H4
...Jumeira 3 19-B3
...Mankhool 23-F6
...Muhaisnah 1 59-C4
...Nadd Al Hamar 56-L6, 56-M6
...Naif 25-D6
...Ras Al Khor Industrial 2 54-M7
...Umm Al Sheif 16-L8
...Umm Suqeim 1 18-J3
...Umm Suqeim 2 17-C3

16D
...Al Barshaa 1 31-F2
...Al Mizhar 1 60-G9
...Al Quoz Industrial 4 32-L7
...Al Satwa 21-F7
...Al Twar 3 51-B8
...Nadd Al Hamar 57-B5
...Umm Al Sheif 16-L8

17
...Abu Hail 26-J6
...Al Baraha 25-F6
...Al Barshaa 1 32-G1
...Al Hamriya 24-K6
...Al Hudaiba 23-A5
...Al Manara 17-E6
...Al Nahda 2 44-G6
...Al Quoz Industrial 1 34-G1
...Al Quoz Industrial 4 33-B7
...Al Qusais 1 43-C9
...Al Qusais Ind 1 44-H9
...Al Satwa 22-L7
...Al Sufouh 2 15-F4
...Al Twar 3 50-M7
...Jumeira 3 19-E2, 19-E3
...Nadd Al Shiba 2 54-H8
...Port Saeed 41-B4
...Ras Al Khor Industrial 1 54-H3
...Riggat Al Buteen 41-B1
...Trade Centre 2 38-K1
...Umm Hurair 2 40-K2
...Umm Ramool 49-D6
...Umm Suqeim 1 18-L7
...Za'abeel 1 39-C5

17A
...Al Bada'a 22-L4
...Al Barshaa 2 32-G4
...Al Barshaa 3 31-D1
...Al Garhoud 49-B1
...Al Karama 24-H9
...Al Khabaisi 41-F2
...Al Mamzar 43-C1
...Al Mizhar 1 59-D9, 67-E1
...Al Mizhar 2 68-J4
...Al Muraqqabat 25-D8
...Al Quoz Industrial 2 34-H5
...Al Quoz Industrial 3 33-A1
...Al Qusais 2 51-D2
...Al Qusais 3 51-C6
...Al Qusais Ind 4 52-L2
...Al Raffa 24-G3
...Al Rashidiya 57-D1
...Al Twar 1 42-M7
...Al Twar 2 51-A2
...Al Wasl 21-A7
...Al Wuheida 26-L7
...Hor Al Anz 26-H9
...Hor Al Anz East 26-M9
...Jumeira 1 22-K3
...Jumeira 2 20-L2
...Jumeira 3 19-D5, 19-E9
...Mankhool 24-G5
...Mirdif 58-H9
...Muhaisnah 1 59-A4
...Muhaisnah 2 60-H1
...Muhaisnah 3 52-H5
...Nadd Al Hamar 56-J8
...Oud Metha 39-F3
...Ras Al Khor Industrial 2 54-M5, 55-A5
...Umm Al Sheif 16-M7
...Umm Suqeim 1 18-L2
...Umm Suqeim 2 17-F2, 17-F3
...Umm Suqeim 3 16-M3

17B
...Al Bada'a 22-L5
...Al Barshaa 2 32-H5

...Al Barshaa 3 31-D2
...Al Garhoud 49-C2
...Al Karama 40-H1
...Al Khabaisi 41-F3
...Al Mamzar 27-B8
...Al Mizhar 1 67-F3
...Al Mizhar 2 68-J5
...Al Muraqqabat 25-C8
...Al Quoz 35-E2
...Al Quoz Industrial 2 34-H8
...Al Quoz Industrial 3 33-A4
...Al Qusais 2 51-D3
...Al Qusais 3 51-C6
...Al Qusais Ind 5 52-M4
...Al Raffa 24-H4
...Al Rashidiya 57-D3
...Al Safa 1 19-E7
...Al Twar 1 42-M9
...Al Twar 2 51-A3
...Al Wasl 21-A8
...Al Wuheida 26-L8
...Hor Al Anz 42-H1
...Hor Al Anz East 42-M1
...Jumeira 1 22-J3, 22-K4
...Jumeira 2 20-M3
...Jumeira 3 19-E7
...Mankhool 24-G7
...Mirdif 66-H1, 66-J1
...Muhaisnah 1 59-D7
...Muhaisnah 2 60-H3
...Muhaisnah 4 52-J8
...Nadd Al Hamar 56-J9
...Nadd Shamma 57-D6
...Oud Metha 40-G4
...Ras Al Khor Industrial 2 55-B7
...Umm Al Sheif 16-M8
...Umm Suqeim 1 18-L4
...Umm Suqeim 2 17-F3
...Umm Suqeim 3 16-M5

17C
...Al Barshaa 2 32-H7
...Al Barshaa 3 31-D6
...Al Garhoud 49-C3
...Al Khabaisi 41-D3
...Al Mamzar 43-B2
...Al Mizhar 2 68-K7
...Al Qusais 2 51-D4
...Al Qusais 3 51-C7
...Al Twar 1 42-M9
...Al Twar 2 51-A5
...Al Wasl 21-A9
...Al Wuheida 26-L8
...Mirdif 66-J1
...Muhaisnah 2 60-H4
...Umm Suqeim 2 17-F5
...Umm Suqeim 3 16-M5

17D
...Al Barshaa 3 31-D7
...Al Garhoud 49-D3
...Al Qusais 3 51-C8
...Mirdif 66-J2
...Muhaisnah 2 60-H4

17E
...Al Barshaa 3 31-D8

18
...Al Baraha 26-G6
...Al Khabaisi 41-E2
...Al Muteèna 25-E8
...Al Quoz 34-M5
...Al Quoz Industrial 1 34-H3
...Al Quoz Industrial 3 33-D3
...Al Qusais 2 51-C4
...Al Raffa 24-H4
...Al Rashidiya 57-E1
...Al Twar 2 50-M4

...Al Wasl 21-A7
...Dubai International Airport 42-J6
...Mankhool 24-J6
...Muhaisnah 3 51-E6
...Muhaisnah 4 52-J4
...Nadd Shamma 57-C5
...Port Saeed 41-A3, 41-A5
...Ras Al Khor Industrial 1 54-L1
...Umm Hurair 2 40-H4
...Umm Suqeim 2 17-D3
...Za'abeel 1 39-C3

18A
...Abu Hail 26-J5, 26-J6
...Al Bada'a 22-M5
...Al Barshaa 1 32-H2
...Al Barshaa 2 31-F5, 32-J6
...Al Barshaa 3 31-D3
...Al Garhoud 41-A9
...Al Hamriya 24-L6
...Al Jafiliya 23-C6
...Al Karama 24-H9
...Al Mamzar 27-A6
...Al Manara 17-F8
...Al Mizhar 2 68-J7
...Al Quoz 19-F9
...Al Quoz Industrial 2 34-L6
...Al Quoz Industrial 4 33-B7
...Al Qusais 1 43-A8
...Al Qusais 3 51-B7
...Al Qusais Ind 1 52-H1
...Al Qusais Ind 3 44-K8
...Al Safa 1 19-F7
...Al Safa 2 18-M7, 19-A7
...Al Satwa 22-J7, 22-L7
...Al Twar 1 42-L7
...Al Twar 3 50-K8
...Al Wuheida 26-L7
...Jumeira 1 21-E4
...Jumeira 2 21-A5
...Jumeira 3 19-F3, 20-G3
...Muhaisnah 1 59-B5
...Muhaisnah 2 60-G3
...Nadd Al Hamar 56-J7
...Nadd Al Shiba 2 53-E6, 53-F7
...Ras Al Khor Industrial 2 55-B6
...Umm Ramool 49-B7
...Umm Suqeim 1 18-M3
...Umm Suqeim 3 17-B4

18B
...Abu Hail 26-K6
...Al Bada'a 22-L5
...Al Barshaa 1 32-G2
...Al Barshaa 2 31-E6
...Al Barshaa 3 31-C2
...Al Hamriya 24-K7
...Al Jafiliya 23-B6
...Al Karama 39-F1
...Al Mamzar 27-D6
...Al Manara 17-D8
...Al Mizhar 1 67-E1
...Al Mizhar 2 68-L3, 999-A5
...Al Quoz Industrial 2 33-E6
...Al Quoz Industrial 4 32-L8, 32-M7
...Al Qusais 1 43-B8
...Al Qusais 3 51-C6
...Al Qusais Ind 1 44-J9
...Al Qusais Ind 3 44-L8
...Al Safa 1 19-D7
...Al Safa 2 18-L7
...Al Twar 1 42-L7
...Al Twar 3 50-L8
...Al Wuheida 26-M7
...Jumeira 1 21-D4
...Jumeira 2 20-L2
...Jumeira 3 19-E3, 19-E9
...Mirdif 66-H1
...Muhaisnah 1 59-C4
...Muhaisnah 2 60-K3
...Nadd Al Hamar 56-L7
...Nadd Al Shiba 2 54-G7

...Ras Al Khor Industrial 2 54-M7
...Umm Ramool 49-E6
...Umm Suqeim 1 18-J4, 18-L3, 18-L4
...Umm Suqeim 3 16-K4

18C
...Al Barshaa 1 31-F2
...Al Barshaa 3 31-A2
...Al Jafiliya 23-B6
...Al Mizhar 1 67-F1
...Al Quoz 19-D9, 35-C1
...Al Safa 1 19-B7
...Al Safa 2 18-K7
...Al Twar 1 42-L7
...Al Twar 3 51-A8
...Jumeira 1 21-C4
...Jumeira 3 19-D3
...Mirdif 58-L7
...Muhaisnah 2 60-M3
...Nadd Al Hamar 56-M6
...Umm Suqeim 1 18-H4

18D
...Al Mizhar 1 60-G9
...Al Safa 2 18-J8
...Al Twar 1 42-M6
...Jumeira 1 21-B4
...Jumeira 3 19-B3
...Nadd Al Hamar 57-B5

18E
...Al Mizhar 1 60-J9
...Al Twar 1 42-M6
...Jumeira 3 19-A3

19
...Abu Hail 26-J6
...Al Barshaa 1 32-G1
...Al Garhoud 49-C2
...Al Hudaiba 23-A5
...Al Jafiliya 23-C6
...Al Karama 40-H1
...Al Mamzar 43-C1
...Al Mizhar 2 68-K6
...Al Muraqqabat 25-C9
...Al Nahda 2 44-H9
...Al Quoz Industrial 1 33-F1
...Al Quoz Industrial 3 33-A2
...Al Raffa 24-G4
...Al Safa 1 19-D6, 19-D7
...Al Satwa 22-L7
...Al Souk Al Kabeer 24-K4
...Al Sufouh 2 15-F4
...Al Twar 3 50-M9
...Al Wasl 21-A7
...Al Wuheida 26-M7
...Dubai International Airport 42-J5
...Muhaisnah 1 59-D7
...Muhaisnah 2 60-J4
...Port Saeed 41-C4
...Ras Al Khor Industrial 1 54-J4
...Ras Al Khor Industrial 2 55-B7
...Trade Centre 1 21-F9
...Umm Hurair 2 40-H4
...Umm Ramool 49-E8
...Umm Suqeim 1 18-L4

19A
...Al Barshaa 2 32-G4
...Al Barshaa 3 31-C1
...Al Khabaisi 41-F2
...Al Manara 17-E6
...Al Mizhar 1 59-E9
...Al Muteena 25-F7
...Al Nahda 2 44-G7
...Al Quoz 19-E9
...Al Quoz Industrial 2 34-H6
...Al Quoz Industrial 4 33-A5
...Al Qusais 1 43-C5

...Al Qusais Ind 2 52-G2
...Al Qusais Ind 4 52-M2
...Al Rashidiya 57-E4
...Al Rigga 25-B6
...Al Safa 2 18-L6
...Al Twar 1 42-M7
...Al Twar 2 51-A2, 51-D3
...Jumeira 2 20-L1
...Jumeira 3 19-E3
...Mankhool 24-G5
...Muhaisnah 4 52-H4
...Nadd Al Hamar 56-H6
...Nadd Al Shiba 2 54-J8, 54-K7
...Nadd Shamma 57-C4
...Umm Al Sheif 16-L7
...Umm Suqeim 3 16-M4
...Za'abeel 1 39-C3

19B
...Al Barshaa 2 32-G5
...Al Barshaa 3 31-B3
...Al Khabaisi 41-F3
...Al Mamzar 43-D2
...Al Manara 17-E8
...Al Mizhar 1 67-E2
...Al Muteena 25-E7, 25-E8
...Al Quoz Industrial 2 34-H8
...Al Quoz Industrial 4 33-B8
...Al Qusais 2 51-D4
...Al Qusais 3 51-D8
...Al Qusais Ind 5 52-M3
...Al Rashidiya 57-E5
...Al Safa 2 18-L7
...Al Twar 1 42-M8
...Al Twar 2 51-A3
...Jumeira 2 20-L3
...Jumeira 3 19-E4, 19-E9
...Mankhool 24-G7
...Mirdif 58-H9
...Muhaisnah 4 52-H5
...Nadd Al Hamar 56-J9
...Nadd Al Shiba 2 54-H9
...Nadd Shamma 57-D6
...Umm Al Sheif 16-M8
...Umm Suqeim 2 17-F4
...Umm Suqeim 3 16-M5

19C
...Al Barshaa 2 32-G7
...Al Barshaa 3 31-C5
...Al Khabaisi 41-D3
...Al Quoz 35-E4
...Al Qusais 1 43-C9, 51-C1
...Al Qusais 3 51-D8
...Al Twar 1 43-A9
...Al Twar 2 51-A5
...Muhaisnah 4 52-H6

19D
...Al Barshaa 2 32-G8
...Al Barshaa 3 31-C7
...Al Qusais 1 51-D1
...Al Twar 1 43-A9
...Muhaisnah 4 52-J7

19E
...Al Barshaa 3 31-C8
...Al Twar 1 51-A1

20
...Al Barshaa 2 31-F6
...Al Barshaa 3 31-B3
...Al Hamriya 24-K7
...Al Jafiliya 23-A7
...Al Khabaisi 42-G3
...Al Muraqqabat 25-C8
...Al Quoz 34-M5
...Al Quoz Industrial 1 34-G3
...Al Qusais 2 51-E4

...Al Twar 3 50-K9
...Al Wasl 21-B7
...Hor Al Anz East 42-M2
...Mankhool 23-E7
...Nadd Shamma 57-C5
...Port Saeed 41-A3
...Ras Al Khor Industrial 3 55-E9
...Umm Hurair 2 40-H5
...Umm Ramool 49-A7
...Umm Suqeim 3 16-M4
...Za'abeel 1 39-D4

20A
...Abu Hail 26-J6
...Al Bada'a 22-L5, 22-M5
...Al Barshaa 1 32-H2
...Al Garhoud 49-A1
...Al Karama 24-H9
...Al Mamzar 27-A7
...Al Manara 18-G8
...Al Mizhar 1 67-E2
...Al Mizhar 2 68-H8
...Al Quoz 35-F1
...Al Quoz Industrial 2 34-L7
...Al Quoz Industrial 3 33-C3
...Al Quoz Industrial 4 33-D7
...Al Qusais 1 43-B8
...Al Qusais 3 51-B7
...Al Qusais Ind 3 44-K8
...Al Qusais Ind 5 52-L3
...Al Raffa 24-H4
...Al Rashidiya 57-C2
...Al Safa 1 19-F7
...Al Satwa 22-J7, 22-L7
...Al Twar 1 42-L7
...Hor Al Anz 26-G8
...Jumeira 1 21-F4
...Jumeira 2 20-M3, 21-A5
...Jumeira 3 19-F3, 20-G3
...Muhaisnah 2 60-H3
...Muhaisnah 3 51-F6
...Nadd Al Hamar 56-H8
...Nadd Al Shiba 2 53-F7
...Ras Al Khor Industrial 1 54-K2
...Ras Al Khor Industrial 2 55-B6, 55-C5
...Umm Suqeim 1 18-L4
...Umm Suqeim 2 17- F4, 18-G3

20B
...Abu Hail 26-K6
...Al Bada'a 22-K6
...Al Barshaa 1 32-H2
...Al Garhoud 41-B9
...Al Karama 40-G1
...Al Mamzar 27-C6
...Al Manara 17-F8
...Al Mizhar 1 68-G1
...Al Mizhar 2 68-K6
...Al Quoz 35-D1
...Al Quoz Industrial 2 34-H7
...Al Quoz Industrial 3 33-A3
...Al Quoz Industrial 4 32-L7
...Al Qusais 3 51-C7
...Al Qusais Ind 3 44-L8
...Al Qusais Ind 5 52-M3
...Al Raffa 24-G4
...Al Rashidiya 57-D2
...Al Safa 1 19-D7
...Al Twar 1 42-L7
...Al Wuheida 26-M7
...Hor Al Anz 26-H8
...Jumeira 1 21-E4
...Jumeira 2 20-K3, 20-L3
...Jumeira 3 19-A3, 19-B3
...Mirdif 66-H1
...Muhaisnah 1 59-B5
...Muhaisnah 2 60-K4
...Muhaisnah 3 52-G6
...Nadd Al Hamar 56-L7
...Nadd Al Shiba 2 54-J9
...Ras Al Khor Industrial 1 54-J3
...Ras Al Khor Industrial 2 54-M8

...Umm Suqeim 1 18-J4
...Umm Suqeim 2 17-E3

20C
...Al Barshaa 1 32-G2
...Al Garhoud 41-C9
...Al Manara 17-D8
...Al Mizhar 2 68-L6
...Al Quoz Industrial 2 33-F7
...Al Quoz Industrial 3 32-L3
...Al Qusais 3 51-D7
...Al Raffa 23-E4
...Al Safa 1 19-C7
...Al Satwa 22-H7
...Jumeira 1 21-C5
...Jumeira 2 20-H3
...Mirdif 66-H1
...Muhaisnah 1 59-C4
...Muhaisnah 2 60-M4
...Nadd Al Hamar 57-B6
...Umm Suqeim 2 17-C4

20D
...Al Barshaa 1 32-G2
...Al Manara 17-C9
...Al Mizhar 2 68-M5
...Al Safa 1 19-B7
...Jumeira 1 21-B4
...Mirdif 58-K9

21

21
...Al Bada'a 22-L5
...Al Hamriya 24-J6
...Al Hudaiba 23-A4
...Al Jafiliya 23-C6
...Al Karama 24-G8
...Al Mamzar 27-C5
...Al Nahda 2 44-H9
...Al Quoz Industrial 1 33-F4
...Al Quoz Industrial 2 34-H6
...Al Quoz Industrial 4 33-A7
...Al Safa 2 18-K6
...Al Satwa 22-K8
...Dubai International Airport 42-K7
...Jumeira 2 20-L3
...Jumeira 3 19-E3
...Mankhool 24-G7
...Muhaisnah 1 59-E7
...Muhaisnah 2 60-J4
...Nadd Al Hamar 56-J8
...Nadd Al Shiba 2 54-J8
...Oud Metha 39-F3
...Port Saeed 41-C4
...Ras Al Khor Industrial 3 55-C9, 63-D2
...Trade Centre 2 38-J1
...Umm Ramool 49-E7
...Umm Suqeim 2 17-E3
...Umm Suqeim 3 16-L5

21A
...Abu Hail 26-J6
...Al Baraha 26-G5
...Al Barshaa 1 16-G8
...Al Barshaa 2 32-G5
...Al Barshaa 3 31-C1
...Al Garhoud 41-B9
...Al Khabaisi 42-G2
...Al Manara 17-E6
...Al Mizhar 1 59-E8
...Al Mizhar 2 68-K4
...Al Muraqqabat 25-D8
...Al Nahda 2 44-G6
...Al Quoz 19-E9
...Al Quoz Industrial 3 16-M9
...Al Qusais 1 43-C6
...Al Qusais 3 51-C6
...Al Qusais Ind 2 52-J1
...Al Raffa 24-G3
...Al Rashidiya 57-D1

...Al Souk Al Kabeer 24-J3
...Al Twar 1 43-A8
...Al Twar 3 50-M7
...Al Wasl 21-A6
...Al Wuheida 26-M7
...Hor Al Anz 26-J8
...Jumeira 1 22-K3
...Jumeira 3 19-D5
...Ras Al Khor Industrial 2 55-A6
...Umm Al Sheif 16-L7
...Umm Suqeim 1 18-K2

21B
...Abu Hail 26-J7
...Al Barshaa 1 32-G1
...Al Barshaa 2 32-G9
...Al Barshaa 3 31-C3
...Al Garhoud 49-B1
...Al Mamzar 43-D2
...Al Manara 17-E8
...Al Mizhar 1 59-E9, 67-F1
...Al Mizhar 2 68-L6
...Al Muraqqabat 25-C9
...Al Quoz 35-E4
...Al Quoz Industrial 3 32-M1
...Al Qusais 1 43-C7, 43-D8, 43-D9
...Al Qusais 3 51-D7
...Al Raffa 24-G4
...Al Rashidiya 57-E2
...Al Twar 1 43-A9, 51-A1
...Al Twar 3 50-M8, 58-M1
...Al Wasl 21-A7
...Al Wuheida 26-M8
...Hor Al Anz 26-J9
...Jumeira 1 22-K4
...Muhaisnah 1 59-B5
...Ras Al Khor Industrial 2 55-B8
...Umm Al Sheif 16-L8
...Umm Suqeim 1 18-K3

21C
...Al Barshaa 3 31-C5
...Al Garhoud 49-C2
...Al Khabaisi 41-D4
...Al Mizhar 1 67-F3
...Al Mizhar 2 68-L6
...Al Quoz Industrial 3 33-A4
...Al Qusais 3 51-D8
...Al Safa 1 19-D7
...Al Twar 3 58-M2
...Al Wasl 21-A9
...Al Wuheida 26-M8
...Hor Al Anz 42-H1
...Umm Suqeim 1 18-K4

21D
...Al Barshaa 3 31-C7
...Al Garhoud 49-D3
...Al Mizhar 1 68-G4
...Al Wasl 37-A1

21E
...Al Barshaa 3 31-C8
...Mirdif 58-H9

22

22
...Al Barshaa 2 31-F6
...Al Jafiliya 23-B7, 23-C6
...Al Karama 40-G1
...Al Khabaisi 42-G2
...Al Quoz 34-M5
...Al Quoz Industrial 2 34-J7
...Al Quoz Industrial 3 33-B3
...Al Quoz Industrial 4 33-B7
...Al Qusais 3 51-D7
...Al Qusais Ind 5 52-K3
...Al Twar 2 51-A4
...Al Twar 3 50-M9
...Al Wuheida 26-L7

...Hor Al Anz 26-G8
...Jumeira 3 19-A3
...Muhaisnah 1 59-C4
...Muhaisnah 3 52-G6
...Muhaisnah 4 52-J4
...Nadd Al Hamar 56-J8
...Nadd Al Shiba 2 53-F8
...Nadd Shamma 57-C5
...Ras Al Khor Industrial 2 55-B7
...Umm Suqeim 1 18-L4
...Umm Suqeim 2 17-C4, 17-E4, 18-G4
...Umm Suqeim 3 17-A4
...Za'abeel 2 38-G3

221-224
...Dubai International Airport 50-H3

22A
...Abu Hail 26-H6
...Al Bada'a 22-L6
...Al Barshaa 1 32-H3
...Al Barshaa 3 31-D3
...Al Garhoud 49-B1
...Al Khabaisi 41-D2
...Al Mamzar 27-B7
...Al Mizhar 2 68-H8
...Al Muraqqabat 25-C8
...Al Muteena 25-D7
...Al Quoz 35-F1
...Al Quoz Industrial 1 34-G4
...Al Qusais 1 43-A9, 43-B8
...Al Qusais 2 51-B4
...Al Qusais Ind 3 44-K9
...Al Rashidiya 57-D2
...Al Safa 1 19-F7
...Al Satwa 22-M7
...Al Twar 1 42-L7
...Al Wasl 21-A7
...Hor Al Anz East 42-L3
...Jumeira 1 22-H4, 22-L4
...Jumeira 2 21-A5
...Mankhool 24-H6
...Muhaisnah 2 60-H4
...Ras Al Khor Industrial 1 54-M1
...Umm Ramool 49-B7

22B
...Abu Hail 26-J6
...Al Bada'a 22-J6
...Al Barshaa 1 31-F2
...Al Barshaa 3 31-B3
...Al Garhoud 41-B9
...Al Khabaisi 41-D3
...Al Mamzar 27-C7
...Al Mizhar 1 67-E2
...Al Mizhar 2 68-K7
...Al Muraqqabat 25-C9
...Al Muteena 25-D7
...Al Quoz 35-F1
...Al Quoz Industrial 1 33-F4
...Al Qusais 1 43-B9, 43-C8
...Al Qusais 2 51-C4
...Al Qusais Ind 3 44-L8
...Al Raffa 24-H4
...Al Rashidiya 57-F1
...Al Safa 1 19-E7
...Al Satwa 22-J7, 22-L7
...Al Twar 1 42-L7
...Al Wasl 20-K5
...Hor Al Anz East 42-M2, 42-M3
...Jumeira 2 20-K3
...Mankhool 24-G7
...Mirdif 66-J1
...Muhaisnah 2 60-K4
...Ras Al Khor Industrial 1 54-K2
...Umm Ramool 49-D7, 49-E7

22C
...Al Bada'a 22-H6
...Al Barshaa 1 31-E1
...Al Barshaa 3 31-A3
...Al Mizhar 1 68-G1
...Al Muraqqabat 41-D1

...Al Muteena 25-F8
...Al Qusais 1 43-C9
...Al Raffa 24-H4
...Al Twar 1 42-M7
...Jumeira 1 22-G4
...Jumeira 2 20-J3
...Mirdif 58-M8
...Muhaisnah 2 60-M4
...Ras Al Khor Industrial 1 54-J3

22D
...Al Barshaa 1 15-C9
...Al Mizhar 1 60-J9
...Al Quoz 35-D1
...Al Satwa 21-F8, 21-F8
...Al Twar 1 42-M7
...Jumeira 2 20-H3

23
...Al Bada'a 22-K5
...Al Baraha 25-F6
...Al Hudaiba 23-A5
...Al Karama 24-G8, 40-H1
...Al Mamzar 43-C2
...Al Nahda 2 44-H6, 44-J9
...Al Quoz 19-E9
...Al Quoz Industrial 1 33-F2
...Al Quoz Industrial 2 34-H7
...Al Quoz Industrial 3 32-M3
...Al Raffa 23-F3
...Al Satwa 22-K7
...Al Sufouh 2 15-E6
...Al Twar 3 58-M2
...Al Wasl 21-A9
...Jumeira 3 19-E3
...Muhaisnah 2 60-J5, 60-K5
...Nadd Al Shiba 2 54-K8
...Port Saeed 41-B5
...Ras Al Khor Industrial 2 54-M6
...Trade Centre 1 21-E9
...Trade Centre 2 38-J1
...Umm Al Sheif 16-L8
...Umm Ramool 49-E8
...Umm Suqeim 1 18-K4
...Umm Suqeim 2 17-E4

23A
...Abu Hail 26-J6
...Al Barshaa 1 15-F8
...Al Barshaa 2 32-G5
...Al Barshaa 3 31-C1
...Al Garhoud 41-B9
...Al Jafiliya 23-C6
...Al Manara 17-E6
...Al Mizhar 1 59-F9
...Al Mizhar 2 68-K4
...Al Muraqqabat 25-D9
...Al Quoz Industrial 4 33-A6
...Al Qusais 3 51-D8
...Al Qusais Ind 2 52-H1
...Al Rashidiya 57-E4
...Al Safa 1 19-C5
...Al Safa 2 18-K6
...Al Wuheida 26-M6
...Hor Al Anz 26-J9
...Jumeira 1 22-J3
...Jumeira 2 20-L1
...Mankhool 23-F5
...Muhaisnah 4 52-J4
...Nadd Al Hamar 56-H6
...Umm Suqeim 3 16-L3

23B
...Al Barshaa 1 15-F9
...Al Barshaa 2 32-G6
...Al Barshaa 3 31-C2
...Al Garhoud 49-B1
...Al Jafiliya 23-C7
...Al Khabaisi 41-D4

...Al Manara 17-E8
...Al Mizhar 1 67-F1
...Al Mizhar 2 68-L5
...Al Muraqqabat 25-C9
...Al Quoz Industrial 4 33-A8
...Al Qusais 3 51-D8
...Al Rashidiya 57-E5
...Al Safa 1 19-D6
...Al Safa 2 18-K7
...Al Wuheida 26-M7
...Hor Al Anz 26-J9
...Jebel Ali Industrial 2-L5, 3-C8
...Jumeira 1 22-J3
...Jumeira 2 20-L3
...Mankhool 23-F7
...Mirdif 58-H9
...Muhaisnah 4 52-J5
...Nadd Al Hamar 56-K9
...Umm Suqeim 3 16-L5

23C
...Al Barshaa 2 32-G8
...Al Barshaa 3 31-C5
...Al Mizhar 1 68-G4
...Al Mizhar 2 68-L6
...Al Muraqqabat 25-C9
...Al Rashidiya 57-F6
...Al Wuheida 26-M8
...Dubai Investment Park 1 7-C1
...Hor Al Anz 42-H1
...Jebel Ali Industrial 0-D2
...Jumeira 1 22-K4
...Mankhool 24-G7
...Mirdif 66-K2
...Muhaisnah 4 52-J5, 52-J7

23D
...Al Barshaa 3 31-C8
...Al Garhoud 49-C2
...Al Muraqqabat 25-B9
...Al Wuheida 26-M9
...Muhaisnah 4 52-J8

24
...Al Barshaa 2 31-E6, 31-F4
...Al Garhoud 49-B1
...Al Karama 40-J1
...Al Mamzar 27-B7
...Al Mizhar 2 68-J7
...Al Muteena 25-F7
...Al Quoz 34-M6, 35-F1
...Al Quoz Industrial 4 33-C8
...Al Qusais 1 43-C8
...Al Qusais Ind 3 44-L9
...Dubai International Airport 42-K7
...Hor Al Anz 26-G8
...Hor Al Anz East 42-L3
...Jebel Ali 6-M2
...Jebel Ali Industrial 2-H3, 2-M4, 3-D5
...Mankhool 23-E7
...Muhaisnah 2 60-M4
...Muhaisnah 3 52-G7
...Nadd Al Shiba 2 53-F7
...Nadd Shamma 57-C5
...Ras Al Khor Industrial 1 54-K3
...Umm Hurair 2 40-G5
...Umm Suqeim 1 18-K4
...Za'abeel 1 39-E4
...Za'abeel 2 38-G3

24A
...Abu Hail 26-H6
...Al Bada'a 22-L6, 22-M6
...Al Barshaa 3 31-D3
...Al Jafiliya 23-B7
...Al Khabaisi 41-D2
...Al Muraqqabat 25-C8
...Al Quoz Industrial 1 34-L3
...Al Quoz Industrial 2 34-L7

...Al Quoz Industrial 3 33-C4
...Al Qusais 2 51-C4
...Al Qusais 3 51-B7
...Al Qusais Ind 5 52-K3
...Al Raffa 24-H4
...Al Rashidiya 57-D2
...Al Satwa 22-H8
...Al Twar 1 42-L7
...Al Twar 2 50-M5
...Al Twar 3 50-M9
...Al Wasl 20-K4
...Al Wuheida 26-K8
...Jumeira 2 20-L5, 20-M3, 21-A5
...Jumeira 3 20-G3
...Nadd Al Hamar 56-H9
...Ras Al Khor Industrial 2 55-C6
...Umm Ramool 49-B8
...Umm Suqeim 2 18-G4
...Umm Suqeim 3 17-B4, 17-B5

24B
...Abu Hail 26-K7
...Al Bada'a 22-K6
...Al Barshaa 3 31-B3
...Al Jafiliya 23-A7
...Al Khabaisi 41-D3
...Al Mizhar 1 67-E2, 68-J1
...Al Quoz Industrial 1 34-G4
...Al Quoz Industrial 2 34-G8
...Al Quoz Industrial 3 32-L4
...Al Qusais 2 51-D4
...Al Qusais 3 51-D7
...Al Qusais Ind 5 52-L3
...Al Raffa 24-H5
...Al Rashidiya 57-F2
...Al Satwa 22-H8
...Al Twar 1 42-M7
...Al Twar 2 51-A4
...Al Twar 3 51-A9, 59-A2
...Al Wasl 20-K5
...Al Wuheida 26-L7
...Jumeira 1 21-D4
...Jumeira 2 20-L3, 20-L3
...Jumeira 3 19-E3
...Mirdif 58-K9
...Muhaisnah 1 59-C4
...Nadd Al Hamar 56-L7
...Ras Al Khor Industrial 2 55-C6
...Umm Ramool 49-C8, 49-D7
...Umm Suqeim 2 17-C4
...Umm Suqeim 3 16-M5

24C
...Al Khabaisi 41-D3
...Al Mizhar 1 67-F2
...Al Muraqqabat 41-C1
...Al Qusais 3 51-D7
...Al Raffa 23-F4
...Al Twar 1 42-M7
...Al Twar 3 51-A9
...Al Wasl 20-J5
...Al Wuheida 26-M8
...Jumeira 1 21-D5
...Jumeira 2 20-J4
...Jumeira 3 19-D3
...Nadd Al Hamar 57-B6
...Ras Al Khor Industrial 2 55-B7
...Umm Suqeim 3 16-K5

24D
...Al Bada'a 21-F6
...Al Wuheida 26-M8
...Jumeira 1 21-C5
...Jumeira 3 19-C4
...Ras Al Khor Industrial 2 55-A8
...Umm Ramool 49-E7

24E
...Al Bada'a 22-H6

24G
...Al Bada'a 21-E6

25

25
...Abu Hail 26-J7
...Al Bada'a 22-K5
...Al Baraha 25-F6
...Al Barshaa 2 31-F8
...Al Hudaiba 23-A5
...Al Karama 24-G9
...Al Khabaisi 41-F3, 42-G2
...Al Mamzar 27-D5, 43-D1
...Al Manara 17-D7
...Al Muraqqabat 25-C9
...Al Quoz 19-E9
...Al Quoz Industrial 2 34-G5
...Al Quoz Industrial 4 32-M7
...Al Qusais Ind 1 44-J8
...Al Raffa 23-F4
...Al Safa 1 19-C6
...Al Safa 2 18-K7
...Al Satwa 22-K8
...Al Twar 3 50-M9
...Jumeira 1 22-J4
...Muhaisnah 2 60-J4
...Nadd Al Hamar 56-K8
...Nadd Al Shiba 2 54-K8
...Naif 25-C5
...Port Saeed 41-C5
...Trade Centre 2 38-J1
...Umm Ramool 49-E6
...Umm Suqeim 2 17-E5
...Umm Suqeim 3 16-L4

25A
...Al Barshaa 1 15-F9
...Al Barshaa 3 31-B2
...Al Jafiliya 23-B6
...Al Mizhar 1 59-F9
...Al Mizhar 2 68-K4
...Al Nahda 2 44-H6
...Al Quoz Industrial 1 33-E1
...Al Quoz Industrial 3 16-L9
...Al Qusais 1 43-C5
...Al Qusais 3 51-D6
...Al Rashidiya 57-D1, 57-E2
...Al Twar 3 50-M7
...Al Wasl 20-M4
...Al Wuheida 26-M6
...Jumeira 2 20-L2
...Jumeira 3 19-D2, 19-E9
...Mankhool 23-F5
...Mirdif 58-J9
...Muhaisnah 1 59-D6
...Muhaisnah 4 52-J6
...Ras Al Khor Industrial 2 54-L5
...Umm Al Sheif 16-L7
...Umm Suqeim 1 18-K2

25B
...Al Barshaa 1 31-F2, 32-L1
...Al Barshaa 3 31-B5
...Al Jafiliya 23-C7
...Al Mamzar 27-C8, 43-C1
...Al Mizhar 1 67-F1
...Al Mizhar 2 68-L5
...Al Muteena 25-E8
...Al Quoz 35-E4
...Al Quoz Industrial 1 33-E4
...Al Qusais 3 51-D7
...Al Rashidiya 57-E4
...Al Souk Al Kabeer 24-J3
...Al Twar 3 50-M9
...Al Wuheida 26-M8
...Jumeira 2 20-L3, 20-M5
...Jumeira 3 19-D3
...Mankhool 23-F7
...Mirdif 58-J9, 66-J1
...Muhaisnah 1 59-E7
...Muhaisnah 4 52-J7
...Ras Al Khor Industrial 2 54-M6

...Umm Al Sheif 16-L8
...Umm Suqeim 1 18-K3, 18-L3

25C
...Al Garhoud 49-D4
...Al Jafiliya 23-C7
...Al Mizhar 1 68-G4
...Al Mizhar 2 68-L6
...Al Quoz Industrial 3 32-M4
...Al Rashidiya 57-F5
...Al Souk Al Kabeer 24-J4
...Al Wuheida 26-M8
...Jumeira 2 20-M5
...Jumeira 3 19-D4
...Mirdif 66-J1, 66-K1
...Muhaisnah 4 52-J8
...Ras Al Khor Industrial 2 55-A8
...Umm Suqeim 1 18-K4

25D
...Al Barshaa 3 31-B8
...Al Rashidiya 57-F6
...Al Twar 3 59-A2
...Al Wuheida 26-M8
...Mirdif 66-K1, 66-K2

26

26
...Al Jafiliya 23-A7
...Al Karama 40-J1
...Al Khabaisi 41-C2
...Al Mamzar 27-A7
...Al Muteena 25-E8
...Al Quoz 34-M6, 35-D1
...Al Quoz Industrial 2 33-F8, 34-J8
...Al Quoz Industrial 4 33-B8
...Al Qusais 2 51-D5
...Al Qusais Ind 3 44-K9
...Al Qusais Ind 5 52-K3
...Al Raffa 24-H4, 24-J3
...Al Souk Al Kabeer 24-J3
...Al Twar 1 42-M8
...Dividing Road 33-E4
...Dubai Investment Park 1 0-E3, 7-D5
...Hor Al Anz 26-G8
...Muhaisnah 1 59-C4
...Muhaisnah 2 60-M4
...Muhaisnah 4 52-H5, 52-J4
...Nadd Al Hamar 56-J8, 56-J9
...Nadd Al Shiba 2 53-F8
...Nadd Shamma 57-C6
...Umm Hurair 2 40-G6
...Umm Suqeim 2 17-D4
...Umm Suqeim 3 16-M5

26A
...Abu Hail 26-H6
...Al Barshaa 2 32-J6
...Al Barshaa 3 31-D4
...Al Mizhar 1 67-E2
...Al Mizhar 2 68-H8
...Al Muraqqabat 25-C8
...Al Qusais 1 43-C9
...Al Qusais 3 51-B7
...Al Rashidiya 57-C3
...Al Satwa 22-J8, 22-K7, 22-M7
...Al Twar 2 50-M5
...Al Twar 3 58-L1
...Al Wuheida 26-K8
...Hor Al Anz East 42-K3
...Jumeira 1 22-H4
...Jumeira 2 21-A6
...Jumeira 3 20-G3
...Mankhool 24-J7
...Muhaisnah 3 51-F7
...Nadd Al Hamar 56-L8
...Ras Al Khor Industrial 1 54-K3
...Ras Al Khor Industrial 2 55-D6
...Umm Ramool 49-D8
...Umm Suqeim 1 18-M4

26B
...*Abu Hail* 26-J7, 26-K7
...*Al Barshaa 2* 32-H6
...*Al Barshaa 3* 31-B4
...*Al Garhoud* 49-C1
...*Al Mamzar* 27-C7
...*Al Mizhar 1* 68-J1
...*Al Mizhar 2* 68-J8
...*Al Muraqqabat* 25-C9
...*Al Qusais 1* 43-B9
...*Al Qusais 3* 51-D7
...*Al Rashidiya* 57-D2
...*Al Satwa* 22-J8
...*Al Twar 3* 58-M1
...*Al Wuheida* 26-L8
...*Hor Al Anz East* 42-L3
...*Jumeira 1* 22-G4
...*Jumeira 2* 20-L3
...*Jumeira 3* 19-D4, 19-E4
...*Mankhool* 24-G7, 24-H6
...*Mirdif* 66-J2
...*Muhaisnah 3* 52-G7
...*Nadd Al Hamar* 56-M7
...*Ras Al Khor Industrial 1* 54-J4
...*Ras Al Khor Industrial 2* 55-C6
...*Umm Al Sheif* 999-C3
...*Umm Ramool* 49-E7
...*Umm Suqeim 1* 18-H4
...*Za'abeel 2* 38-H4

26C
...*Al Barshaa 2* 31-F6
...*Al Garhoud* 41-C9
...*Al Mizhar 1* 60-K9
...*Al Mizhar 2* 68-K7
...*Al Muraqqabat* 41-C1
...*Al Qusais 1* 43-C9
...*Al Twar 2* 51-A5
...*Al Twar 3* 51-A9
...*Al Wuheida* 26-M8
...*Hor Al Anz East* 42-M3
...*Jumeira 1* 21-D5
...*Jumeira 2* 20-L3
...*Jumeira 3* 19-A4
...*Mankhool* 23-F7
...*Mirdif* 58-M9
...*Nadd Al Hamar* 57-A7

26D
...*Al Qusais 1* 43-C9
...*Al Wuheida* 26-M8
...*Jumeira 1* 21-B5
...*Jumeira 2* 20-K4, 20-K4
...*Mankhool* 23-E7
...*Nadd Al Hamar* 57-B6

26E
...*Jumeira 2* 20-J4

27

27
...*Abu Hail* 26-J8
...*Al Barshaa 2* 31-F8
...*Al Khabaisi* 42-G3
...*Al Mamzar* 27-C6, 43-E1
...*Al Mizhar 2* 68-M5
...*Al Nahda 2* 44-J9
...*Al Quoz Industrial 2* 34-G6
...*Al Quoz Industrial 3* 32-L2
...*Al Quoz Industrial 4* 32-M6
...*Al Raffa* 23-F4
...*Al Safa 2* 18-K7
...*Al Satwa* 22-K8
...*Ayal Nasir* 25-B4
...*Hor Al Anz* 42-J1
...*Jumeira 2* 20-K2
...*Jumeira 3* 19-D4
...*Mankhool* 23-F6
...*Muhaisnah 1* 59-B4, 59-E6, 59-E7

...*Nadd Al Hamar* 56-J6
...*Nadd Al Shiba 2* 54-K9
...*Port Saeed* 41-C5
...*Trade Centre 2* 38-H1
...*Umm Suqeim 3* 16-L4

27A
...*Al Baraha* 26-G6
...*Al Barshaa 1* 15-F8
...*Al Barshaa 3* 31-B1
...*Al Garhoud* 41-B9
...*Al Jafiliya* 23-B6
...*Al Karama* 24-G8
...*Al Manara* 17-D6
...*Al Mizhar 1* 59-F8
...*Al Muraqqabat* 25-D9
...*Al Quoz* 19-E9
...*Al Qusais 3* 51-D6
...*Al Qusais Ind 2* 52-J1
...*Al Rashidiya* 57-E2
...*Al Safa 1* 19-C5
...*Al Souk Al Kabeer* 24-H3
...*Al Twar 3* 50-M6
...*Al Wasl* 20-M4
...*Al Wuheida* 27-A7
...*Jumeira 1* 22-J3
...*Muhaisnah 2* 60-K1
...*Ras Al Khor Industrial 2* 54-L6
...*Umm Al Sheif* 16-K7
...*Umm Suqeim 1* 18-K2

27B
...*Al Bada'a* 22-K5
...*Al Barshaa 1* 31-E1
...*Al Barshaa 3* 31-B2
...*Al Jafiliya* 23-C7
...*Al Karama* 24-G9
...*Al Manara* 17-D7
...*Al Mizhar 1* 68-G2
...*Al Muraqqabat* 25-C9
...*Al Muteena* 25-F7
...*Al Quoz* 35-E2
...*Al Rashidiya* 57-F5
...*Al Safa 1* 19-C6
...*Al Twar 3* 51-A9, 59-A1
...*Al Wasl* 20-M5
...*Jumeira 1* 22-J3
...*Mirdif* 66-K1
...*Muhaisnah 2* 60-K3
...*Muhaisnah 4* 52-J3
...*Ras Al Khor Industrial 2* 54-M8
...*Umm Al Sheif* 16-K8
...*Umm Suqeim 1* 18-K4
...*Umm Suqeim 2* 17-E3

27C
...*Al Barshaa 3* 31-B3
...*Al Garhoud* 49-C1
...*Al Karama* 40-G1
...*Al Manara* 17-D8
...*Al Qusais 3* 51-D8
...*Al Safa 1* 19-C7
...*Al Twar 3* 59-A2
...*Al Wuheida* 26-M8
...*Jumeira 1* 22-J4
...*Mirdif* 66-K2, 66-K3
...*Muhaisnah 2* 60-K3
...*Muhaisnah 4* 52-K5
...*Ras Al Khor Industrial 2* 55-A8
...*Umm Suqeim 2* 17-E5

27D
...*Al Garhoud* 49-D2
...*Al Qusais 3* 51-D8
...*Muhaisnah 4* 52-K7

27E
...*Muhaisnah 2* 60-K4
...*Muhaisnah 4* 52-J8

28

28
...*Al Barshaa 3* 31-D4
...*Al Jafiliya* 23-A7
...*Al Karama* 40-J1
...*Al Quoz Industrial 2* 34-J8
...*Al Qusais 3* 51-C8
...*Al Qusais Ind 5* 52-L4
...*Al Rashidiya* 57-E2
...*Hor Al Anz East* 42-L3
...*Muhaisnah 3* 51-F7
...*Nadd Al Shiba 2* 53-E7
...*Nadd Shamma* 57-D6
...*Ras Al Khor Industrial 1* 54-K4
...*Umm Hurair 2* 40-G7
...*Umm Suqeim 2* 17-F4
...*Za'abeel 2* 38-M3

28A
...*Abu Hail* 26-J7
...*Al Garhoud* 49-A2
...*Al Khabaisi* 41-C2
...*Al Mamzar* 27-A7
...*Al Mizhar 1* 67-F2
...*Al Mizhar 2* 68-L6
...*Al Muteena* 25-D7
...*Al Quoz* 35-F1
...*Al Quoz Industrial 1* 34-J4
...*Al Quoz Industrial 3* 33-C4
...*Al Qusais 1* 43-B9
...*Al Satwa* 22-K8, 22-L8
...*Al Twar 1* 42-L8, 42-L9
...*Al Twar 3* 58-K1
...*Al Wasl* 21-A7
...*Al Wuheida* 26-K8
...*Dubai International Airport* 50-M5
...*Hor Al Anz* 26-G8
...*Jumeira 1* 22-G5
...*Jumeira 3* 19-E4
...*Mankhool* 24-H7
...*Nadd Al Hamar* 56-J8
...*Ras Al Khor Industrial 2* 55-D6
...*Umm Ramool* 49-B8
...*Umm Suqeim 1* 18-M4
...*Umm Suqeim 3* 17-A5
...*Za'abeel 1* 39-C4

28B
...*Abu Hail* 26-K7
...*Al Garhoud* 49-B1
...*Al Khabaisi* 41-C3
...*Al Mamzar* 27-C7
...*Al Mizhar 1* 68-J1
...*Al Quoz* 35-E1
...*Al Quoz Industrial 1* 34-G4
...*Al Quoz Industrial 3* 32-L4
...*Al Qusais 1* 43-C9
...*Al Satwa* 22-H8
...*Al Twar 1* 42-M8, 42-M9
...*Al Twar 2* 51-A5
...*Al Twar 3* 58-L1
...*Al Wasl* 20-M5
...*Al Wuheida* 26-L8
...*Hor Al Anz* 26-H9
...*Jumeira 1* 21-D5
...*Jumeira 3* 19-C4
...*Mankhool* 24-G7
...*Mirdif* 66-J3
...*Muhaisnah 1* 59-B6
...*Nadd Al Hamar* 56-M7
...*Ras Al Khor Industrial 2* 55-C7
...*Umm Ramool* 49-C8, 49-D8
...*Umm Suqeim 1* 18-J4, 18-J4
...*Umm Suqeim 3* 16-L5

28C
...*Al Garhoud* 49-C1
...*Al Khabaisi* 41-D4
...*Al Mamzar* 27-B7, 27-C7

...Al Twar 3 51-A6
...Jumeira 1 22-J4
...Jumeira 3 19-C3
...Mirdif 58-J8
...Muhaisnah 2 60-L2
...Ras Al Khor Industrial 3 63-B2
...Umm Suqeim 1 18-J1
...Umm Suqeim 2 17-D2
...Umm Suqeim 3 16-K3

31B
...Al Barshaa 2 31-E6
...Al Barshaa 3 31-B6
...Al Garhoud 49-D2
...Al Jafiliya 23-B7
...Al Manara 17-D7
...Al Muraqqabat 25-D9
...Al Quoz 35-D2, 35-F4
...Al Qusais 3 51-D6
...Al Rashidiya 57-F3
...Al Safa 2 18-J7
...Al Twar 3 51-A7
...Jumeira 1 22-J4
...Jumeira 3 19-C4
...Mirdif 58-J8
...Muhaisnah 2 60-L2
...Umm Suqeim 1 18-J3
...Umm Suqeim 2 17-D4
...Umm Suqeim 3 16-K4

31C
...Al Barshaa 2 31-E8
...Al Manara 17-D8
...Al Qusais 3 51-D8
...Al Rashidiya 57-F4
...Al Twar 3 51-A9, 59-A1
...Mirdif 58-J9, 58-K9
...Muhaisnah 2 60-L3
...Umm Suqeim 1 18-J5

31D
...Al Rashidiya 57-F5
...Mirdif 58-K9

32

32
...Abu Hail 26-K8
...Al Barshaa 2 31-F6
...Al Jafiliya 23-B8
...Al Khabaisi 41-C2
...Al Qusais 3 51-B8
...Al Rashidiya 57-D3
...Al Twar 2 51-A5
...Al Twar 3 58-L2
...Al Wuheida 26-K8
...Mirdif 66-M1
...Nadd Al Shiba 2 53-E7, 53-E8
...Umm Suqeim 2 17-C5

32A
...Al Barshaa 3 31-D5
...Al Garhoud 49-B2
...Al Mamzar 27-A8
...Al Mizhar 1 67-E4
...Al Quoz 35-F2
...Al Qusais 1 51-B1
...Al Qusais Ind 1 51-F1
...Al Qusais Ind 5 52-K4
...Al Satwa 22-K8
...Al Twar 1 42-L8
...Hor Al Anz 26-G9
...Jumeira 1 22-G5
...Jumeira 3 19-E4, 19-E4
...Muhaisnah 3 51-F8
...Nadd Al Hamar 56-J9
...Ras Al Khor Industrial 2 55-D7
...Umm Ramool 49-B9
...Umm Suqeim 1 18-M5

32B
...Al Barshaa 3 31-B5

...Al Garhoud 49-B2
...Al Mamzar 27-B8
...Al Mizhar 1 68-G3
...Al Quoz 35-E2
...Al Qusais 1 51-C1
...Al Qusais Ind 1 52-G1
...Al Qusais Ind 5 52-L4
...Al Satwa 22-J8
...Al Twar 1 42-M8
...Jumeira 1 21-E5
...Jumeira 3 19-B4, 19-B5, 19-D4
...Muhaisnah 3 52-G8
...Nadd Al Hamar 56-L8
...Ras Al Khor Industrial 2 55-C7
...Umm Ramool 49-C9
...Umm Suqeim 1 18-K5
...Umm Suqeim 3 16-L6

32C
...Al Garhoud 49-D1
...Al Mizhar 1 68-H2
...Al Quoz 35-D2
...Al Qusais Ind 1 44-G9, 52-G1
...Al Satwa 22-H8
...Al Twar 1 42-M8
...Jumeira 1 21-B5, 21-D5
...Jumeira 3 19-A5
...Nadd Al Hamar 56-M8
...Umm Ramool 49-E8
...Umm Suqeim 1 18-H5

32D
...Al Mizhar 1 68-L1
...Al Satwa 21-E8
...Nadd Al Hamar 57-A7

32E
...Nadd Al Hamar 57-C7

33

33
...Al Bada'a 22-J5
...Al Barshaa 2 31-E6
...Al Barshaa 3 31-A4
...Al Garhoud 49-E4
...Al Khabaisi 42-J3
...Al Mamzar 27-D7, 43-C1
...Al Manara 17-C8
...Al Safa 1 19-C7
...Al Safa 2 18-J6
...Jumeira 1 22-J4
...Jumeira 2 20-K3
...Mankhool 23-E7
...Muhaisnah 1 59-D5
...Nadd Al Hamar 56-K6
...Trade Centre 2 38-H1
...Umm Suqeim 2 17-D2

33A
...Al Barshaa 1 15-D9, 15-E8
...Al Jafiliya 23-B6
...Al Karama 23-F9
...Al Mizhar 1 59-F8
...Al Mizhar 2 68-M3
...Al Quoz Industrial 2 33-F5
...Al Raffa 23-E3
...Al Rashidiya 49-E9
...Al Satwa 22-J7
...Al Sufouh 2 15-C4
...Al Twar 3 51-A6
...Jumeira 2 20-L4
...Jumeira 3 19-C2
...Mirdif 58-K9, 66-K1
...Umm Suqeim 1 18-J1
...Umm Suqeim 3 16-K4

33B
...Al Barshaa 3 31-B7
...Al Jafiliya 23-B6
...Al Karama 39-F1
...Al Mizhar 1 60-G9

...Al Mizhar 2 68-M4
...Al Muraqqabat 41-C1
...Al Quoz 35-D1
...Al Quoz Industrial 2 33-F7
...Al Raffa 23-E4
...Al Rashidiya 57-F1
...Al Satwa 22-J8
...Al Souk Al Kabeer 24-J4
...Al Sufouh 2 15-C5
...Al Twar 3 51-A7
...Jumeira 2 20-L5
...Jumeira 3 19-C3
...Mirdif 66-K1, 66-L1
...Umm Suqeim 1 18-J4
...Umm Suqeim 3 16-K6

33C
...Al Mizhar 1 68-G1
...Al Mizhar 2 999-A5
...Al Muraqqabat 41-B1
...Al Raffa 24-K5
...Al Rashidiya 57-F4
...Al Twar 3 51-A8
...Mirdif 66-L1
...Umm Suqeim 1 18-J5

33D
...Al Mizhar 1 68-H2
...Al Rashidiya 57-F5
...Al Twar 3 51-B9, 59-B1
...Mirdif 66-L5

33E
...Al Rashidiya 58-G6

34

34
...Abu Hail 26-H7
...Al Barshaa 2 32-J6
...Al Jafiliya 23-C7
...Al Mizhar 1 67-E4
...Al Qusais 1 51-C1, 51-D1
...Al Qusais 3 51-C8
...Al Qusais Ind 5 52-L4
...Al Rashidiya 57-F2
...Al Satwa 21-B8
...Al Souk Al Kabeer 24-K3
...Al Twar 3 58-L2
...Jumeira 1 22-L4
...Muhaisnah 1 59-E4
...Ras Al Khor Industrial 2 55-D7
...Umm Ramool 57-B1
...Umm Suqeim 2 17-E5
...Za'abeel 2 38-J4

34A
...Al Barshaa 3 31-D5
...Al Garhoud 49-C2
...Al Khabaisi 41-C2
...Al Mamzar 27-B8
...Al Muraqqabat 25-B8
...Al Quoz 35-F2
...Al Satwa 22-G8
...Al Twar 1 42-L8
...Hor Al Anz 26-G9
...Mirdif 66-K2
...Muhaisnah 3 51-F8
...Muhaisnah 4 52-J5
...Nadd Al Hamar 56-L8
...Umm Suqeim 1 18-M5
...Za'abeel 1 39-C5

34B
...Al Barshaa 3 31-B5
...Al Garhoud 49-C1
...Al Khabaisi 41-C3
...Al Mamzar 27-C8
...Al Muraqqabat 25-B8
...Al Quoz 35-E2
...Al Qusais Ind 5 52-K4
...Al Satwa 21-F8

...Al Twar 1 42-M8, 42-M9
...Al Wuheida 26-L8
...Hor Al Anz 42-H1
...Muhaisnah 3 52-G8
...Nadd Al Hamar 57-A7
...Umm Suqeim 1 18-L5

34C
...Al Muraqqabat 41-C1
...Al Quoz 35-D2
...Al Satwa 21-E9
...Hor Al Anz 42-H1
...Nadd Al Hamar 57-C7
...Umm Suqeim 1 18-J5

34D
...Hor Al Anz 42-J1
...Umm Suqeim 1 18-J5

34E
...Hor Al Anz 42-K2

35

35
...Al Garhoud 49-E3
...Al Jafiliya 23-B6
...Al Karama 23-F9
...Al Mamzar 43-D1
...Al Muraqqabat 25-E9
...Al Raffa 23-E4
...Al Safa 1 19-B6
...Al Safa 2 18-H6
...Al Sufouh 2 15-C4
...Al Wasl 20-L5
...Hor Al Anz 42-J1
...Jumeira 2 20-K3
...Jumeira 3 19-A2
...Muhaisnah 1 59-D4
...Muhaisnah 2 60-M4
...Nadd Al Hamar 56-K8
...Trade Centre 2 38-H1
...Umm Al Sheif 999-C3

35A
...Al Bada'a 22-J5
...Al Barshaa 1 15-D8
...Al Barshaa 2 31-E6
...Al Barshaa 3 31-A2
...Al Mamzar 27-E4
...Al Manara 17-C6
...Al Mizhar 1 60-G8
...Al Mizhar 2 68-M3
...Al Quoz 19-D8
...Al Quoz Industrial 2 33-F5
...Al Qusais 3 51-E6
...Al Satwa 22-J7
...Al Twar 3 51-A6
...Jumeira 1 22-H3
...Jumeira 3 19-C3
...Mankhool 23-E5
...Umm Suqeim 1 18-J1
...Umm Suqeim 2 17-D3

35B
...Al Bada'a 22-J6
...Al Barshaa 1 15-D9
...Al Barshaa 2 31-E7
...Al Barshaa 3 31-A4
...Al Mizhar 1 68-H1
...Al Mizhar 2 68-M4
...Al Quoz 19-D9
...Al Quoz Industrial 2 33-F7
...Al Qusais 3 51-B7, 51-E8
...Al Rashidiya 57-F1
...Al Satwa 22-J8
...Jumeira 1 22-H4
...Jumeira 3 19-C4
...Mankhool 23-E7
...Mirdif 66-M3
...Umm Suqeim 1 18-J3
...Umm Suqeim 2 17-D3

35C
...Al Barshaa 3 31-A5
...Al Mizhar 1 68-H3, 68-J3
...Al Mizhar 2 999-A5
...Al Quoz 19-D9
...Al Rashidiya 57-F2
...Al Twar 3 51-B9, 59-A2
...Umm Suqeim 2 17-D5

35D
...Al Barshaa 3 31-A7
...Al Quoz 35-D1, 35-D2, 35-D3
...Al Rashidiya 57-F4
...Mirdif 66-M5
...Umm Suqeim 2 17-D5

35E
...Al Rashidiya 58-G5

36

36
...Al Barshaa 2 32-J7
...Al Garhoud 49-C2
...Al Jafiliya 23-B8, 23-C7, 23-D6
...Al Khabaisi 41-C2
...Al Qusais 1 51-C1
...Al Qusais 3 51-D8
...Al Rashidiya 57-E2
...Al Twar 1 43-A8
...Al Twar 3 58-L2
...Mirdif 66-K2
...Muhaisnah 3 51-F8
...Muhaisnah 4 52-K5
...Za'abeel 2 38-M3

36A
...Abu Hail 26-G7
...Al Barshaa 3 31-C5
...Al Mamzar 27-B8
...Al Mizhar 1 67-E4
...Al Muraqqabat 25-B9
...Al Quoz 35-F2
...Al Wasl 21-A8
...Al Wuheida 26-K8
...Hor Al Anz 26-G9
...Jebel Ali Industrial 3-E7
...Mirdif 66-J2
...Nadd Al Hamar 57-B8
...Ras Al Khor Industrial 2 55-D7
...Umm Suqeim 2 17-F5

36B
...Abu Hail 26-H7
...Al Barshaa 3 31-B5
...Al Mamzar 27-B8
...Al Mizhar 1 68-G3
...Al Muraqqabat 41-B1
...Al Quoz 35-E2
...Al Qusais Ind 5 52-M4
...Al Wasl 20-M6
...Al Wuheida 26-L8
...Hor Al Anz 42-H1
...Jebel Ali Industrial 2-L4, 3-C7
...Muhaisnah 1 59-D5
...Nadd Al Hamar 57-C7
...Ras Al Khor Industrial 2 55-C8
...Umm Suqeim 2 17-D5

36C
...Abu Hail 26-K8
...Al Mizhar 1 68-H2
...Al Quoz 35-D2
...Al Wuheida 26-M8
...Hor Al Anz 42-J2
...Ras Al Khor Industrial 2 55-A9

36D
...Al Mizhar 1 68-K1

36E
...Al Mizhar 1 68-L1

37

37
...Al Barshaa 3 31-A7
...Al Hamriya Port 27-D4
...Al Manara 17-C8
...Al Muraqqabat 41-C1
...Al Raffa 23-E4
...Al Sufouh 2 15-C4
...Al Wasl 20-L5
...Dividing Road 33-E5
...Hor Al Anz 42-J2
...Jumeira 1 22-H4
...Jumeira 2 20-K3
...Mirdif 58-K9
...Muhaisnah 1 59-E4
...Muhaisnah 2 60-M4
...Trade Centre 2 38-H1
...Umm Suqeim 1 18-H6

37A
...Al Bada'a 22-J5
...Al Barshaa 1 15-D8
...Al Barshaa 2 31-D6
...Al Garhoud 49-C1
...Al Jafiliya 23-A6
...Al Karama 23-F8
...Al Mizhar 1 60-G7, 60-G8
...Al Mizhar 2 68-M3
...Al Muteena 25-F8
...Al Quoz 19-D9
...Al Rashidiya 58-G5
...Al Safa 1 19-B5
...Al Safa 2 18-H6
...Al Satwa 22-J7
...Jumeira 3 19-C2
...Mankhool 23-E5
...Nadd Al Hamar 56-L8
...Umm Suqeim 1 18-H2
...Umm Suqeim 2 17-D3

37B
...Al Barshaa 1 15-D8
...Al Barshaa 2 31-E7
...Al Garhoud 49-D1
...Al Jafiliya 23-B6
...Al Karama 23-F9
...Al Mizhar 1 68-H1
...Al Mizhar 2 999-A3
...Al Muteena 25-F9
...Al Quoz 19-D9
...Al Rashidiya 58-G6
...Al Safa 1 19-B6
...Al Safa 2 18-H7
...Al Satwa 22-J8
...Jumeira 3 19-C3
...Mankhool 23-E7
...Nadd Al Hamar 56-L9
...Umm Suqeim 1 18-H3

37C
...Al Quoz 35-D1
...Al Safa 1 19-B7
...Al Souk Al Kabeer 24-H3
...Umm Suqeim 1 18-H5

37D
...Al Souk Al Kabeer 24-J4

38

38
...Al Barshaa 2 31-F7
...Al Barshaa 3 31-B6
...Al Garhoud 49-D2
...Al Khabaisi 41-C2
...Al Muraqqabat 25-B8
...Al Qusais 1 51-A1
...Al Qusais Ind 5 52-L5

...*Muhaisnah 3* 52-G9
...*Muhaisnah 4* 52-J5
...*Za'abeel 1* 39-C6

38A
...*Al Jafiliya* 23-D6
...*Al Mamzar* 27-A9
...*Al Mizhar 1* 67-F4
...*Al Quoz* 35-F2
...*Al Qusais 3* 51-C8
...*Al Rashidiya* 57-D3
...*Al Twar 3* 58-L2
...*Al Wuheida* 26-K9
...*Hor Al Anz* 25-F9
...*Muhaisnah 1* 59-C6
...*Nadd Al Hamar* 56-J9
...*Umm Suqeim 2* 17-F5

38B
...*Al Jafiliya* 23-C8
...*Al Mamzar* 27-B9
...*Al Mizhar 1* 68-G3
...*Al Quoz* 35-E2
...*Al Rashidiya* 57-D3
...*Al Twar 3* 58-M2
...*Al Wuheida* 26-L9
...*Hor Al Anz* 42-H1
...*Mirdif* 66-J3
...*Muhaisnah 1* 59-E5
...*Nadd Al Hamar* 56-K9, 56-L9
...*Umm Suqeim 2* 17-D5

38C
...*Al Mamzar* 27-C9
...*Al Mizhar 1* 68-H2
...*Al Quoz* 35-D2
...*Al Qusais 3* 51-E8
...*Al Wuheida* 26-M9
...*Hor Al Anz* 42-J2

38D
...*Al Mizhar 1* 68-J2
...*Al Wuheida* 26-M8

39

39
...*Al Bada'a* 22-J6
...*Al Karama* 23-F9
...*Al Mamzar* 43-E1
...*Al Quoz Industrial 2* 33-E5
...*Al Safa 1* 19-B5, 19-B6
...*Al Sufouh 2* 15-C5
...*Hor Al Anz* 42-J2
...*Jumeira 2* 20-L5
...*Muhaisnah 1* 59-C3
...*Nadd Al Hamar* 56-K7
...*Trade Centre 2* 38-H1
...*Umm Suqeim 1* 18-M2

39A
...*Al Barshaa 1* 15-D8
...*Al Barshaa 2* 31-D6
...*Al Garhoud* 41-C9
...*Al Jafiliya* 23-A6
...*Al Manara* 17-C6
...*Al Mizhar 1* 60-G7
...*Al Quoz* 19-D9
...*Al Rashidiya* 58-G4
...*Al Safa 2* 18-H6
...*Al Satwa* 22-J7
...*Jumeira 1* 22-H3
...*Jumeira 2* 20-J2
...*Jumeira 3* 19-B2
...*Mankhool* 23-E5
...*Mirdif* 66-M3
...*Umm Suqeim 1* 18-H2
...*Umm Suqeim 2* 17-C3

39B
...*Al Barshaa 1* 15-C9
...*Al Barshaa 2* 31-D7

...*Al Jafiliya* 23-B7
...*Al Manara* 17-C8
...*Al Mizhar 1* 68-H1
...*Al Quoz* 35-D1
...*Al Rashidiya* 58-G5
...*Al Safa 2* 18-H7, 19-A7
...*Al Satwa* 22-J8
...*Jumeira 1* 22-H4
...*Jumeira 2* 20-K3, 20-K4
...*Jumeira 3* 19-B3
...*Mankhool* 23-E7
...*Mirdif* 66-M5
...*Umm Suqeim 1* 18-H3, 18-H7
...*Umm Suqeim 2* 17-C5

39C
...*Al Barshaa 2* 31-D8
...*Al Quoz* 35-D2
...*Al Rashidiya* 58-G6
...*Jumeira 3* 19-B4

39D
...*Al Quoz* 35-D3

40

40
...*Al Barshaa 2* 32-J7
...*Al Jafiliya* 23-D6
...*Al Mamzar* 27-A9, 27-C9
...*Al Qusais 1* 51-C1
...*Al Qusais Ind 5* 52-L5
...*Al Twar 1* 42-M9
...*Hor Al Anz* 26-G9, 42-G1
...*Mirdif* 66-J3
...*Ras Al Khor Industrial 3* 63-E3
...*Za'abeel 2* 38-M6

40A
...*Al Barshaa 3* 31-C6
...*Al Garhoud* 49-A3
...*Al Mizhar 1* 68-L1
...*Al Muraqqabat* 25-B8
...*Al Quoz* 35-F2
...*Al Rashidiya* 57-D3
...*Al Twar 3* 58-M3
...*Al Wasl* 20-M6
...*Al Wuheida* 26-L9
...*Jumeira 2* 20-M6
...*Nadd Al Hamar* 57-A8
...*Umm Suqeim 2* 18-G5

40B
...*Al Barshaa 3* 31-B6
...*Al Mizhar 1* 68-L1
...*Al Muraqqabat* 25-B8
...*Al Quoz* 35-D3
...*Al Rashidiya* 57-F3
...*Al Twar 3* 59-A1
...*Al Wasl* 20-J6
...*Al Wuheida* 26-M9
...*Muhaisnah 1* 59-C7
...*Nadd Al Hamar* 57-B8, 57-C8
...*Umm Suqeim 2* 17-F5

40C
...*Al Muraqqabat* 41-B1
...*Al Wuheida* 26-M9
...*Muhaisnah 1* 59-D6
...*Umm Suqeim 2* 17-D5

40D
...*Muhaisnah 1* 59-E5
...*Umm Suqeim 2* 17-C5

41

41
...*Al Bada'a* 22-J5
...*Al Barshaa 1* 15-C8

...*Al Garhoud* 41-C9
...*Al Jafiliya* 23-A6
...*Al Karama* 23-F9
...*Al Quoz* 35-D1
...*Al Safa 1* 19-A6
...*Al Safa 2* 18-M7
...*Al Satwa* 22-J7, 22-J8
...*Al Souk Al Kabeer* 24-J5
...*Al Sufouh 2* 15-B4
...*Al Wasl* 20-K5
...*Jumeira 2* 20-J3
...*Jumeira 3* 19-B3
...*Trade Centre 2* 38-G1
...*Umm Suqeim 1* 18-H3
...*Za'abeel 1* 39-C5

41A
...*Al Mizhar 1* 60-H8
...*Al Muraqqabat* 41-C1
...*Al Rashidiya* 49-F9
...*Hor Al Anz* 26-K9
...*Jumeira 1* 22-G4
...*Jumeira 3* 19-B3
...*Mankhool* 23-E5
...*Mirdif* 66-M3
...*Nadd Al Hamar* 56-K6
...*Umm Suqeim 1* 18-H7
...*Umm Suqeim 2* 17-C3

41B
...*Al Garhoud* 41-C9
...*Al Mizhar 1* 68-J2
...*Al Muraqqabat* 41-B1
...*Al Rashidiya* 57-F1
...*Hor Al Anz* 26-K9
...*Jebel Ali Industrial* 2-K5, 3-B8
...*Jumeira 1* 22-H4
...*Mankhool* 23-E7
...*Mirdif* 66-M5
...*Nadd Al Hamar* 56-L8
...*Umm Suqeim 1* 18-H7
...*Umm Suqeim 2* 17-C5

41C
...*Al Muraqqabat* 41-B1
...*Al Rashidiya* 58-G4

41D
...*Hor Al Anz* 42-K1

41E
...*Hor Al Anz* 42-K1

42

42
...*Al Barshaa 2* 31-F7
...*Al Barshaa 3* 31-C6
...*Al Jafiliya* 23-C7, 23-D7
...*Al Mamzar* 27-C9
...*Al Mizhar 1* 67-F4
...*Al Qusais 3* 51-D9
...*Al Qusais Ind 5* 52-L5
...*Jebel Ali Industrial* 2-H5, 3-A8, 3-F7
...*Mirdif* 66-J3
...*Muhaisnah 1* 59-E5
...*Muhaisnah 4* 52-J5

42A
...*Al Barshaa 2* 32-H9
...*Al Garhoud* 49-C2
...*Al Mizhar 1* 67-F4
...*Al Muraqqabat* 25-B9
...*Al Quoz* 36-G3
...*Al Rashidiya* 57-D4
...*Al Twar 1* 42-L9
...*Al Twar 3* 58-M3
...*Hor Al Anz* 25-F9

42B
...*Al Garhoud* 49-D2
...*Al Mizhar 1* 68-G4
...*Al Quoz* 35-F3

...Al Rashidiya 57-D4
...Al Twar 1 42-M9
...Hor Al Anz 42-H1

42C
...Al Mizhar 1 68-J3
...Al Quoz 35-E3
...Al Twar 1 42-M9, 43-A9
...Hor Al Anz 42-K2

42D
...Al Mizhar 1 68-L2
...Al Quoz 35-D3

43

43
...Al Garhoud 49-D1
...Al Jafiliya 23-A6
...Al Mamzar 27-D5
...Al Muraqqabat 41-C1
...Al Rashidiya 57-F1
...Al Sufouh 2 15-B4
...Hor Al Anz 42-J2
...Jebel Ali Industrial 2-J3, 3-A7
...Jumeira 2 20-J3

43A
...Al Barshaa 1 15-C8
...Al Garhoud 41-B7
...Al Karama 23-E9
...Al Mizhar 1 60-H8
...Al Quoz 19-D8
...Al Souk Al Kabeer 24-H3
...Al Wasl 20-K4
...Jumeira 1 22-G3
...Jumeira 3 19-A6, 19-B3
...Mankhool 23-D5
...Mirdif 58-K8, 58-M7
...Nadd Al Hamar 56-K6
...Umm Suqeim 1 18-H3

43B
...Al Bada'a 22-J6
...Al Barshaa 1 15-B9, 15-C8
...Al Garhoud 41-D9
...Al Karama 39-F1
...Al Mizhar 1 68-J2
...Al Quoz 19-D9
...Al Safa 1 19-A7
...Al Wasl 20-K5
...Jumeira 3 19-A7, 19-B4
...Mankhool 23-E7
...Mirdif 58-K8
...Nadd Al Hamar 56-L7
...Umm Suqeim 1 18-H5
...Umm Suqeim 2 17-C5

43C
...Al Mizhar 1 68-J3, 68-K2
...Al Quoz 35-D1, 35-D3
...Mirdif 58-K8
...Nadd Al Hamar 56-L8

43D
...Mirdif 58-K9, 58-L8

44

44
...Al Barshaa 2 32-J7
...Al Barshaa 3 31-C6
...Al Jafiliya 23-D7
...Al Mamzar 43-A1, 43-C1
...Al Qusais Ind 5 52-L6
...Jebel Ali Industrial 2-M5, 3-C9
...Muhaisnah 1 59-E5

44A
...Al Mizhar 1 68-L2
...Al Quoz 35-F3

...Al Rashidiya 57-D3
...Al Twar 1 42-M9
...Al Wasl 21-B8
...Hor Al Anz 25-F9
...Muhaisnah 1 59-D6

44B
...Al Mizhar 1 68-L2
...Al Quoz 35-E3
...Al Raffa 24-J4
...Al Rashidiya 57-F3
...Al Wasl 21-A8
...Hor Al Anz 42-G1
...Mirdif 66-J3

44C
...Al Quoz 35-C3
...Hor Al Anz 42-K3

45

45
...Al Bada'a 22-J6
...Al Barshaa 3 31-C7
...Al Garhoud 41-B8
...Al Mamzar 27-D5
...Al Rashidiya 49-F9
...Al Wasl 20-K6, 20-K7
...Jumeira 2 20-J3
...Trade Centre 2 38-G1
...Umm Suqeim 2 17-C5

45A
...Al Bada'a 22-J5
...Al Jafiliya 23-A6
...Al Karama 23-E9
...Al Mizhar 1 60-H8
...Al Muraqqabat 41-D1
...Al Quoz 19-C9
...Al Safa 2 19-A6
...Al Sufouh 2 15-C7
...Jumeira 1 22-G4
...Jumeira 3 19-A2
...Mirdif 58-L9
...Nadd Al Hamar 56-L6

45B
...Al Barshaa 1 15-C8
...Al Jafiliya 23-A7
...Al Karama 23-E9, 39-E1
...Al Mizhar 1 60-H8
...Al Muraqqabat 41-C1
...Al Quoz 19-C9
...Al Satwa 22-H7
...Jumeira 1 22-G5
...Jumeira 3 19-B4
...Mirdif 58-L9
...Nadd Al Hamar 56-M8

45C
...Al Mizhar 1 68-J1
...Al Muraqqabat 41-C2
...Al Quoz 35-C3
...Mirdif 58-L9

45D
...Mirdif 66-L1

46

46
...Al Barshaa 2 31-E7
...Al Jafiliya 23-D7
...Al Mamzar 43-A2
...Al Qusais Ind 5 52-M5, 52-M6
...Al Rashidiya 57-F3
...Hor Al Anz 41-F1
...Muhaisnah 4 52-J5

46A
...Al Garhoud 49-C3

...Al Mizhar 1 67-F5
...Al Quoz 35-F3
...Al Twar 1 50-L1
...Muhaisnah 1 59-D7

46B
...Al Garhoud 49-D2
...Al Mizhar 1 68-H4, 68-M2
...Al Quoz 35-E3
...Al Twar 1 50-M1
...Muhaisnah 1 59-E5

46C
...Al Mizhar 1 68-L2
...Al Twar 1 50-M1, 51-A1

47

47
...Al Bada'a 22-H6
...Al Barshaa 1 15-B8
...Al Garhoud 41-C9
...Al Mamzar 27-D5
...Al Satwa 22-H7
...Jumeira 2 20-J2
...Mirdif 66-M3
...Nadd Al Hamar 56-L7
...Trade Centre 2 38-G1

47A
...Al Jafiliya 23-A6
...Al Karama 23-E9
...Al Mizhar 1 60-H7
...Al Quoz 19-C9
...Al Rashidiya 58-G4
...Al Wasl 20-J4
...Jumeira 1 22-G3
...Jumeira 3 19-A2
...Umm Suqeim 2 17-B3

47B
...Al Jafiliya 23-B8
...Al Karama 39-E1
...Al Mizhar 1 60-J8
...Al Rashidiya 58-H6
...Al Wasl 20-K5
...Jumeira 1 22-G4
...Jumeira 3 19-A4
...Umm Suqeim 2 17-B5

47C
...Al Karama 39-E1
...Al Wasl 20-K6
...Jumeira 1 22-G4

48

48
...Al Barshaa 2 32-H8
...Al Barshaa 3 31-C7
...Al Garhoud 49-D2
...Al Jafiliya 23-D7
...Al Quoz 35-C3
...Al Qusais Ind 5 52-L6
...Al Twar 1 50-M1

48A
...Al Mamzar 43-B2
...Al Qusais Ind 5 999-B8
...Al Rashidiya 57-D4, 57-D5
...Al Wasl 21-A9
...Muhaisnah 1 59-D7

48B
...Al Mamzar 43-C2
...Al Rashidiya 57-D4
...Al Wasl 20-L6, 21-A7
...Muhaisnah 1 59-E5

48C
...Al Rashidiya 57-E4

48D
...Al Rashidiya **57-F3**
48E
...Al Rashidiya **57-F3, 58-G3**

49

49
...Al Bada'a **22-H6**
...Al Garhoud **41-B8**
...Al Jafiliya **23-A7**
...Al Mamzar **27-D4**
...Al Wasl **20-J5**
...Jumeira 2 **20-H2**
...Trade Centre 2 **38-G1**
...Za'abeel 1 **39-B5**

49A
...Al Mizhar 1 **60-H6**
...Jumeira 3 **19-A3**
...Mirdif **66-M2**
...Nadd Al Hamar **56-L5**

49B
...Al Mizhar 1 **60-H7**
...Al Quoz **35-C3**
...Jumeira 3 **19-A4**
...Mirdif **66-M3, 67-A3**
...Nadd Al Hamar **56-M7**

49C
...Al Mizhar 1 **60-J8**
...Mirdif **66-M3, 67-A3**
...Nadd Al Hamar **56-M8**

49D
...Al Mizhar 1 **60-J9**
...Mirdif **66-M4, 67-A4**

49E
...Al Mizhar 1 **68-K1**
...Mirdif **67-A5**

50

50
...Al Barshaa 2 **31-E8**
...Al Barshaa 3 **31-B7**
...Al Garhoud **49-D2**
...Al Mamzar **43-A3**
...Al Quoz **35-F3**
...Al Qusais Ind 5 **52-M6**
...Al Twar 1 **50-M1**
...Al Wasl **21-C9**
...Jebel Ali Industrial **0-B2**
...Muhaisnah 4 **52-J5**

50A
...Al Jafiliya **23-D7**
...Al Rashidiya **57-E5**

50B
...Al Jafiliya **23-C8**
...Al Rashidiya **57-E4**
...Muhaisnah 1 **59-E6**

50C
...Al Rashidiya **57-F4**
...Muhaisnah 1 **59-F5**

50D
...Al Rashidiya **58-G4**

51

51
...Al Bada'a **22-H5**
...Al Garhoud **41-C6, 41-C8**
...Al Jafiliya **23-A6**
...Al Mizhar 1 **60-J8, 68-K1**

...Al Safa 2 **18-M7**
...Jumeira 1 **21-F4**
...Jumeira 2 **20-J5**
...Jumeira 3 **19-A2**
...Mirdif **67-A5**
...Trade Centre 2 **38-G1**

51A
...Al Mamzar **27-E4**
...Al Quoz **35-C2**
...Al Shindagha **24-J2**
...Jumeira 2 **20-H3**
...Nadd Al Hamar **56-L5**

51B
...Al Mamzar **27-E5**
...Al Quoz **35-C3**
...Jebel Ali Industrial **2-J5, 3-A9**
...Jumeira 2 **20-H3**
...Nadd Al Hamar **56-M7**

51C
...Nadd Al Hamar **56-M8**

52

52
...Al Barshaa 2 **32-H8**
...Al Barshaa 3 **31-B7**
...Al Jafiliya **23-D8**
...Al Mamzar **43-D1**
...Al Quoz **35-E3, 35-E4**
...Al Rashidiya **57-E4**
...Al Twar 1 **51-A1**

52A
...Al Garhoud **49-C3**
...Al Wasl **21-B9**
...Muhaisnah 1 **59-E7**

52B
...Al Garhoud **49-D3**
...Al Wasl **21-A9**
...Mirdif **66-M1**
...Muhaisnah 1 **59-F6**

52C
...Al Wasl **20-K7**
...Mirdif **67-A1**

53

53
...Al Bada'a **22-H5**
...Al Garhoud **41-B7**
...Al Jafiliya **23-A6**
...Al Mamzar

Al Mamzar **27-E4**
...Al Satwa **22-H7**
...Al Wasl **20-J5**
...Mirdif **67-A5**
...Trade Centre 2 **38-G1**
...Umm Suqeim 1 **18-M2**

53A
...Jumeira 1 **21-F3**
...Jumeira 2 **20-H3**
...Nadd Al Hamar **56-L5**

53B
...Al Mizhar 1 **68-K1**
...Jumeira 1 **21-F4**
...Jumeira 2 **20-H3**
...Nadd Al Hamar **56-M6**

53C
...Al Mizhar 1 **68-L2**
...Nadd Al Hamar **57-A8**

54

54
...Al Barshaa 2 **31-E8**
...Al Garhoud **49-C3**
...Al Jafiliya **23-B8**
...Al Mamzar **43-B3, 43-D1**
...Al Quoz **35-E4**
...Muhaisnah 1 **59-F5**

54A
...Al Barshaa 3 **31-C8**
...Al Rashidiya **57-E5**
...Muhaisnah 4 **52-J6**

54B
...Al Barshaa 3 **31-B8**
...Al Rashidiya **57-E5**
...Mirdif **67-A1**
...Muhaisnah 4 **52-K6**

54C
...Al Rashidiya **57-F4**

54D
...Al Rashidiya **58-G4**

54E
...Al Rashidiya **58-G4**

55

55
...Al Garhoud **41-B6**
...Al Satwa **22-H8**
...Al Wasl **20-H4, 20-J5, 20-J7**
...Jumeira 2 **20-J5**
...Nadd Al Hamar **56-M5**

55A
...Al Jafiliya **23-A7**
...Al Mizhar 1 **68-K1**
...Jumeira 1 **21-F3**
...Jumeira 2 **20-H3**
...Mirdif **67-A3**
...Trade Centre 2 **38-G1**

55B
...Al Jafiliya **23-A8**
...Al Mamzar **27-E5**
...Al Mizhar 1 **68-L2**
...Jumeira 1 **21-F4**
...Jumeira 2 **20-H4**
...Mirdif **67-A4**
...Za'abeel 2 **38-G3**

55C
...Mirdif **67-A5**
...Za'abeel 2 **38-J4**

55D
...Za'abeel 2 **38-J5**

56

56
...Al Garhoud **49-E4**
...Al Mamzar **43-B3**
...Al Quoz **35-E4, 35-F3**
...Al Rashidiya **58-G4, 58-G5, 58-H4, 58-H5**
...Al Wasl **21-A9**

56A
...Al Barshaa 2 **32-H8**
...Al Barshaa 3 **31-C8**
...Muhaisnah 1 **59-F7**

56B
...Al Barshaa 2 **31-E8**
...Al Barshaa 3 **31-B8**

...*Mirdif* 67-A2
...*Muhaisnah 1* 59-F6
56C
...*Mirdif* 67-B1

57

57
...*Al Bada'a* 22-G6
...*Al Garhoud* 41-C6
...*Al Mizhar 1* 68-L1
...*Al Safa 2* 18-M8, 19-A7
...*Al Satwa* 22-H7
...*Jumeira 1* 21-E4
...*Mirdif* 67-B5
...*Trade Centre 2* 37-F1
...*Umm Suqeim 1* 18-K4

57A
...*Al Jafiliya* 23-A6
...*Al Mamzar* 27-E4
...*Nadd Al Hamar* 56-M4

57B
...*Al Jafiliya* 23-A7
...*Al Mamzar* 27-F5
...*Nadd Al Hamar* 57-A7

57C
...*Al Jafiliya* 23-A8

58

58
...*Al Barshaa 3* 31-B8
...*Al Garhoud* 49-E4
...*Al Mamzar* 43-D2
...*Al Quoz* 35-F4
...*Muhaisnah 1* 59-F6, 60-G6
...*Muhaisnah 4* 52-J6

58A
...*Al Rashidiya* 57-D5
...*Al Wasl* 20-M7
...*Nadd Shamma* 57-D6

58B
...*Al Rashidiya* 57-E5
...*Al Wasl* 20-J7
...*Mirdif* 66-M3

58C
...*Al Rashidiya* 57-E5
...*Mirdif* 67-A2

58D
...*Al Rashidiya* 57-F5
58E
...*Al Rashidiya* 58-G5

59

59
...*Al Bada'a* 22-G6
...*Al Garhoud* 41-C6
...*Al Mamzar* 27-F4
...*Al Mizhar 1* 68-L1
...*Al Satwa* 22-G7
...*Mirdif* 67-B4
...*Nadd Al Hamar* 57-A8
...*Trade Centre 2* 37-F1

59A
...*Al Safa 2* 19-A7
...*Jumeira 1* 21-E4
59B
...*Jumeira 1* 21-E5

60

60
...*Dubai Investment Park 1* 7-C1
...*Jebel Ali Industrial* 0-D3
...*Muhaisnah 1* 59-C6
60A
...*Al Barshaa 2* 32-H8
...*Al Barshaa 3* 31-C9
...*Al Raffa* 24-K4
...*Al Rashidiya* 57-F5
...*Mirdif* 66-M5

60B
...*Al Barshaa 2* 31-F9
...*Al Barshaa 3* 31-B8
...*Al Rashidiya* 58-H5
...*Mirdif* 66-M4
...*Muhaisnah 1* 59-E8

60C
...*Al Barshaa 2* 31-E9
...*Mirdif* 67-B3, 67-C3
...*Muhaisnah 1* 59-F7
60D
...*Muhaisnah 1* 60-G6

61

61
...*Al Mamzar* 27-F5
...*Al Mizhar 1* 60-L9
...*Al Satwa* 22-G8
...*Nadd Al Hamar* 57-A7
...*Trade Centre 2* 37-F1

61A
...*Al Garhoud* 41-C6
...*Jumeira 1* 21-E3
61B
...*Al Garhoud* 41-C7
...*Al Mizhar 1* 68-M1
...*Jumeira 1* 21-E4
...*Mirdif* 67-B4

62

62
...*Al Barshaa 2* 31-E9
...*Muhaisnah 4* 52-J6
62A
...*Al Rashidiya* 57-D6
62B
...*Al Rashidiya* 57-F5
...*Mirdif* 67-A4

63

63
...*Al Bada'a* 22-G6
...*Al Garhoud* 41-C5
...*Al Satwa* 22-G7
...*Jumeira 1* 21-E4
...*Nadd Al Hamar* 57-A5
...*Trade Centre 2* 37-F1
63B
...*Mirdif* 67-A2
63C
...*Mirdif* 67-A2
63E
...*Mirdif* 67-B4

64

64
...*Al Rashidiya* 58-H5, 58-H6
64B
...*Mirdif* 66-M4
64C
...*Mirdif* 67-B4

65

65
...*Al Bada'a* 22-G6
...*Al Garhoud* 41-C6
...*Al Satwa* 22-G8
...*Trade Centre 2* 37-F2
65A
...*Mirdif* 58-J6, 58-K8
...*Nadd Al Hamar* 57-A5
65B
...*Jumeira 1* 21-E5
...*Mirdif* 58-L9
...*Nadd Al Hamar* 57-B7
65C
...*Mirdif* 66-M1

66

66
...*Muhaisnah 4* 52-K6
66A
...*Al Rashidiya* 57-E6
66B
...*Al Rashidiya* 57-E6
...*Mirdif* 67-A4
66C
...*Al Rashidiya* 58-G6
66D
...*Al Rashidiya* 58-H5

67

67
...*Al Bada'a* 22-G6
...*Al Satwa* 22-G7
...*Nadd Al Hamar* 57-B7
...*Trade Centre 2* 37-F1
67A
...*Jumeira 1* 21-D3
...*Mirdif* 67-A1
67B
...*Jumeira 1* 21-D4
...*Mirdif* 67-B3
67C
...*Jumeira 1* 21-D5
...*Mirdif* 67-B3
67D
...*Mirdif* 67-C4

68

68A
...*Al Rashidiya* 57-E6
68B
...*Al Rashidiya* 57-E6

68C
...*Al Rashidiya* **58-G6**

69

69
...*Al Bada'a* **21-F6**
...*Al Satwa* **22-G8**
...*Trade Centre 2* **37-F1**

69A
...*Jumeira 1* **21-D4**
...*Mirdif* **58-K7**
...*Nadd Al Hamar* **57-A5**

69B
...*Jumeira 1* **21-D5**
...*Mirdif* **58-L8**
...*Nadd Al Hamar* **57-B7**

69C
...*Mirdif* **58-M9**

69D
...*Mirdif* **67-A2**

69E
...*Mirdif* **67-B3, 67-C4**

70

70
...*Mirdif* **66-M5**
...*Muhaisnah 4* **52-K7**

70A
...*Al Rashidiya* **57-E6**

70B
...*Al Rashidiya* **57-F6**

70C
...*Al Rashidiya* **58-G6**

71

71
...*Al Bada'a* **21-F6**
...*Mirdif* **67-B2**

71A
...*Al Satwa* **21-F7**
...*Jumeira 1* **21-D3**
...*Nadd Al Hamar* **57-B5**

71B
...*Al Satwa* **22-G8**
...*Jumeira 1* **21-D5**
...*Nadd Al Hamar* **57-B7**

72

72A
...*Al Rashidiya* **57-E7**

72B
...*Al Rashidiya* **57-F6**

72C
...*Al Rashidiya* **58-G6**

73

73
...*Al Bada'a* **21-F6**
...*Nadd Al Hamar* **57-C7**

73A
...*Al Satwa* **21-F7**

...*Jumeira 1* **21-D4**
...*Trade Centre 2* **37-E1**

73B
...*Al Satwa* **21-F8**
...*Jumeira 1* **21-D5**
...*Mirdif* **58-L7**

73C
...*Mirdif* **58-L7**

73D
...*Mirdif* **58-L8, 58-M8**

74

74
...*Muhaisnah 4* **52-J7**

74A
...*Al Rashidiya* **57-F7**

74B
...*Al Rashidiya* **58-G6**

75

75
...*Al Bada'a* **21-F6**

75A
...*Jumeira 1* **21-C3**
...*Mirdif* **58-M8**
...*Nadd Al Hamar* **57-A4**

75B
...*Jumeira 1* **21-C4**
...*Mirdif* **58-M9**
...*Nadd Al Hamar* **57-B5**

75C
...*Jumeira 1* **21-D5**
...*Mirdif* **58-M9**
...*Nadd Al Hamar* **57-C6**

75D
...*Mirdif* **58-M9**

76

76
...*Muhaisnah 4* **52-J7**
...*Nadd Shamma* **57-D6, 57-D7**

76A
...*Mirdif* **66-M6**

76B
...*Mirdif* **67-A5**

76C
...*Mirdif* **67-C4**

77

77
...*Al Bada'a* **21-E6**

77A
...*Al Satwa* **21-F7**
...*Jumeira 1* **21-C3**
...*Mirdif* **67-A1**

77B
...*Al Satwa* **21-F7**
...*Jumeira 1* **21-C4**
...*Mirdif* **67-B1, 67-B2**

77C
...*Al Satwa* **21-F8**
...*Mirdif* **67-B2**

78

78
...*Mirdif* **67-B5**
...*Muhaisnah 4* **52-J7**

79

79
...*Al Bada'a* **21-E6**
...*Jumeira 1* **21-C5**

79A
...*Al Satwa* **21-F7**
...*Mirdif* **67-B2**

79B
...*Al Satwa* **21-F8**
...*Mirdif* **67-B3, 67-C3**

79C
...*Mirdif* **67-C3**

79D
...*Mirdif* **67-C4**

81

81
...*Al Bada'a* **21-E6**
...*Za'abeel 2* **37-F3**

81A
...*Al Satwa* **21-E7**

81B
...*Jumeira 1* **21-C5**
...*Mirdif* **58-L7**

81C
...*Mirdif* **59-A9**

81D
...*Mirdif* **67-A1**

83

83
...*Al Bada'a* **21-E6**
...*Mirdif* **58-M8**

83A
...*Al Satwa* **21-E7**
...*Jumeira 1* **21-B4**
...*Trade Centre 2* **37-E2**

83B
...*Al Satwa* **21-E8**
...*Jumeira 1* **21-B5**

83C
...*Jumeira 1* **21-C6**

85

85
...*Al Bada'a* **21-E6**
...*Al Satwa* **21-E7**

85A
...*Mirdif* **67-B1**

85B
...*Mirdif* **67-C3**

87

87
...*Al Bada'a* 21-E6
...*Al Satwa* 21-E8

87A
...*Jumeira 1* 21-B4
...*Mirdif* 58-L7

87B
...*Mirdif* 58-L7, 58-M7

87C
...*Jumeira 1* 21-B5
...*Mirdif* 58-L7, 58-M7

87D
...*Jumeira 1* 21-B5
...*Mirdif* 58-M8

89

89
...*Al Bada'a* 21-D6
...*Al Satwa* 21-D8
...*Jumeira 1* 21-B5

89A
...*Mirdif* 58-M8

89B
...*Mirdif* 58-M8, 59-A8

89C
...*Mirdif* 59-A9

89D
...*Mirdif* 59-A9

91

91
...*Al Bada'a* 21-D6
...*Jumeira 1* 21-A4

91A
...*Al Satwa* 21-D7

91B
...*Al Satwa* 21-E9
...*Mirdif* 58-M7

91C
...*Mirdif* 59-A8

91D
...*Mirdif* 67-B1

93

93
...*Al Bada'a* 21-D6

94

94
...*Muhaisnah 4* 52-J8

98

98A
...*Muhaisnah 1* 59-C8

A

A P I World Tower
...*Trade Centre 1* 22-M8

Aaesha Preparatory School for Girls
...*Al Karama* 24-J8

Abattoir & Cattle Market
...*Al Qusais Ind 2* 52-H2

ABN Amro Bank
...*Mankhool* 24-H6

Abu Dhabi Commercial Bank
...*Ayal Nasir* 25-B4

Abu Dhabi National Bank
...*Riggat Al Buteen* 25-A8

Abu Hail
...*Abu Hail* 26-H6

Abu Hail Centre
...*Hor Al Anz East* 42-K3

Abu Hail Rd
...*Dividing Road* 26-K7

Ace Hardware
...*Al Quoz* 19-B8

Admiral Plaza
...*Al Souk Al Kabeer* 24-J3

Ahmad Bin Sulaim Elementary School for Boys
...*Al Baraha* 25-F6

Ahud Private School
...*Al Baraha* 25-F6

Airlines Centre
...*Al Khabaisi* 41-C3

Airport Hotel
...*Al Garhoud* 41-C7

Airport Rd
...*Dividing Road* 49-E3

Airshow Exhibition
...*Dubai International Airport* 50-G8

Al Adhid Rd
...*Dividing Road* 23-D6

Al Ahli Club
...*Al Nahda 1* 43-A5

Al Ahmadiyyah School & Heritage House
...*Hor Al Anz* 42-J2

Al Ain Centre
...*Mankhool* 24-J5

Al Amal Hospital
...*Al Wasl* 21-B7

Al Aqsa Elementary School for Boys
...*Al Rashidiya* 57-F5

Al Athar Rd
...*Jumeira 3* 20-G2

Al Attar
...*Trade Centre 2* 38-G1

Al Awir Rd
...*Dividing Road* 55-F9

Al Bada'a
...*Al Bada'a* 22-J5

Al Baraha
...*Al Baraha* 26-G6

Al Baraha Hospital
...*Al Baraha* 25-F5

Al Barshaa 1
...*Al Barshaa 1* 31-F1

Al Barshaa 2
...*Al Barshaa 2* 32-G7

Al Barshaa 3
...*Al Barshaa 3* 31-B4

Al Boom Tourist Village
...*Umm Hurair 2* 40-J9

Al Bustan Centre
...*Al Twar 1* 43-A7

Al Bustan Cinema
...*Al Qusais 1* 43-A7

Al Bustan Rotana
...*Al Garhoud* 41-C8

Al Buteen
...*Al Buteen* 24-M3

Al Daghaya
...*Al Daghaya* 25-A3

Al Dhiyafa Rd
...*Dividing Road* 23-A7

Al Durrah
...*Trade Centre 1* 22-J8

Al Emam Abu Hanifa Elementary School
...*Al Quoz* 35-F1

Al Emam Al Shafei Preparatory School for Boys
...*Al Wasl* 20-L6

Al Emarat Preparatory School for Boys
...*Al Rashidiya* 57-F6

Al Fahidi Roundabout
...*Al Raffa* 24-L4

Al Falah Model School
...*Mankhool* 23-E6

Al Farooq Pakistani Islamic School
...*Al Qusais 3* 51-B6

Al Garhoud
...*Al Garhoud* 49-B1

Al Garhoud Bridge
...*Dividing Road* 40-L9

Al Garhoud Complex
...*Al Garhoud* 41-B8

Al Garhoud Rd
...*Dividing Road* 41-A7

Al Ghadier
...*Trade Centre 2* 38-H1

Al Ghubaiba St
...*Dividing Road* 24-H2

Al Ghurair City
...*Al Muraqqabat* 25-C7

Al Hadiqa Rd
...*Al Safa 1* 20-G5

Al Hamar Rd
...*Dividing Road* 49-D9

Al Hamriya
...*Al Hamriya* 24-K5

Al Hamriya Port
...*Al Hamriya Port* 27-A3

Al Hamriya Shopping Complex
...*Hor Al Anz East* 26-K9

Al Hamriya St
...*Al Wuheida* 26-M6

Al Hana Centre
...*Al Satwa* 23-A5

Al Hikma Kindergarten
...*Al Rashidiya* 57-F2

Al Hudaiba
...*Al Hudaiba* 23-B4

Al Hudaiba Elementary School for Girls
...Al Twar 2 50-M4

Al Hudaiba St
...Jumeira 1 22-K3

Al Ittihad Private School
...Al Mamzar 27-C7

Al Ittihad Rd
...Dividing Road 41-F3, 42-G3, 43-C3

Al Ittihad Secondary School
...Hor Al Anz East 42-K1

Al Jaddaf
...Al Jaddaf 48-G2

Al Jafiliya
...Al Jafiliya 23-C6

Al Jahiz Elementary School for Boys
...Al Rashidiya 57-E1

Al Jawhara Hotel
...Al Rigga 25-B6

Al Jazeira St
...Al Muraqqabat 25-C8

Al Karama
...Al Karama 23-F8

Al Karama Kindergarten
...Al Karama 24-J8

Al Karama Shopping Complex
...Al Karama 39-F1

Al Kawakeb
...Trade Centre 2 37-F1

Al Khabaisi
...Al Khabaisi 41-E2

Al Khabeese
...Al Khabaisi 42-G3

Al Khaleej Centre
...Al Souk Al Kabeer 24-H5

Al Khaleej Holiday Hotel
...Riggat Al Buteen 24-M4

Al Khaleej National School
...Al Garhoud 49-A4

Al Khaleej Palace Hotel
...Riggat Al Buteen 25-A8

Al Khaleej Rd
...Al Mamzar 27-D4
...Al Shindagha 24-H2
...Al Wuheida 26-L5
...Dividing Road 25-F4, 26-L5, 27-A5,
27-B5, 27-E4

Al Khawaneej Rd
...Al Mizhar 2 68-G9

Al Khor St
...Al Ras 24-L2

Al Kifaf
...Al Kifaf 23-D9

Al Koufa
...Oud Metha 40-G3

Al Kuwait Elementary School for Girls
...Al Twar 1 42-M7

Al Maarif Secondary School for Boys
...Al Baraha 25-F6

Al Maktoum Bridge
...Umm Hurair 2 40-M2

Al Maktoum Hospital
...Naif 25-C6

Al Maktoum Hospital Rd
...Naif 25-B6

Al Maktoum Preparatory School for
Boys
...Al Wasl 20-J6

Al Maktoum Rd
...Dividing Road 25-A6, 25-B9, 25-B9

Al Mamzar
...Al Mamzar 27-A8

Al Mamzar Beach
...Al Mamzar 27-D7

Al Mamzar Centre
...Al Mamzar 43-A3

Al Mamzar Intermediate School
...Al Mamzar 43-B2

Al Mamzar Rd
...Al Mamzar 27-B6

Al Manal Centre
...Naif 25-A4

Al Manara
...Al Manara 17-E7

Al Manara Rd
...Al Manara 18-H6
...Umm Suqeim 2 18-G3

Al Manara Secondary School for Boys
...Al Manara 17-F7

Al Manhal Kindergarten
...Al Satwa 22-G7

Al Mankhool
...Mankhool 23-E6

Al Mankhool School
...Mankhool 23-E5

Al Marqadh
...Al marqadh 45-B3

Al Mateena St
...Al Muteena 25-E7

Al Mawakeb School
...Al Barshaa 2 31-F3
...Al Garhoud 49-B4

Al Mazhar Primary School for Girls
...Al Twar 3 59-A1

Al Mina
...Al Mina 23-F2

Al Mina Al Siyahi
...Al Mina Al Siyahi 13-D2, 13-D2

Al Mina Rd
...Al Hudaiba 23-F3

Al Mizhar 1
...Al Mizhar 1 60-H9

Al Mizhar 2
...Al Mizhar 2 68-K5

Al Moosa
...Trade Centre 1 21-F9

Al Moosa 2
...Trade Centre 1 21-F9

Al Muhallab Preparatory School for
Boys
...Al Mamzar 27-B8

Al Mulla Plaza
...Al Qusais 1 43-A4

Al Muraqqabat
...Al Muraqqabat 25-D9, 41-B1

Al Muraqqabat Rd
...Al Muraqqabat 25-C9

Al Murar
...Al Murar 25-C4

Al Murooj Complex
...Trade Centre 2 37-E2

Al Musallah Rd
...Dividing Road 25-B5

Al Mussalla Towers
...Al Hamriya 24-J5

Al Mustaqbal Elementary School for
Girls
...Umm Suqeim 2 17-E4

Al Muteena
...Al Muteena 25-D6

Al Nahda 1
...Al Nahda 1 43-D4

Al Nahda 2
...Al Nahda 2 43-F6

Al Nahda Interchange
...Al Mamzar 43-A3

Al Nahda Rd
...Dividing Road 51-B8

Al Nakhal Rd
...Naif 25-C6

Al Nasr Cinema
...Oud Metha 40-G2

Al Nasr Club
...Oud Metha 40-G2

Al Nasr Leisureland
...Oud Metha 40-G3

Al Nuwaibi Police Post
...Jebel Ali Free Zone 3-A3

Al Qataiyat Rd
...Dividing Road 23-E9

Al Qiadan Interchange
...Dividing Road 42-K3

Al Quds Rd
...Dubai International Airport 42-L9

Al Quoz
...Al Quoz 35-D1

Al Quoz Elementary School for Girls
...Al Quoz 19-F9

Al Quoz Industrial 1
...Al Quoz Industrial 1 34-H2

Al Quoz Industrial 2
...Al Quoz Industrial 2 34-H6

Al Quoz Industrial 3
...Al Quoz Industrial 3 33-B2

Al Quoz Industrial 4
...Al Quoz Industrial 4 33-B6

Al Qusais 1
...Al Qusais 1 43-B9

Al Qusais 2
...Al Qusais 2 51-B3

Al Qusais 3
...Al Qusais 3 51-C7

Al Qusais Industrial 1
...Al Qusais Ind 1 43-E9, 43-F9, 51-F1

Al Qusais Industrial 2
...Al Qusais Ind 2 51-F2

Al Qusais Industrial 3
...Al Qusais Ind 3 44-K8

Al Qusais Industrial 4
...Al Qusais Ind 4 52-L1

Al Qusais Industrial 5
...Al Qusais Ind 5 52-L4

Al Qusais Labour Accomodation
...Muhaisnah 2 60-J3

Al Qusais Rd
...Dividing Road 51-F1

Al Qusais Shopping Complex
...Al Qusais 1 51-A1

Al Rabee Kindergarten
...*Jumeira 1* **21-C4**

Al Raffa
...*Al Raffa* **23-F4**

Al Rais Centre
...*Mankhool* **24-H5**

Al Ras
...*Al Ras* **24-K3**

Al Rasheed Rd
...*Hor Al Anz* **26-J8**
...*Hor Al Anz East* **26-L9**

Al Rashidiya
...*Al Rashidiya* **57-E3**

Al Rashidiya Park
...*Al Rashidiya* **58-G3**

Al Rashidiya Public Library
...*Al Rashidiya* **57-F4**

Al Rashidiya Rd
...*Dividing Road* **50-K8**

Al Raya Secondary School for Girls
...*Al Wasl* **20-M4**

Al Rigga
...*Al Rigga* **25-B6**

Al Rigga Rd
...*Al Muraqqabat* **25-C9**

Al Rolla Rd
...*Al Raffa* **24-H4**

Al Rostamani
...*Trade Centre 1* **21-F9**

Al Sabkha Rd
...*Dividing Road* **25-A4**

Al Sadiq Islamic English School
...*Al Qusais 2* **51-B4**

Al Saeediya Preparatory School for Boys
...*Al Karama* **24-G8**

Al Safa
...*Trade Centre 1* **22-G9**

Al Safa 1
...*Al Safa 1* **19-C6**

Al Safa 2
...*Al Safa 2* **18-L6**

Al Safa Secondary School for Boys
...*Al Wasl* **20-K6**

Al Safa St
...*Al Wasl* **21-D7**

Al Salam
...*Trade Centre 1* **21-E9**

Al Salam Preparatory School
...*Al Qusais 3* **51-C8**

Al Satwa
...*Al Satwa* **22-L6**

Al Satwa Rd
...*Al Satwa* **22-H7, 22-K6**
...*Dividing Road* **22-H6**

Al Seef Rd
...*Al Hamriya* **24-M7**

Al Shabab Club
...*Al Mamzar* **27-B9**

Al Shabab Stadium
...*Al Mamzar* **27-B9**

Al Shindagha
...*Al Shindagha* **24-H1**

Al Shindagha Market
...*Al Shindagha* **24-J2**

Al Shorooq Kindergarten
...*Al Twar 3* **59-A1**

Al Souk Al Kabeer
...*Al Souk Al Kabeer* **24-J3**

Al Sufouh 1
...*Al Sufouh 1* **14-J4**

Al Sufouh 2
...*Al Sufouh 2* **15-D6**

Al Thanya Rd
...*Dividing Road* **17-B4**

Al Twar 1
...*Al Twar 1* **42-M9**

Al Twar 2
...*Al Twar 2* **51-A4**

Al Twar 3
...*Al Twar 3* **50-M8**

Al Twar Rd
...*Dividing Road* **42-K4, 50-L3**

Al Urouba St
...*Jumeira 1* **21-B4**

Al Waheeda Secondary School for Boys
...*Al Wuheida* **26-M6**

Al Warqaa 1
...*Al Warqaa 1* **64-M5**

Al Warqaa 2
...*Al Warqaa 2* **65-D1**

Al Warqaa 3
...*Al Warqaa 3* **65-C6**

Al Wasl
...*Al Wasl* **19-L4**

Al Wasl Club
...*Al Jaddaf* **39-D8**

Al Wasl Elementary School for Girls
...*Al Satwa* **22-H7**

Al Wasl Hospital
...*Al Jaddaf* **39-E7**

Al Wasl Park
...*Al Bada'a* **22-H5**

Al Wasl Rd
...*Al Bada'a* **21-F5**
...*Al Manara* **17-D6**
...*Al Safa 1* **19-C5**
...*Al Safa 2* **18-K5**
...*Al Wasl* **20-J4**

Al Wuheida
...*Al Wuheida* **26-L6**

Al Wuheida Rd
...*Al Wuheida* **27-A6**
...*Dividing Road* **27-A8**

Alexandria Rd
...*Al Mamzar* **27-E6, 27-F7**

Allama Iqbal Islamic School
...*Al Quoz* **35-E2**

Alliance Francaise
...*Oud Metha* **40-G5**

Ambassador Hotel
...*Al Souk Al Kabeer* **24-H2**

American Hospital
...*Oud Metha* **40-G3**

American School of Dubai
...*Al Bada'a* **21-F5**

American School of Dubai, The
...*Jumeira 1* **21-E5**

American University in Dubai
...*Al Sufouh 1* **14-G5**

Amina Bint Wahab Secondary School for Girls
...*Al Baraha* **25-F6**

Arab Bank for Investment & Foreign Trade
...*Riggat Al Buteen* **25-A7**

Arab Unity School
...*Al Mizhar 1* **59-C9**

Arabian Ranches
... **10-J7**

Archies Library
...*Al Karama* **24-H8**

Arif Castle
...*Al Raffa* **24-G3**

Arif Castle Hotel
...*Al Raffa* **24-G2**

Arrivals
...*Dubai International Airport* **41-E9**

Ascot Hotel
...*Al Raffa* **24-H3**

Asma Bint Abu Baker Multi Level for Girls
...*Al Twar 3* **50-M8**

Astoria Hotel
...*Al Souk Al Kabeer* **24-J3**

Atrium Centre
...*Mankhool* **24-J6**

Australia Consulate
...*Al Wasl* **20-L7**

Autodrome
... **10-G6**

Avari Dubai International
...*Al Muraqqabat* **41-C1**

Ayal Nasir
...*Ayal Nasir* **25-B3, 25-B3**

B

Bader Preparatory School for Boys
...*Muhaisnah 1* **59-A6**

Bangladesh Consulate
...*Al Muteena* **25-C7**

Baniyas Rd
...*Al Buteen* **24-M4**
...*Riggat Al Buteen* **41-A1**

Baniyas Square
...*Naif* **25-A5**

Bank Banorab
...*Al Muraqqabat* **25-B8**

Bank Melli Iran
...*Al Garhoud* **41-A7**

Bank of Sharjah
...*Al Garhoud* **41-A7**

Bank Pariba
...*Riggat Al Buteen* **25-A6**

Bank Saderat Iran
...*Riggat Al Buteen* **25-A5**

Banque Du Caire S.A.E.
...*Al Muteena* **25-D7**

Banque Indosuez
...*Trade Centre 2* **22-M9**

Banque Libannaise Pour Le Commerce
...*Al Muraqqabat* **25-A7**

Baraha St
...*Al Baraha* **25-F5**

Barclays Bank Plc
...*Oud Metha* 39-E3

Beach Centre, The
...*Jumeira 1* 22-G3

Beirut Rd
...*Al Qusais 2* 51-B5

Belhoul International Hospital Centre
...*Al Satwa* 23-A7

Bilal Bin Rabah Elemetary School for Boys
...*Al Satwa* 22-G7

Bin Sougat Centre
...*Al Rashidiya* 57-F1

Blue Diamond Hotel
...*Al Daghaya* 25-A3

British Council
...*Umm Hurair 2* 40-K2

British Council Library
...*Umm Hurair 2* 40-K2

Bu Kidra Country Club
...*Bukadra* 46-H6

Bukadra
...*Bukadra* 46-H9, 46-H9

Bur Juman Centre
...*Mankhool* 24-J7

Burj Al Arab
...*Umm Suqeim 3* 16-L2

Burj Dubai
...*Trade Centre 2* 37-C2

Butterflies & Busy Bees Nursery
...*Jumeira 1* 21-B4

C

Cairo Rd
...*Al Mamzar* 27-B6

Cambridge High School
...*Al Garhoud* 49-A4

Cambridge High School, The
...*Al Garhoud* 49-A2

Canada Consulate
...*Mankhool* 24-J6

Capitol Hotel
...*Al Mina* 23-B3

Capricorn
...*Trade Centre 2* 38-J1

Cargo Mega Terminal
...*Dubai International Airport* 41-D5

Cargo Village
...*Dubai International Airport* 41-D5

Carlton Tower
...*Al Rigga* 25-B6

Carrefour - Al Shindagha
...*Al Shindagha* 24-J2

Carrefour - Deira City Centre
...*Al Garhoud* 41-B4

Casablanca Hotel
...*Naif* 25-B5

Casablanca Rd
...*Al Garhoud* 41-C8

Cemetery
...*Al Hamriya* 24-L6
...*Al Raffa* 23-F3, 24-G4, 24-G5, 24-H3
...*Al Rigga* 25-B6
...*Al Twar 1* 42-K6
...*Jebel Ali* 5-C3

...*Muhaisnah 2* 60-J1

Center, The
...*Al Muteena* 25-E9

Central Lab
...*Al Karama* 40-H1

Central Post Office
...*Al Karama* 40-H1

Central Prison
...*Al Wasl* 21-C7

Centre for American Education
...*Al Garhoud* 49-A2

Century Cinemas
...*Jumeira 1* 21-B4

Century Plaza
...*Jumeira 1* 22-G3

Century Village
...*Al Garhoud* 41-A8

Champlain College
...*Al Garhoud* 41-B6

Chillis
...*Al Garhoud* 41-B7

China Consulate
...*Al Jafiliya* 23-D7

Cine Club
...*Oud Metha* 40-G5

Cinestar
...*Port Saeed* 41-B4

Citibank
...*Umm Hurair 2* 39-F7

Claridge Hotel
...*Al Muteena* 25-C7

Clinic
...*Jebel Ali Village* 4-G4

Clock Tower
...*Dividing Road* 41-B2

Coaster Berth
...*Al Shindagha* 24-H1

Comfort Inn
...*Al Muraqqabat* 25-B7

Compumall
...*Al Karama* 24-H8

Computer Plaza
...*Mankhool* 24-H5

Connection Sports Management
...*Trade Centre 1* 22-M8

Corniche Deira
...*Corniche Deira* 25-E3

Courtyard, The
...*Al Quoz Industrial 1* 33-E1

Crowne Plaza
...*Trade Centre 1* 22-J8

D

D56
...*Route Number* 60-H5, 66-L1

D57
...*Route Number* 6-M3

D59
...*Route Number* 4-J4

D61
...*Route Number* 13-F4

D62
...*Route Number* 56-K5

D63
...*Route Number* 16-K7, 32-K2

D65
...*Route Number* 18-G3

D67
...*Dividing Road* 63-C5
...*Route Number* 54-K5, 63-C5

D69
...*Route Number* 12-M2, 20-G2, 20-G7, 36-G2

D70
...*Route Number* 41-B8

D71
...*Route Number* 21-D6

D73
...*Route Number* 23-A4, 38-M6

D74
...*Route Number* 41-E3

D75
...*Route Number* 23-D5

D77
...*Route Number* 24-G7

D78
...*Route Number* 26-G6

D79
...*Route Number* 24-K7, 40-G4

D80
...*Route Number* 42-H2

D81
...*Route Number* 40-J6

D82
...*Route Number* 26-H8

D83
...*Route Number* 66-H5

D84
...*Route Number* 24-L8, 39-F1

D85
...*Route Number* 25-D3, 41-A4, 41-A5, 49-A6

D88
...*Route Number* 23-D8, 24-H7, 25-E5

D89
...*Route Number* 25-A8, 49-F7, 67-C2

D90
...*Route Number* 21-E7, 24-G5

D91
...*Route Number* 42-K2

D92
...*Route Number* 21-E5, 23-D3, 26-J5

D93
...*Route Number* 59-F5, 68-M1

D94
...*Route Number* 14-G4, 15-E4, 22-L3

D95
...*Route Number* 43-B1, 43-D9

D97
...*Route Number* 43-F5

Dallas
...*Al Souk Al Kabeer* 24-H4

Damascus Rd
...*Al Qusais 2* 51-C2

Deira Cinema
...*Al Muraqqabat* 25-B7

Deira City Centre Cinema
...*Al Garhoud* 41-B4

Deira City Centre Mall
...*Al Garhoud* 41-B4

Deira Old Souq
...*Al Buteen* 24-M3

Deira Park Hotel
...*Naif* 25-B5

Denmark Consulate
...*Al Rigga* 25-B7

Department of Civil Aviation
...*Dubai International Airport* 41-E7

Department of Economic Development
...*Riggat Al Buteen* 25-A8

Department of Health & Medical Services
...*Al Jafiliya* 23-D8

Department of HH the Ruler's Affairs & Protocol Affairs
...*Al Mina* 23-F2

Department of Ports & Customs
...*Al Mina* 23-D1

Department of Tourism & Commerce Marketing
...*Riggat Al Buteen* 25-A8

Departures
...*Dubai International Airport* 49-E2

Desert Spring Village
...*Al Sufouh 2* 15-A7

Development Board
...*Riggat Al Buteen* 25-A7

DEWA - Al Qusais
...*Al Twar 1* 42-M8

DEWA - Al Rashidiya
...*Al Rashidiya* 57-E2

DEWA - Al Satwa
...*Al Hudaiba* 23-C3

DEWA - Ayal Nasser
...*Riggat Al Buteen* 25-A6

DEWA - Burj Nahar
...*Al Muteena* 25-D6

DEWA - HQ
...*Umm Hurair 2* 40-G7

DEWA - Jebel Ali
...*Jebel Ali Free Zone* 2-H8

DEWA - Jumeira
...*Al Wasl* 21-D9

DEWA - Safia
...*Hor Al Anz* 42-J1

DEWA - Steam Power Station
...*Jebel Ali* 4-J1

DM Medical & Hazardous Waste Treatment Plant
...*Jebel Ali* 5-C5

DNATA
...*Al Quoz* 20-K8

Doha
...*Trade Centre 1* 21-F9

Driving Licence Office - Al Safa
...*Jumeira 3* 19-F4

Dubai - Al Ain Rd
...*Dividing Road* 53-E4

Dubai Airport Free Zone Authority
...*Dubai International Airport* 50-L2

Dubai Auto Parts City
...*Warsan 1* 64-H6

Dubai Aviation Club
...*Al Garhoud* 41-A9

Dubai Aviation College
...*Al Garhoud* 41-A8

Dubai Bank
...*Trade Centre 2* 22-M9

Dubai Camel Racecourse
...*Al Marqadh* 36-L9

Dubai Chamber of Commerce & Industry
...*Al Rigga* 24-M8

Dubai Cinema
...*Hor Al Anz* 25-F9

Dubai Civil Aviation Department
...*Dubai International Airport* 41-E7

Dubai College
...*Al Sufouh 2* 15-A4

Dubai Commercial Bank
...*Mankhool* 24-J5

Dubai Country Club
...*Al Bukadra* 46-H8

Dubai Courts
...*Umm Hurair 2* 40-L2

Dubai Creek
...*Al Souk Al Kabeer* 24-M5

Dubai Creek Golf & Yacht Club
...*Umm Hurair 2* 40-M7

Dubai Creek Marina
...*Umm Hurair 2* 40-M6

Dubai Creek Park
...*Umm Hurair 2* 40-K6

Dubai Development & Investment Authority
...*Trade Centre 2* 22-J9

Dubai Diving Centre
...*Jumeira 1* 22-J2

Dubai Drydocks
...*Al Mina* 23-C1

Dubai English College
...*Al Safa 1* 19-F6

Dubai English Speaking School
...*Umm Hurair 2* 40-H4

Dubai Equestrian Centre
...*Nadd Al Shiba 1* 45-B2

Dubai Exiles Rugby Club
...*Al Bukadra* 46-J7

Dubai Festival City
...*Ras Al Khor* 48-K7, 48-L2

Dubai First School
...*Al Quoz* 36-G2

Dubai Flower Centre
...*Dubai International Airport* 41-E4

Dubai Folklore Theatre Society
...*Al Mamzar* 43-A1

Dubai Garden Centre
...*Al Quoz Industrial 3* 17-C9

Dubai Gas Bottling Plant
...*Jebel Ali Free Zone* 3-B2

Dubai Gem Private Nursery & School
...*Oud Metha* 40-H4

Dubai Gem Private School
...*Oud Metha* 40-G4

Dubai Government Workshop
...*Al Jaddaf* 47-E2

Dubai Grand Hotel
...*Al Qusais 1* 51-C1

Dubai Healthcare City
...*Umm Hurair 2* 40-H6

Dubai Hospital
...*Al Baraha* 26-G5

Dubai Infants School
...*Oud Metha* 40-H4

Dubai International Airport
...*Dubai International Airport* 50-H2

Dubai International Airport Hotel
...*Dubai International Airport* 41-E9

Dubai International Art Centre
...*Jumeira 1* 22-G3

Dubai International Conference Centre
...*Trade Centre 2* 38-L1

Dubai International Exhibition Centre
...*Trade Centre 2* 38-M1

Dubai International Marine Club
...*Al Mina Al Siyahi* 13-D3

Dubai International Seafarer's Centre
...*Mankhool* 23-E5

Dubai Internet City
...*Al Sufouh 1* 14-H5

Dubai Investment Park
...*Dubai Investment Park 1* 0-K5

Dubai Investment Park 1
...*Dubai Investment Park 1* 7-E3

Dubai IT Academy
...*Al Wasl* 37-B1

Dubai Kart Club
...*Jebel Ali* 1-D3

Dubai Lending Library
...*Jumeira 1* 22-H3

Dubai Marina
...*Al Mina Al Siyahi* 13-D4

Dubai Marine Beach Resort & Spa
...*Jumeira 1* 22-K2

Dubai Maritime City
...*Al Shindagha* 24-G1

Dubai Media City
...*Al Sufouh 1* 14-G4

Dubai Mega Mall
... 999-C999

Dubai Metals & Commodities Centre
...*Emirates Hills 1* 13-B6

Dubai Municipality
...*Al Rigga* 25-A7

Dubai Municipality - Advertising Section
...*Umm Ramool* 49-E5

Dubai Municipality - Emergency Office
...*Riggat Al Buteen* 25-A7

Dubai Municipality - Fees & Revenues Section
...*Riggat Al Buteen* 25-A7

Dubai Municipality - Garage Transport Department
...*Al Garhoud* 49-D4

Dubai Municipality - HQ
...*Riggat Al Buteen* 25-A7

Dubai Municipality - Legal Affairs Department
...*Riggat Al Buteen* 25-A7

Dubai Municipality - Public Relations Section
...*Riggat Al Buteen* 25-A7

Dubai Municipality - Public Transport (Inquiries)
...*Riggat Al Buteen* 25-A7

Dubai Municipality - Rent Committee
...*Riggat Al Buteen* 25-A7

Dubai Municipality - Store
...*Al Garhoud* 49-D3

Dubai Municipality - Umm Ramool
Offices
...*Umm Ramool* 49-E5

Dubai Municipality - Used Car
Exhibitions Complex
...*Ras Al Khor Industrial 3* 55-B9

Dubai Museum
...*Al Raffa* 24-K4

Dubai National School
...*Al Barshaa 1* 31-E1
...*Al Satwa* 22-M7

Dubai Palm Hotel
...*Al Muteena* 25-D7

Dubai Pearl
...*Al Sufouh 1* 14-4H

Dubai Petroleum Company
...*Al Satwa* 21-D7

Dubai Police - Air Wing
...*Dubai International Airport* 41-D5

Dubai Police - Airport
...*Dubai International Airport* 41-E9

Dubai Police - Al Muraqqabat
...*Al Muraqqabat* 25-E9

Dubai Police - Al Rafaa
...*Al Souk Al Kabeer* 24-H3

Dubai Police - Al Rashidiya
...*Ras Al Khor Industrial 3* 55-B9

Dubai Police - Bur Dubai
...*Al Jafiliya* 23-B8

Dubai Police - Club
...*Al Jaddaf* 39-F8

Dubai Police - Criminal Investigation
Department (CID)
...*Al Twar 1* 42-L4

Dubai Police - General Ports & Airport
Department
...*Dubai International Airport* 41-E9

Dubai Police - Headquarters
...*Al Twar 1* 42-L4

Dubai Police - Naif Rd
...*Naif* 25-B4

Dubai Police - Rashidiya
...*Al Rashidiya* 57-F2

Dubai Ports Authority
...*Al Mina* 23-D1

Dubai Secondary School
...*Al Mamzar* 43-A2

Dubai T.V.
...*Umm Hurair 2* 40-K2

Dubai Tennis Stadium
...*Al Garhoud* 41-A8

Dubai Textile City
... 999-C999
...*Warsan 1* 63-D7

Dubai Traffic
...*Al Jafiliya* 23-B8

Dubai Traffic Police - HQ
...*Al Quoz Industrial 3* 16-L9

Dubai Traffic Police - Qusais
...*Al Twar 1* 42-K5

Dubai University College
...*Riggat Al Buteen* 25-A8

Dubai Wildlife & Waterbird Sanctuary
...*Al Jaddaf* 46-K5

Dubai World Trade Centre
...*Trade Centre 1* 22-M9

Dubailand
... 10-K9

DUBAL Aluminium Smelter
...*Jebel Ali Free Zone* 3-B2

Ducab (Cable Works)
...*Jebel Ali* 1-B5

DUGAS (Natural Gas)
...*Jebel Ali Free Zone* 3-A2

Dune Centre
...*Al Bada'a* 22-M5

Dusit Dubai
...*Trade Centre 2* 37-E1

E

E11
...*Al Twar 1* 42-L4
...*Route Number* 14-K6, 22-H9, 40-G8

E31
...*Route Number* 64-L3

E44
...*Route Number* 37-E5, 46-L8, 64-K6

E66
...*Route Number* 39-C7, 53-D5

Economic Department
...*Al Muraqqabat* 25-A8

Egypt Consulate
...*Umm Hurair 1* 24-K7

Electric Sub Station
...*Mirdif* 58-K6

Emarat Atrium
...*Al Wasl* 20-L7

Embassy Suites
...*Al Muteena* 25-E8

Emirates Airlines
...*Dubai International Airport* 49-F4

Emirates Bank International
...*Al Buteen* 24-M4

Emirates Billiards Centre
...*Hor Al Anz East* 42-L3

Emirates Golf Club
...*Al Sufouh 1* 14-G8

Emirates Hills
...*Emirates Hills 3* 29-E3

Emirates Hills 1
...*Emirates Hills 1* 13-C7

Emirates Hills 2
...*Emirates Hills 2* 14-H7

Emirates Hills 3
...*Emirates Hills 3* 29-E3

Emirates International School
...*Umm Al Sheif* 17-B8

Emirates Montessory Nursery
...*Jumeira 1* 21-B4

Emirates Post - Abu Hail
...*Abu Hail* 26-H5

Emirates Post - Airport
...*Dubai International Airport* 49-E2

Emirates Post - Airport Free Zone
...*Dubai International Airport* 50-L2

Emirates Post - Al Mussalla
...*Al Souk Al Kabeer* 24-K5

Emirates Post - Al Sanaweya
...*Al Rigga* 25-A6

Emirates Post - Al Twar
...*Al Twar 2* 51-A5

Emirates Post - Deira
...*Al Rigga* 25-A6

Emirates Post - Deira Main Office
...*Hor Al Anz East* 42-L2

Emirates Post - DNATA
...*Al Khabaisi* 41-C3

Emirates Post - Hor Al Anz
...*Hor Al Anz* 26-G9

Emirates Post - HQ
...*Al Karama* 24-J9

Emirates Post - Satwa
...*Jumeira 1* 21-F5

Emirates Post - Trade Centre
...*Trade Centre 2* 23-A9

Emirates Snooker Centre
...*Hor Al Anz East* 42-L3

Emirates Towers
...*Trade Centre 2* 38-J1

Emirates Towers Boulevard
...*Trade Centre 2* 31-J1

Emirates Towers Offices
...*Trade Centre 2* 38-J1

Emirates Training Centre
...*Al Garhoud* 41-A9

English Speaking School, The
...*Umm Hurair 2* 40-H4

ENOC
...*Oud Metha* 39-F3

EPPCO
...*Oud Metha* 39-F3

Etisalat - Al Khaleej
...*Al Raffa* 24-J5

Etisalat - Al Wasl
...*Trade Centre 2* 37-E1

Etisalat - HQ
...*Riggat Al Buteen* 25-A8

Etisalat - Jebel Ali
...*Jebel Ali Free Zone* 3-A4

Exhibition Halls
...*Trade Centre 1* 22-M9

Explorer Publishing
...*Al Mina Al Siyahi* 13-F4

F

Fairmont Dubai
...*Trade Centre 1* 22-M8

Falcon Chemicals
...*Al Mina Al Siyahi* 13-E4

Fatima English School
...*Al Rashidiya* 57-E4

Finland Consulate
...*Al Garhoud* 41-C5

Fish, Meat & Vegetable Market – Deira
...*Al Shindagha* 25-A2

Four Points Sheraton
...*Al Hamriya* 24-K6

France Consulate
...*Trade Centre 1* 22-L8

French Children's Nursery House
...*Jumeira 1* 22-K3

G

Galleria Cinema
...*Al Shindagha* 25-C3

Galleria Shopping Mall
...*Al Shindagha* 25-C3

Gardens Mall
...*Jebel Ali* 4-H3

Gardens, The
...*Jebel Ali* 4-J4

Gate, The
...*Trade Centre 2* 38-J1

Germany Consulate
...*Mankhool* 24-K8

Gharnata Elementary School for Girls
...*Al Rashidiya* 57-F2

Ghaya Residence
...*Trade Centre 2* 38-G1

Godolphin Gallery
...*Nadd Al Shiba 1* 45-A5

Gold & Diamond Museum
...*Al Quoz Industrial 3* 16-M9

Gold & Diamond Park
...*Al Quoz Industrial 3* 17-A9

Golden Sands Area
...*Mankhool* 24-H6

Grammar School
...*Al Garhoud* 49-A4

Grand Cinecity
...*Al Muraqqabat* 25-C7

Grand Cineplex
...*Umm Hurair 2* 40-G8

Grand Hyatt Dubai
...*Umm Hurair 2* 40-H8

Greek School
... 999-C999

Green Community
...*Dubai Investment Park 1* 7-E5

Greens, The
...*Emirates Hills 2* 14-K7

Gulf Inn Hotel
...*Al Muraqqabat* 25-B8

Gulf Montessori Centre
...*Mankhool* 24-J6

Gulf Montessori Nursery
...*Al Garhoud* 41-C9

H

Habib Bank AG Zurich
...*Al Hamriya* 24-K7

Hamarain Centre
...*Al Muraqqabat* 41-E1

Hamriya Port
...*Al Hamriya Port* 27-A3

Happy Home Nursery
...*Al Karama* 24-J8

Hard Rock Café
...*Al Sufouh 1* 13-F5

Heritage & Diving Village
...*Al Shindagha* 24-L1

Heritage International Hotel
...*Mankhool* 24-J5

Hessa Preparatory School for Girls
...*Za'abeel 1* 39-D4

HH. The Ruler's Court
...*Al Souk Al Kabeer* 24-L4

HH. The Ruler's Guesthouse
...*Jumeira 1* 22-M2

Higher Colleges of Technology (Men's)
...*Al Nahda 2* 44-H7

Higher Colleges of Technology (Women's)
...*Al Nahda 2* 44-E7

Hilton
...*Al Mina Al Siyahi* 4-M2

Hilton Apartments
...*Trade Centre 1* 22-L9

Hilton Dubai Creek
...*Riggat Al Buteen* 25-A9

Hilton Dubai Jumeira
...*Al Mina Al Siyahi* 13-A3

Holiday Centre Shopping Mall
...*Trade Centre 1* 22-K8

Holiday Inn Bur Dubai
...*Oud Metha* 39-F4

Holiday Inn Downtown
...*Al Muraqqabat* 41-C1

Hor Al Anz
...*Hor Al Anz* 26-H9

Hor Al Anz East
...*Hor Al Anz East* 42-L2

Hor Al Anz Public Library
...*Hor Al Anz East* 42-M2

Hor Al Anz St
...*Abu Hail* 26-H6, 26-H7
...*Hor Al Anz* 26-G9

Horse Racecourse
...*Za'abeel 2* 38-K3

Housing, Police
...*Al Qusais 3* 51-D9

Howard Johnson Hotel
...*Al Muraqqabat* 25-B8

HSBC Bank Middle East
...*Al Souk Al Kabeer* 24-K3

Hyatt Golf Park
...*Al Daghaya* 25-C3

Hyatt Regency
...*Al Shindagha* 25-C3

Hydropolis
...*Marsa Dubai* 13-C1

I

Ibis
...*Trade Centre 2* 38-L1, 38-M2

Iman Private School
...*Al Rashidiya* 58-G2

Imperial Suites Hotel
...*Al Raffa* 24-H4

India Consulate
...*Umm Hurair 1* 24-K8

Indian High School
...*Oud Metha* 40-H3

Indian Village
...*Al Quoz Industrial 3* 17-A9

Inter-Continental
...*Al Rigga* 25-A7

Interchange No.1
...*Dividing Road* 37-C1

Interchange No.4
...*Dividing Road* 16-J9

Interchange No.7
...*Dividing Road* 3-B3

InterContinental Dubai
...*Al Rigga* 25-A6

International Private Hospital
...*Al Rigga* 25-A5

International School of Choueifat
...*Umm Suqeim 1* 18-M2

International School of Dubai
...*Al Quoz* 36-G4

Iran Consulate
...*Umm Hurair 1* 24-L7

Iranian Hospital
...*Al Bada'a* 22-K4

Irish Village
...*Al Garhoud* 41-A8

Islamic Preparatory School
...*Al Mamzar* 27-B8

Islamic School for Education
...*Muhaisnah 1* 59-D4

Italy Consulate
...*Trade Centre 2* 22-M9

J

Jamal Abdulnasir Elementary School for Boys
...*Al Satwa* 22-M7

Japan Consulate
...*Trade Centre 2* 22-M9

Japanese School
...*Al Wasl* 20-L6

Jebel Ali Beach
...*Jebel Ali* 1-D2

Jebel Ali Free Zone
...*Jebel Ali Free Zone* 2-J8

Jebel Ali Golf Resort
...*Jebel Ali* 1-E3

Jebel Ali Harbour
...*Jebel Ali* 2-L2

Jebel Ali Horse Racecourse
...*Jebel Ali* 30-J3

Jebel Ali Hotel
...*Jebel Ali* 1-E3

Jebel Ali Hotel Beach
...*Jebel Ali* 1-D2

Jebel Ali Industrial
...*Jebel Ali Industrial* 2-L3

Jebel Ali Interchange No.6
...*Dividing Road* 4-G2

Jebel Ali Primary School
...*Jebel Ali Village* 4-G3

Jebel Ali Sailing Club
...*Al Mina Al Siyahi* 13-C3

Jebel Ali Village
...*Jebel Ali Village* 4-G4

Jebel Ali Village Clinic
...*Jebel Ali Village* 4-G4

Jebel Ali Water Reservoir
...*Jebel Ali* 4-G5

Jordan Consulate
...*Umm Hurair 1* 24-K8

Juma Al Majid Cultural Centre
...*Hor Al Anz* 42-G1

Jumeira 1
...*Jumeira 1* 21-E4

Jumeira 2
...*Jumeira 2* 20-K2

Jumeira 3
...*Jumeira 3* 19-D3

Jumeira Beach Club, The
...*Jumeira 2* **20-L1**

Jumeira Beach Corniche
...*Jumeira 1* **22-H2**

Jumeira Beach Hotel
...*Umm Suqeim 3* **16-M3**

Jumeira Beach Residence
...*Al Mina Al Siyahi* **13-A3**

Jumeira Centre
...*Jumeira 1* **22-J3**

Jumeira College
...*Al Safa 1* **19-A5**

Jumeira English Speaking School
...*Al Safa 1* **19-E7**

Jumeira Fire Station
...*Al Wasl* **21-B6**

Jumeira Mosque
...*Jumeira 1* **22-L3**

Jumeira Plaza
...*Jumeira 1* **22-H3**

Jumeira Plaza Mall
...*Jumeira 1* **22-H3**

Jumeira Primary School
...*Jumeira 1* **19-A5**

Jumeira Rd
...*Jumeira 2* **20-H2**
...*Jumeira 3* **19-B2, 19-F2**
...*Umm Suqeim 1* **18-J3, 18-L3, 18-M3**
...*Umm Suqeim 2* **17-C3, 17-D3, 17-F3**

Jumeira Rotana Hotel
...*Al Bada'a* **22-M4**

Jumeirah Islands
...*Al Sufouh 1* **13-A8**

Jumeirah Lake Towers
...*Emirates Hills 1* **13-A6**

Jumeria Beach
...*Jumeira 1* **22-H2**

Jumeriah Beach Park
...*Jumeira 2* **20-J1**

JW. Marriott
...*Al Muraqqabat* **41-E1**

K

Kalantar
...*Trade Centre 1* **21-E9**

Karama Centre
...*Al Karama* **24-G9**

Kendah House
...*Trade Centre 2* **38-H1**

Khalid Al Attar
...*Trade Centre 1* **22-H9**

Khalid Bin Al Waleed Rd
...*Dividing Road* **24-J5**

Khalid Ibn Al Waleed School
...*Al Garhoud* **49-A2**

Khattab Rd
...*Dividing Road* **25-D6**

Khawla Bint Al Azwar Elementary
School for Girls
...*Al Satwa* **21-E8**

Kid's Island Nursery
...*Jumeira 2* **20-K4**

Kindergarten Nursery School
...*Port Saeed* **41-A4**

Kuwait Consulate
...*Umm Hurair 1* **24-L8**

L

Lady Bird Nursery
...*Al Wasl* **20-M4**

Ladybird Nursery
...*Al Bada'a* **21-D6**

Lakes, The
...*Emirates Hills 2* **30-G1**

Lamcy Cinema
...*Oud Metha* **39-E3**

Lamcy Plaza
...*Oud Metha* **39-F3**

Lands Department
...*Riggat Al Buteen* **25-A8**

Latifa Bin Hamdan Multi Level for Girls
...*Al Karama* **24-H9**

Le Meridien Hotel
...*Al Garhoud* **41-D8**

Le Meridien Mina Seyahi
...*Al Mina Al Siyahi* **13-F3**

Le Royal Meridien Beach Resort & Spa
...*Al Mina Al Siyahi* **13-B3**

Lebanon Consulate
...*Umm Hurair 1* **24-L8**

Little Land Nursery
... **999-z**

Little Princess Nursery
...*Al Qusais 2* **51-C3**

Little Star Nursery
...*Al Satwa* **22-M7**

Lloyds TSB Bank Plc
...*Jumeira 2* **20-H4**

London Crown Hotel
...*Mankhool* **24-J6**

Lords Hotel
...*Al Muraqqabat* **25-B8**

Lotus
...*Al Muraqqabat* **25-B8**

Lotus Hotel
...*Al Muraqqabat* **25-B8**

M

Madinat Badr
...*Muhaisnah 1* **59-A6**

Madinat Jumeirah
...*Al Sufouh 1* **16-J3**

Magrudy Shopping Mall
...*Jumeira 1* **22-J3**

Malaysia Consulate
...*Oud Metha* **39-F2**

Mall of the Emirates
...*Al Barshaa 1* **32-J1**

Mankhool
...*Mankhool* **23-E6**

Mankhool Rd
...*Al Jafiliya* **23-F5**

Marco Polo Hotel
...*Al Muteena* **25-D6**

Marine Control Tower
...*Jebel Ali Free Zone* **2-H5**

Marks & Spencer
...*Al Muraqqabat* **25-E9**

Marriott Executive Apartments
...*Al Rigga* **41-B1**
...*Riggat Al Buteen* **41-B1**

Marsa Dubai
...*Marsa Dubai* **13-C5**

Mashreq Bank
...*Al Muraqqabat* **25-C7**

Mayfair Hotel
...*Al Muraqqabat* **41-B1**

Mazaya Centre
...*Trade Centre 1* **21-D9**

Meadows, The
...*Emirates Hills* **13-B8**

Mercato
...*Jumeira 1* **21-D4**

Metroplex Cinema
...*Trade Centre 2* **20-H8**

Metropolitan Deira
...*Al Khabaisi* **41-C2**

Metropolitan Hotel
...*Trade Centre 2* **20-J8**

Metropolitan Palace Hotel
...*Al Muraqqabat* **25-B9**

Metropolitan Resort & Beach Club Hotel
...*Al Mina Al Siyahi* **13-C3**

Middle East Bank
...*Al Buteen* **24-M4**

Middle East Hotel
...*Ayal Nasir* **25-A4**

Millenium School, The
...*Al Qusais Ind 1* **43-E8**

Mina A'Salam
...*Al Sufouh 2* **16-K3**

Mina Al Seyahi Beach
...*Al Mina Al Siyahi* **13-D3**

Ministry of Agriculture & Fisheries
...*Al Muraqqabat* **41-B2**

Ministry of Communication
...*Al Khabaisi* **41-D3**

Ministry of Defence
...*Al Souk Al Kabeer* **24-K4**

Ministry of Economy & Commerce
...*Al Khabaisi* **41-C2**

Ministry of Education & Youth
...*Al Twar 1* **42-J4**

Ministry of Electricity & Water
...*Al Muteena* **25-E9**

Ministry of Finance & Industry
...*Al Souk Al Kabeer* **24-H2**

Ministry of Health
...*Al Karama* **24-H7**

Ministry of Information & Culture
...*Al Qusais 1* **42-M7**

Ministry of Labour & Social Affairs
...*Hor Al Anz East* **42-L3**

Ministry of Planning
...*Al Muteena* **25-C7**

Ministry of Public Works & Housing
...*Al Qusais 1* **43-A8**

Ministry of Youth & Sports
...*Hor Al Anz East* **42-K2**

Mirdif
...*Mirdif* **66-L2**

Mirdif 251
...*Mirdif* **66-L2**

Modern High School
...*Al Wasl* **20-K6, 20-K6**

Modern International School
...*Al Rashidiya* **57-F2**

Montgomerie, The
...*Al Barshaa 3* **13-C8**

Mother to Mother Tykes
...*Trade Centre 2* **22-M9**

Muhaisnah 1
...*Muhaisnah 1* **59-C5**

Muhaisnah 2
...*Muhaisnah 2* **60-G3**

Muhaisnah 3
...*Muhaisnah 3* **52-G6**

Muhaisnah 4
...*Muhaisnah 4* **52-J3**

Musallah Al Eid
...*Al Baraha* **25-E5**
...*Mankhool* **23-E7**

Mushrif National Park
...*Mushrif Park* **67-E8**

Mushrif Park
...*Mushrif Park* **66-M8**

Nad Al Hamar
...*Nadd Al Hamar* **57-A7**

Nad Al Sheba Camel Racetrack
...*Al marqadh* **45-B4**

Nadd Al Hamar
...*Nadd Al Hamar* **56-J7**

Nadd Al Hamar Rd
...*Dividing Road* **56-H6**

Nadd Al Shiba 1
...*Nadd Al Shiba 1* **53-A2**

Nadd Al Shiba 2
...*Nadd Al Shiba 2* **54-G5**

Nadd Al Shiba 3
...*Nadd Al Shiba 3* **62-K4**

Nadd Al Shiba 4
...*Nadd Al Shiba 4* **61-E4**

Nadd Al Shiba Golf Course
...*Nadd Al Shiba 1* **45-B8**

Nadd Al Shiba Golf Course & Horse Racecourse
...*Nadd Al Shiba 1* **45-C8**

Nadd Al Shiba Palace
...*Nadd Al Shiba 1* **53-A9**

Nadd Al Shiba Rd
...*Nadd Al Shiba 1* **53-D1**

Nadd Shamma
...*Nadd Shamma* **57-B4, 57-C4**

Naif
...*Naif* **25-C5**

Naif Park
...*Naif* **25-B4**

Naif Rd
...*Dividing Road* **25-C4**

Naif Souk
...*Naif* **25-A4**

National Bank of Dubai
...*Al Muraqqabat* **25-A8**

National Bank of Ras Al Khaimah
...*Riggat Al Buteen* **41-B1**

National Charity School for Girls
...*Al Garhoud* **49-A1**

Nautilus Academy, The
...*Al Hamriya* **24-J5**

Netherlands Consulate
...*Mankhool* **24-J6**

New Indian Model School
...*Al Garhoud* **49-A3**

Nido Nursery
...*Al Quoz* **19-D9**

Nihal Rotana Inn
...*Al Muraqqabat* **41-B1**

Norway Consulate
...*Al Souk Al Kabeer* **24-J2**

Novotel
...*Trade Centre 2* **38-L2**

Number One Tower Apartments
...*Trade Centre 1* **21-F9**

Nursery Modern School
...*Al Twar 1* **42-M7**

Oasis
...*Trade Centre 2* **37-F1**

Oasis Beach Hotel
...*Al Mina Al Siyahi* **13-A3**

Oasis Centre
...*Al Quoz* **19-C8**

Oman Consulate
...*Umm Hurair 1* **24-K8**

Omar Bin Al Khattab Rd
...*Dividing Road* **25-B7**

Omer Al Mukhtar School for Boys
...*Al Bada'a* **22-H6**

One&Only Royal Mirage, The
...*Al Sufouh 1* **14-G3**

Oud Al Muteena
...*Oud Al Muteena* **60-M8**

Oud Metha
...*Oud Metha* **39-F2**

Oud Metha Rd
...*Dividing Road* **40-H4, 46-J2**

Our Own English High School
...*Oud Metha* **40-G4**

Oxford School, The
...*Al Bada'a* **22-K5**

P

Pakistan Consulate
...*Umm Hurair 1* **24-K8**

Pakistan Islamic School
...*Umm Hurair 2* **40-J3**

Palestine Consulate
...*Hor Al Anz East* **42-K2**

Palm Beach Rotana Inn
...*Al Raffa* **24-H3**

Palm Hotel, The
...*Al Sufouh 1* **13-F5**

Palm Jebel Ali, The
...*Jebel Ali* **1-A1**

Palm Jumeirah, The
...*Al Sufouh 1* **14-J1**

Palm Strip
...*Jumeira 1* **22-K3**

Palm's Nursery School
...*Jumeira 3* **20-G4**

Panorama Hotel
...*Al Raffa* **24-G5**

Park & Shop
...*Al Safa 1* **19-D5**

Passport & Immigration Department
...*Al Jafiliya* **23-B8**

Phoenicia Hotel
...*Naif* **25-A5**

Planet Hollywood
...*Umm Hurair 2* **39-F6**

Plant Street
...*Al Bada'a* **22-K5**

Plaza Cinema
...*Al Souk Al Kabeer* **24-J2**

Police Training College
...*Al Sufouh 1* **16-G6**

Port Administration
...*Al Mina* **23-E2**

Port Saeed
...*Port Saeed* **41-B3**

Ports & Customs Department (Car Storage)
...*Ras Al Khor Industrial 3* **63-C2**

President Hotel
...*Al Karama* **24-J7**

Princess Flamingo
...*Al Qusais 2* **51-A2**

Princeton Hotel
...*Al Garhoud* **41-B6**

Public Library
...*Al Ras* **24-K2**

Public Prosecution
...*Umm Hurair 2* **40-L3**

Pyramids
...*Umm Hurair 2* **40-G6**

Q

Qatar Consulate
...*Al Jafiliya* **23-D7**

Qortuba Preparatory School for Girls
...*Al Satwa* **21-D8**

Quality Inn
...*Al Muraqqabat* **25-B9**

R

Ramada Continental Hotel
...*Hor Al Anz East* **42-K3**

Ramada Hotel
...*Mankhool* **24-H5**

Ramee International Hotel
...*Naif* **25-A5**

Ras Al Khor
...*Ras Al Khor* **48-K9**

Ras Al Khor Industrial 1
...*Ras Al Khor Industrial 1* **55-A2**

Ras Al Khor Industrial 2
...*Ras Al Khor Industrial 2* **55-A5**

Ras Al Khor Industrial 3
...*Ras Al Khor Industrial 3* 63-D1

Ras Al Khor Rd
...*Dividing Road* 55-A2

Rashid Hospital
...*Umm Hurair 2* 40-J5

Rashidiya Rd
...*Dividing Road* 52-J3

Regal Plaza Hotel
...*Mankhool* 24-J5

Regent Palace Hotel
...*Al Karama* 24-J7

Regent School
...*Jumeira 3* 19-F3

Renaissance Dubai
...*Al Muteena* 25-E8

Rex Drive-in Cinema
...*Muhaisnah 1* 59-B8

Riggat Al Buteen
...*Riggat Al Buteen* 25-A6

Ring Rd
...*Dividing Road* 58-G7
...*Muhaisnah 2* 52-J9
...*Nadd Al Shiba 3* 62-M8

Ritz-Carlton, Dubai, The
...*Al Mina Al Siyahi* 13-B3

Riviera Hotel
...*Al Rigga* 25-A6

Romania Consulate
...*Jumeira 3* 19-A4

Rydges Plaza Hotel
...*Al Jafiliya* 23-A6

S

Saeed
...*Trade Centre 1* 22-K8

Safa Park
...*Al Wasl* 20-H6

Safestway
...*Al Wasl* 37-A1

Sahara
...*Trade Centre 1* 21-F9

Salahuddin Rd
...*Dividing Road* 25-D8

Salma Al Ansariya Elementary School for Girls
...*Al Satwa* 21-E8

San Marco Hotel
...*Al Murar* 25-D4

Saudi Arabia Consulate
...*Umm Hurair 1* 24-L8

Saudi Arabia Ministry of Labour
...*Hor Al Anz East* 42-L3

School of Research Science
...*Al Qusais Ind 1* 43-E8

Sea Rock Hotel
...*Naif* 25-C6

Sea Shell Inn
...*Al Raffa* 24-H4

Sea View Hotel
...*Al Raffa* 23-F3

Second of December Secondary School for Girls
...*Al Twar 1* 42-M7

Shangri-La Hotel
...*Trade Centre 1* 21-F9

Sheikh Mohammed Centre for Cultural Understanding
...*Jumeira 1* 22-G3

Sheikh Saeed Al Maktoum's House
...*Al Shindagha* 24-L1

Sheikh Zayed Rd
...*Dividing Road* 4-H2, 14-J6, 19-C7, 22-K9

Sheikha Sulaiman Mohammad Sulaiman School
...*Nadd Al Hamar* 56-K6

Sheraton Deira
...*Al Muteena* 25-F8

Sheraton Dubai Creek Hotel & Towers
...*Al Rigga* 25-A7

Sheraton Jumeira Beach Resort & Towers
...*Al Mina Al Siyahi* 4-M1

Shooting Club
...*Jebel Ali* 1-C7

Shurahbeel Elementary School
...*Al Qusais 2* 51-C4

Sikkat Al Khail St
...*Dividing Road* 24-M3

Sky
...*Trade Centre 2* 38-H1

Small World Nursery
...*Jumeira 1* 22-K3

Sofitel City Centre Hotel & Residence
...*Al Garhoud* 41-B5

Solid Waste Dumping Area
...*Al Qusais Ind 5* 52-M8

South Africa Consulate
...*Al Karama* 24-K7

Spinneys
...*Al Safa 2* 19-A5
...*Jumeira 1* 22-J3
...*Mankhool* 24-H5

Spinneys (Umm Suqeim)
...*Umm Suqeim 1* 19-A5

Spinneys Centre
...*Al Safa 2* 19-A5

Springs, The
...*Emirates Hills 3* 29-D7

Sri Lanka Consulate
...*Al Hudaiba* 23-C4

St. George Hotel
...*Al Ras* 24-K3

St. Mary's Catholic High School
...*Umm Hurair 2* 40-H4

Standard Chartered
...*Mankhool* 24-G5

Standard Chartered Grindlays
...*Mankhool* 24-G5

Strand Cinema
...*Al Karama* 24-K8

Sun & Sand Hotel
...*Al Muraqqabat* 41-B1

Sun Rock Hotel
...*Mankhool* 23-D5

Sweden Consulate
...*Al Mina* 23-D2

Swiss Plaza Hotel
...*Al Souk Al Kabeer* 24-J3

Switzerland Consulate
...*Trade Centre 2* 23-A9

Syria Consulate
...*Al Wuheida* 26-L6

T

Taj Palace Hotel
...*Al Muraqqabat* 25-B9

Tariq Bin Ziad Preparatory School for Boys
...*Al Baraha* 25-E5

TechnoCampus
...*Port Saeed* 41-A5

Terminal 1
...*Dubai International Airport* 41-E9

Terminal 2
...*Dubai International Airport* 42-J7

Thailand Consulate
...*Jumeira 2* 20-K3

The One
...*Jumeira 1* 22-K3

The Ritz-Carlton, Dubai
...*Al Mina Al Siyahi* 13-B3

Thunderbowl
...*Al Wasl* 21-C9

Tiny Home Montessori Nursery
...*Jumeira 1* 22-G5

Toulaitilah Primary School
...*Hor Al Anz* 42-H2

Towers Rotana Hotel
...*Trade Centre 1* 21-F9

Town Centre
...*Jumeira 1* 21-C4

Trade Centre
...*Trade Centre 2* 22-M9

Trade Centre 1
...*Trade Centre 1* 21-F9

Trade Centre 2
...*Trade Centre 2* 37-E1

Trade Centre Rd
...*Al Karama* 23-F9
...*Dividing Road* 23-E8

Trade School
...*Port Saeed* 41-B2, 41-B2

Traffic Police Desk - Al Awir Used Cars Showroom
...*Ras Al Khor Industrial 3* 55-B9

Traffic Police Desk - DUCAMZ
...*Ras Al Khor Industrial 3* 55-C9

Traffic Police Desk - Mazda
...*Dubai International Airport* 42-J4

Turkey Consulate
...*Trade Centre 2* 22-M8

Twin Towers
...*Al Rigga* 25-A6

U

UAE Radio & TV - Dubai
...*Umm Hurair 2* 40-K2

UK Consulate
...*Al Hamriya* 24-L6

Um Hani Preparatory School for Girls
...*Al Rashidiya* 57-F5

Turkey Consulate
...*Trade Centre 2* **22-M8**
Twin Towers
...*Al Rigga* **25-A6**

U

UAE Radio & TV - Dubai
...*Umm Hurair 2* **40-K2**
UK Consulate
...*Al Hamriya* **24-L6**
Um Hani Preparatory School for Girls
...*Al Rashidiya* **57-F5**
Umm Al Sheif
...*Umm Al Sheif* **16-M8**
Umm Al Sheif Rd
...*Umm Suqeim 1* **19-A3**
Umm Hurair 1
...*Umm Hurair 1* **24-K8**
Umm Hurair 2
...*Umm Hurair 2* **40-G7**
Umm Hurair Rd
...*Dividing Road* **40-G1**
Umm Ramool
...*Umm Ramool* **49-C6**
Umm Ramool Rd
...*Dividing Road* **57-B5**
Umm Suqeim 1
...*Umm Suqeim 1* **18-J4**
Umm Suqeim 2
...*Umm Suqeim 2* **17-D4**
Umm Suqeim 3
...*Umm Suqeim 3* **17-A4**
Umm Suqeim Beach
...*Umm Suqeim 3* **17-B2**
Umm Suqeim Prep. School for Girls
...*Al Safa 2* **18-J7**
Umm Suqeim Rd
...*Dividing Road* **32-K4**
Union Co-op/Choithram
...*Jumeira 3* **20-G4**
Union House

...*Jumeira 1* **22-M3**
Union National Bank
...*Al Muraqqabat* **25-B7**
Union Square
...*Al Rigga* **25-B7**
United Arab Bank
...*Riggat Al Buteen* **25-A8**
University of Wollongong
...*Jumeira 3* **19-A2**
USA Consulate
...*Trade Centre 2* **22-M9**
Used Cars Showroom
...*Ras Al Khor Industrial 3* **55-B9**

V

Vasantam Hotel
...*Al Souk Al Kabeer* **24-J3**
Vendome Plaza Hotel
...*Al Muraqqabat* **41-B1**

W

Wafi City
...*Umm Hurair 2* **39-F6**
Warba Centre
...*Al Muraqqabat* **41-E1**
Warsan 1
...*Warsan 1* **64-G7**
Water Jet Ski Area
...*Ras Al Khor* **48-M1**
Water Tank
...*Nadd Shamma* **57-C2**
Welcare Hospital
...*Al Garhoud* **41-B7**
West Hotel
...*Al Murar* **25-B4**
Western Hotel
...*Al Raffa* **24-G5**
White Crown
...*Trade Centre 1* **22-L8**

White Swan
...*Trade Centre 1* **22-L8**
Wholesale Fruit & Vegetable Market
...*Corniche Deira* **26-G4**
...*Ras Al Khor Industrial 3* **63-E4**
Wild Wadi
...*Umm Suqeim 3* **16-L3**
Wollongong Beach
...*Jumeira 3* **19-A2**
Wonder Land
...*Umm Hurair 2* **40-J8**
World Trade Centre Hotel
...*Trade Centre 2* **22-M9**

Y

Yemen Consulate
...*Al Hamriya* **24-K7**
York International Hotel
...*Al Raffa* **24-J5**

Z

Za'abeel 1
...*Za'abeel 1* **39-D5**
Za'abeel 2
...*Za'abeel 2* **38-G6**
Za'abeel Palace
...*Za'abeel 1* **39-B4**
Za'abeel Park
...*Za'abeel 1* **39-C1**
Za'abeel Rd
...*Dividing Road* **39-A3**
...*Za'abeel 1* **39-F1**
Za'abeel Roundabout
...*Za'abeel 1* **39-B2**
Za'abeel Secondary School for Girls
...*Za'abeel 1* **39-D4**
Zayed University
...*Al Twar 3* **50-K9**

Al Futtaim Motors

Parts Centres
...*Ramoul,* **49-B5,** Tel 286 0018
...*Al Quoz,* **19-C8,** Tel 338 6414
Service Centres
...*Ramoul,* **49-B5,** Tel 286 2200
...*Sheikh Zayed Road,* **19-C8,** Tel 338 1113
Showrooms
...*Deira City Centre,* **41-A4,** Tel 295 4231
...*Sheikh Zayed Road,* **19-C8,** Tel 338 6341
Tyres, Batteries and Accessories Division
...*Ramoul,* **49-B5,** Tel 285 9717
Tyre Express Service Centres
Managed by Al-Futtaim Motors at these Emarat Stations

...*Al Garhoud,* **39-F8,** Tel 324 0425
...*Al Madares,* **49-A3,** Tel 282 3399
...*Al Safa,* **19-C7,** Tel 342 2692
...*Al Nahrawan,* **51-B4,** Tel 261 3202
...*Al Rajhan,* **23-C9,** Tel 398 8031
...*Lamtara,* **20-K7,** Tel 343 7317
Workshop Equipment
...*Ramoul,* **49-B5,** Tel 285 9881

Dubai Municipality

Advertising Section
...*Umm Ramool,* **49-E5,** Tel 285 8661
Emergency Office
...*Riggat Al Buteen,* **25-A7,** Tel 223 2323
Fees & Revenues Section
...*Riggat Al Buteen,* **25-A7,** Tel 206 3274
Garage Transport Department
...*Al Garhoud,* **49-D4,** Tel 285 0700
Headquarters
.. .*Riggat Al Buteen,* **25-A7,** Tel 221 5555
Legal Affairs Department
...*Riggat Al Buteen,* **25-A7,** Tel 206 3331
Public Relations Section
...*Riggat Al Buteen,* **25-A7,** Tel 206 4678
Rent Committee
...*Riggat Al Buteen,* **25-A7,** Tel 221 5555
Store
...*Al Garhoud,* **49-D3,** Tel 286 3999
Umm Ramool Offices
...*Umm Ramool,* **49-E5,** Tel 286 3366
Used Car Exhibitions Complex
...*Ras Al Khor Industrial 3,* **55-B9,** Tel 333 3800

A guide to the addressing system in Dubai

Dubai is in the process of completing a Comprehensive Addressing System that consists of two complementary number systems – the Route Numbering System and the Community, Street & Building Numbering System. The former helps an individual to develop and follow simple series of directions for travelling from one area to another in Dubai, the latter helps a visitor to locate a particular building or house in the city.

Routes Numbering System

Various routes connecting Dubai to other Emirates of the UAE or main cities within an Emirate are classified as 'Emirate-Routes' or 'E-Routes'. They possess two digit numbers on a falcon emblem as shown on the UAE Map. Four E-Routes pass through Dubai.

 Dubai with Abu Dhabi and Sharjah.

 Dubai with Hatta.

 Dubai with Al Ain.

 Jebel Ali with Lahbab.

Routes connecting main communities within Dubai are designated as 'Dubai-Routes' or 'D-Routes'. They possess two digit numbers on a fort emblem. D-Routes parallel to the coast are even numbered starting from D94 and decreases as one goes away from the coast. D-Routes perpendicular to coast are odd numbered starting from D53 and decreases as one goes away from the Abu Dhabi border.

Community, Street & Building Numbering System

This system helps an individual to locate a particular building or house in Dubai. The Emirate is divided into nine sectors.

Sectors 1, 2, 3, 4, and 6 represent urban areas.

Sector 5 represent Jebel Ali.

Sector 7, 8 and 9 represent rural areas (inclusive of Hatta).

Sectors are sub-divided into communities, which are bounded by main roads. A three digit number identifies each community. The first is the number of the Sector, while the following two digits denote the location of the community in relation to neighbouring communities in sequential order.

Buildings on the left hand side of the street have odd numbers while those on the right hand side take even numbers. Again, building numbers increase as one goes away from the city centre. The complete address of a building in Dubai is given as Community Number, Street Number and Building Number.

Emirates Safe Driving Handbook

Road safety is a very serious issue and a subject that the **Emirates Motor Sports Federation (EMSF) and Explorer Publishing** feel very strongly about. In their continuous effort to promote safety on the streets of the UAE, they have produced the **Safe Driving Handbook**. We firmly believe that the information in this book will help to make our roads safer.

Considering we have the advantage of a highly sophisticated road network system, all we now require to keep our roads safe is for all drivers to respect the rules of the road and to show common courtesy to other motorists.

We hope that the contents of this book will serve as a constant reminder to those who are already aware of road rules, and to others, as a source of valuable information. Obeying road rules as a matter of habit is all that's required to make driving more pleasurable, and definitely a whole lot safer.

With a 12% annual increase in the number of vehicles on UAE roads, the need for educated and safety-conscious drivers becomes even more important. Traffic accidents have become a daily phenomenon on UAE roads.

An average of 548 people have lost their lives every year for the last five years. More than 50% of the total road fatalities are associated with speeding.

Speed Limits

• You MUST NOT exceed the maximum speed limits for the road and for your vehicle.

• The speed limit is the absolute maximum and does not mean it is safe to drive at that speed irrespective of conditions. Driving at speeds too fast for the road and traffic conditions can be dangerous. You should always reduce your speed when:
- the road layout or condition presents hazards, such as bends
- sharing the road with pedestrians and cyclists, particularly children, and motorcyclists
- weather conditions make it safer to do so
- driving at night as it is harder to see other road users.

• Conversely, it is also important to maintain a speed which is not slower than the regular flow of traffic. If you are significantly holding up traffic, either on the road or highway, pull over and allow others to pass before continuing.

Stopping Distances

• Drive at a speed that will allow you to stop well within the distance you can see to be clear.

You should:
- Leave enough space between you and the vehicle in front so that you can pull up safely if it suddenly slows down or stops. The safe rule is never to get closer than the overall stopping distance (see Typical Stopping Distances diagram below and on the facing page).
- Allow at least a three second gap between you and the vehicle in front on roads carrying fast traffic. The gap should be at least doubled on wet roads

- Remember, large vehicles and motorcycles need a greater distance to stop.
- Use a fixed point to help measure a three second gap.

Keep The Hard Shoulder Clear

Dhs. 500 FINE — **6 PENALTY POINTS**

NEVER drive along the hard shoulder. Not only is it very dangerous, it is also ILLEGAL.

Keep Right

Dhs. 200 FINE — **3 PENALTY POINTS**

ALWAYS move over as **far right** as possible, as soon as it is safe to do so.

Keep Your Distance

Dhs. 100 FINE — **1 PENALTY POINT**

NEVER drive too close to the vehicle in front. Always leave at least a three second gap between you and the next vehicle.

Box Junctions

Dhs. 100 FINE — **1 PENALTY POINT**

NEVER enter a box junction until your exit is clear.

And **REMEMBER, keep to** the speed limit, **do not** jump red lights, and **always** be courteous to other road users.

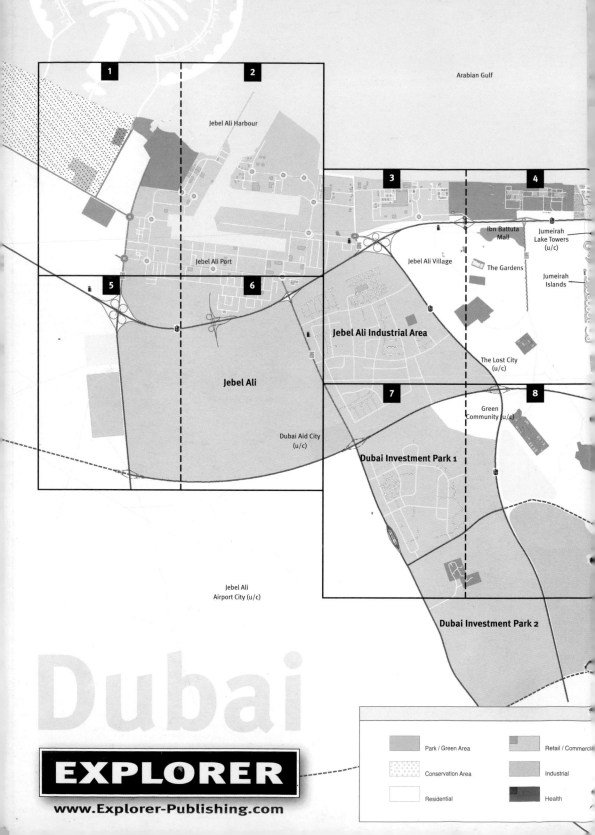

Palm Jebel Ali (u/c)

1

2

Jebel Ali Harbour

Arabian Gulf

3

4

Ibn Battuta
Mall

Jumeirah
Lake Towers
(u/c)

Jebel Ali Village

The Gardens

Jumeirah
Islands

Jebel Ali Port

5

6

Jebel Ali Industrial Area

The Lost City
(u/c)

Jebel Ali

7

8

Green
Community (u/c)

Dubai Aid City
(u/c)

Dubai Investment Park 1

Jebel Ali
Airport City (u/c)

Dubai Investment Park 2

Dubai

EXPLORER

www.Explorer-Publishing.com

	Park / Green Area		Retail / Commercial
	Conservation Area		Industrial
	Residential		Health